Roslyn Cookbook

Compiler as a Service, Static Code Analysis, Code Quality, Code Generation, and more

Manish Vasani

BIRMINGHAM - MUMBAI

Roslyn Cookbook

Copyright © 2017 Packt Publishing

All rights reserved. No part of this book may be reproduced, stored in a retrieval system, or transmitted in any form or by any means, without the prior written permission of the publisher, except in the case of brief quotations embedded in critical articles or reviews.

Every effort has been made in the preparation of this book to ensure the accuracy of the information presented. However, the information contained in this book is sold without warranty, either express or implied. Neither the author, nor Packt Publishing, and its dealers and distributors will be held liable for any damages caused or alleged to be caused directly or indirectly by this book.

Packt Publishing has endeavored to provide trademark information about all of the companies and products mentioned in this book by the appropriate use of capitals. However, Packt Publishing cannot guarantee the accuracy of this information.

First published: July 2017

Production reference: 1260717

Published by Packt Publishing Ltd.
Livery Place
35 Livery Street
Birmingham
B3 2PB, UK.
ISBN 978-1-78728-683-2

www.packtpub.com

Credits

Author
Manish Vasani

Reviewers
Ovais Mehboob Ahmed Khan

Commissioning Editor
Aaron Lazar

Acquisition Editor
Nitin Dasan

Content Development Editor
Jason Pereira

Technical Editor
Prashant Mishra

Copy Editor
Charlotte Carneiro

Project Coordinator
Sheejal Shah

Proofreader
Safis Editing

Indexer
Rekha Nair

Graphics
Jason Monteiro

Production Coordinator
Melwyn Dsa

About the Author

Manish Vasani is a senior software developer working for Microsoft Corporation based in Redmond, WA, USA. He is extremely passionate about working on extensible compiler platforms designed to enable rich analysis scenarios. He did his master's in Computer Science at Columbia University, New York, with a focus on compiler design under the guidance of Professor Alfred V. Aho.

He has roughly 10+ years of work experience at Microsoft, and has been on the Roslyn Managed Languages team since mid-2011. During this time, he has worked on the Roslyn compiler and IDE teams, as well as on the new Roslyn project system for .Net Core projects.

He is currently working on the Roslyn analyzers team and was part of the design team for the analyzer and code fix API and implemented the analyzer driver that executes the analyzers in the compiler and VS IDE. They are also working towards porting FxCop code analysis rules to FxCop analyzers.

Acknowledgments

First, I would like to thank my parents for all their unconditional love and support throughout all these years. They taught me to never give up on my dreams, no matter how difficult the circumstances. I would never be the person I am today without them being on my side all this time. I would like to thank my elder sister and my late elder brother for their love and care throughout our childhood. No matter however far apart we are, you all will always live in my heart.

I would also like to thank all my teachers, right from my elementary schooling up to my graduation. You showed me value of knowledge and the true way to live life, which is to learn and spread knowledge every single day.

I would like to thank all my friends, who have helped me gather and cherish all the beautiful and fun memories in life. I would especially like to thank Arjun Singri and Karthik Murthy, my college friends who first got me interested in compiler design. It is amazing how a small school project transformed into a lifelong passion and work, and has got me to this place where I can author a book on this topic.

I would like to thank my employers, Microsoft, and all my team members and leads till date. Microsoft is and will always be my second home. I cannot imagine working at any other place. I hope they can carry my burden for few more years and help me retire at this company.

I would like to thank Packtpub, for giving me the opportunity to write this book and publishing it. Thank you for believing in me and trusting that I am the right person to author this book.

Last, and by no means the least, I would like to thank my daughter, Inara, and my wife, Someeni. You both are the reason that I live every day, smile every day, enjoy every day.

Inara, you are the most beautiful miracle of my life. Being a father has given me more pride and joy, then anything else in life. Seeing you grow and take every step forward, gives me a reason to wait for the next day, so that I can see the pleasant surprises that you bring along with it. I will always remember the image of you clapping and jumping with joy "My daddy is writing a book, clap for daddyyyy…".

Someeni, you are my eternal pillar of support and strength. You have helped me through all the ups and downs of life. Stayed up late nights with me while I dabbled at the book. I had second thoughts about whether I can manage to write this book, but you never doubted it even once. You are the prettiest person I know, with the most beautiful heart and soul. I can never forget or repay the numerous sacrifices you have made as a wife and a mother. You have always unwaveringly chosen family over your own career and happiness. I am extremely grateful to have you as a life partner, I couldn't have asked for anyone better. I would like to dedicate this book to you and our journey together.

About the Reviewer

Ovais Mehboob Ahmed Khan is a seasoned programmer and solution architect with more than 14 years of software development experience. He has worked in different organizations across Pakistan, the USA, and the Middle East. Currently, he is working for a government entity based in Dubai, and also provides consultancy services to a Microsoft gold partner firm based in New Jersey.

He is a Microsoft MVP in Visual Studio and Development Technologies and specializes mainly in Microsoft .NET, cloud, and web development. He is a prolific writer and has published numerous technical articles on different websites, such as MSDN, TechNet, and DZone; he also has a personal blog at (`http://OvaisMehboob.com`) and is the author of two books, titled as *JavaScript for .NET Developers and Enterprise Application Architecture with .NET Core*, published by Packt. He is an active speaker and group leader of Microsoft Developers UAE Meetup, Microsoft Technology Practices, and Developers and Enterprise Practices user groups, and has presented various technical sessions at various events and conferences.

In short, Ovais is a passionate developer and an architect, who is always interested in learning new technologies. He can be reached at `ovaismehboob@hotmail.com`, and on Twitter at `@ovaismehboob`.

www.PacktPub.com

For support files and downloads related to your book, please visit `www.PacktPub.com`.

Did you know that Packt offers eBook versions of every book published, with PDF and ePub files available? You can upgrade to the eBook version at `www.PacktPub.com` and as a print book customer, you are entitled to a discount on the eBook copy. Get in touch with us at `service@packtpub.com` for more details.

At `www.PacktPub.com`, you can also read a collection of free technical articles, sign up for a range of free newsletters and receive exclusive discounts and offers on Packt books and eBooks.

`https://www.packtpub.com/mapt`

Get the most in-demand software skills with Mapt. Mapt gives you full access to all Packt books and video courses, as well as industry-leading tools to help you plan your personal development and advance your career.

Why subscribe?

- Fully searchable across every book published by Packt
- Copy and paste, print, and bookmark content
- On demand and accessible via a web browser

Customer Feedback

Thanks for purchasing this Packt book. At Packt, quality is at the heart of our editorial process. To help us improve, please leave us an honest review on this book's Amazon page at "https://www.amazon.com/dp/1787286835".

If you'd like to join our team of regular reviewers, you can e-mail us at customerreviews@packtpub.com. We award our regular reviewers with free eBooks and videos in exchange for their valuable feedback. Help us be relentless in improving our products!

In loving memory of my elder brother, Hitesh.

Table of Contents

Preface	1
Chapter 1: Writing Diagnostic Analyzers	9
Introduction	9
Creating, debugging, and executing an analyzer project in Visual Studio	11
Getting ready	11
How to do it…	12
How it works…	17
Creating a symbol analyzer to report issues about symbol declarations	19
Getting ready	20
How to do it…	20
How it works…	22
There's more…	23
See also	24
Creating a syntax node analyzer to report issues about language syntax	24
Getting ready	24
How to do it…	25
How it works…	27
Creating a syntax tree analyzer to analyze the source file and report syntax issues	28
Getting ready	29
How to do it…	29
How it works…	32
Creating a method body analyzer to analyze whole method and report issues	32
Getting ready	33
How to do it…	33
How it works…	35
Creating a compilation analyzer to analyze whole compilation and report issues	38
Getting ready	39
How to do it…	39
How it works…	42
Writing unit tests for an analyzer project	46

Getting ready	46
How to do it...	46
How it works...	50
See also	53
Publishing NuGet package and VSIX for an analyzer project	54
Getting ready	54
How to do it...	55

Chapter 2: Consuming Diagnostic Analyzers in .NET Projects — 57

Introduction	57
Searching and installing analyzers through the NuGet package manager	58
Getting ready	58
How to do it...	59
Searching and installing VSIX analyzers through the VS extension gallery	65
Getting ready	66
How to do it...	66
Viewing and configuring analyzers in solution explorer in Visual Studio	71
Getting ready	71
How to do it...	72
How it works...	75
Using the ruleset file and Rule Set editor to configure analyzers	76
Getting ready	76
How to do it...	76
How it works...	79
There's more...	79

Chapter 3: Writing IDE Code Fixes, Refactorings, and Intellisense Completion Providers — 81

Introduction	82
Creating, debugging, and executing a CodeFixProvider to fix a compiler warning	82
Getting ready	83
How to do it...	84
How it works...	87
Applying batch code fixes (FixAll) across different scopes: document, project, and solution	93
Getting ready	93
How to do it...	94

Creating a custom FixAllProvider to fix all occurrences of an issue across a scope	96
Getting ready	97
How to do it…	98
How it works…	101
Creating a CodeRefactoringProvider to refactor source code to recommend using C# 7.0 tuples	105
Getting ready	106
How to do it…	107
How it works…	112
There's more…	116
Creating a CompletionProvider to provide additional intellisense items while editing code.	116
Getting ready	118
How to do it…	118
How it works…	120
Writing unit tests for a CodeFixProvider	125
Getting ready	125
How to do it…	126
How it works…	129
Chapter 4: Improving Code Maintenance of C# Code Base	131
Introduction	131
Configuring C# code style rules built into Visual Studio 2017	132
Getting ready	133
How to do it…	133
How it works…	138
There is more...	139
Using the .editorconfig file for configuration of code style rules	140
Getting ready	140
How to do it…	140
How it works…	144
Using the public API analyzer for API surface maintenance	145
Getting ready	146
How to do it…	146
How it works…	150
There's more…	150
Using third-party StyleCop analyzers for code style rules	150
Getting ready	150
How to do it…	151

How it works... 154

Chapter 5: Catch Security Vulnerabilities and Performance Issues in C# Code — 157

Introduction — 158
Identifying configuration-related security vulnerabilities in web applications — 158
- Getting ready — 159
- How to do it... — 160
- How it works... — 163

Identifying cross-site scripting vulnerabilities in view markup files (.cshtml, .aspx files) in web applications — 164
- Getting ready — 164
- How to do it... — 165
- How it works... — 167

Identifying insecure method calls that can lead to SQL and LDAP injection attacks — 168
- Getting ready — 168
- How to do it... — 168
- How it works... — 171

Identifying weak password protection and management in web applications — 171
- Getting ready — 171
- How to do it... — 172

Identifying weak validation of data from external components to prevent attacks such as cross-site request forgery and path tampering — 174
- Getting ready — 174
- How to do it... — 175

Identifying performance improvements to source code using FxCop analyzers — 177
- Getting ready — 177
- How to do it... — 178
- How it works... — 181

Chapter 6: Live Unit Testing in Visual Studio Enterprise — 183

Introduction — 183
Running live unit tests in Visual Studio for unit test projects based on NUnit, XUnit, and MSTest frameworks — 185
- Getting started — 186
- How to do it... — 186

Viewing and navigating live unit test results	191
Getting started	191
How to do it...	191
Understanding incremental live unit test execution with code changes	193
Getting started	193
How to do it...	194
How it works...	197
Understanding Start/Stop/Pause/Continue/Restart functionality for fine grain control of LUT	197
Getting started	198
How to do it...	198
Including and excluding subset of tests for live execution	201
Getting started	201
How to do it...	202
Configuring different options for live unit testing using the Tools Options dialog	205
Getting started	205
How to do it...	206

Chapter 7: C# Interactive and Scripting — 209

Introduction	209
Writing a simple C# script and evaluating it within the Visual Studio interactive window	210
Getting started	210
How to do it…	211
How it works...	212
Using script directives and REPL commands in the C# interactive window	214
Getting started	214
How to do it…	214
Using keyboard shortcuts for evaluating and navigating through script sessions in the C# interactive window	217
Getting started	217
How to do it…	217
Initializing the C# interactive session from the existing C# project	219
Getting started	219
How to do it…	219
Executing the C# script on a Visual Studio developer command prompt using csi.exe	222
Getting started	222

How to do it…	222
Using the Roslyn scripting API to execute C# code snippets	**225**
Getting started	225
How to do it…	225
How it works…	226

Chapter 8: Contribute Simple Functionality to Roslyn C# Compiler Open Source Code — 231

Introduction	**232**
Setting up Roslyn enlistment	**233**
Getting Started	234
How to do it…	234
Implementing a new syntax error in the C# compiler code base	**235**
Getting Started	237
How to do it…	237
How it works…	238
Implementing a new semantic error in the C# compiler code base	**240**
Getting Started	240
How to do it…	241
How it works…	243
Writing unit tests for a new error in the C# compiler code base	**244**
Getting Started	245
How to do it…	245
Using Roslyn Syntax Visualizer to view Roslyn syntax tokens and nodes for a source file	**247**
Getting Started	247
How to do it…	247
Sending a Roslyn pull request to contribute to next version of C# compiler and VS IDE	**251**
Getting Started	251
How to do it…	251

Chapter 9: Design and Implement a New C# Language Feature — 253

Introduction	**253**
New language feature: Switch Operator (?::)	257
Designing syntax and grammar for a new C# language feature	**258**
Getting Started	258
How to do it…	258
How it works…	262
Implementing parser support for a new C# language feature	**264**

Getting Started	265
How to do it...	265
How it works...	268
Implementing binding/semantic analysis support for a new C# language feature	**270**
Getting Started	270
How to do it...	270
How it works...	273
There's more...	276
Implementing lowering/code generation support for a new C# language feature	**278**
Getting Started	278
How to do it...	279
How it works...	281
Writing unit tests for C# parsing, binding, and codegen phases	**284**
Getting Started	285
How to do it...	285

Chapter 10: Command-Line Tools Based on Roslyn API — 293

Introduction	**293**
Writing an application based on the Compiler Syntax API to parse and transform source files	**295**
Getting started	295
How to do it...	295
How it works...	297
Writing an application based on the Compiler Semantic API to display diagnostics and overload resolution results	**301**
Getting started	301
How to do it...	301
How it works...	303
Writing an application based on the Compiler Analyzer API to execute diagnostic analyzers and display analyzer diagnostics	**306**
Getting started	306
How to do it...	306
How it works...	307
Writing an application based on the Workspaces API to format and simplify all source files in the solution	**312**
Getting started	312
How to do it...	312
How it works...	314

Writing an application based on the Workspaces API to edit projects in a solution and display project properties 318
    Getting started 318
    How to do it… 318
    How it works... 320

Index 325

Preface

Software developers deal with source code on a day-to-day basis. Regardless of the technology or the programming language that they work on, there are a bunch of routine tasks that they must perform on their code:

- Compile source code into the runtime-specific binary format
- Analyze source code to identify issues in the source code
- Edit source code to fix issues or refactor to improve maintenance, understandability, performance, security, and so on
- Navigate source code to search patterns, references, definitions, and relationships
- Debug source code to observe and fix runtime behavior for functionality, performances, security, and so on
- Visualize collections of source components (projects), their properties, configuration, and so on

The .NET Compiler Platform (code named *Roslyn*) is a platform for .NET programming languages, C# and Visual Basic, to enable building tools and extensions to perform these routine programming tasks. Notably, this platform is shared between Microsoft's .NET compilers and the Visual Studio IDE for .NET development.

Roslyn is divided into multiple programming layers, with each layer exposing public APIs to write customized tools and extensions:

- **CodeAnalysis** layer: Core syntax and semantic representation layer of source code. C# and Visual Basic compilers (*csc.exe* and *vbc.exe*) are written on top of this layer.
- **Workspaces** layer: Project and solution layer that collects a set of logically related source files. These are not coupled to any specific host, such as Visual Studio.
- **Features** layer: Set of IDE features built on top of the CodeAnalysis and Workspaces API such as code fixes, refactorings, IntelliSense, completion, finding references, and navigating to definition and so on. These are not coupled to any specific host, such as Visual Studio.
- **Visual Studio** layer: Visual Studio workspace and project system that brings together and lights up all the compiler and IDE features.

Preface

Roslyn is essentially a stack of services that has been written with two core design principles: **Extensibility** (for layers above and third-party plugins) and **Maintainability** (it has well-documented and supported public APIs across these layers). External developers or third parties can do bunch of cool stuff on top of these services:

- Write their own tools for any specific programming layer to accomplish any of the programming tasks noted previously.
- Write simple plugins (for example diagnostic analyzers, code fixes and refactorings, completion and IntelliSense providers) for specific layers.
- Perform advanced scenarios at any specific layer, such as implementing their own compiler, Workspace, IDE, or project system, and all the other functionality across the stack lights up automagically.

What this book covers

Chapter 1, *Writing Diagnostic Analyzers*, enables developers to write diagnostic analyzer extensions to the C# compiler and Visual Studio IDE to analyze source code and report warnings and errors. End users will see these diagnostics on building the project from the command line or Visual Studio and see them live while editing the source code in the Visual Studio IDE.

Chapter 2, *Consuming Diagnostic Analyzers in .NET Projects*, enables developers in the C# community to harness third-party Roslyn diagnostic analyzers for their C# projects. You will learn how to search, install, view, and configure diagnostic analyzers in Visual Studio.

Chapter 3, *Writing IDE Code Fixes, Refactorings, and IntelliSense Completion Providers*, enables developers to write code fix and code refactoring extensions to the Visual Studio IDE to edit C# source code to fix compiler/analyzer diagnostics and refactor source code, respectively. It also enables developers to write completion provider extensions to the C# IntelliSense in the Visual Studio IDE for an enhanced code editing experience.

Chapter 4, *Improving Code Maintenance of C# Code Base*, enables developers in the C# community to improve the code maintenance and readability of their source code by using the analyzers and code fixes that are built into the Visual Studio IDE, as well as some popular third-party implementations.

Chapter 5, *Catch Security Vulnerabilities and Performance Issues in C# Code*, enables C# community developers to catch security and performance issues in their C# code base by using popular third-party analyzers such as PUMA scan analyzers and FxCop analyers.

Chapter 6, *Live Unit Testing in Visual Studio Enterprise*, enables developers to use the new Roslyn-based feature in the Visual Studio 2017 Enterprise edition that enables smart live unit test (LUT) execution in the background. LUT automatically runs the impacted unit tests in the background as you edit code, and visualizes the results and code coverage live, in the editor, in real-time.

Chapter 7, *C# Interactive and Scripting*, enables developers to use C# interactive and scripting features in Visual Studio. C# scripting is a tool for quickly testing out C# and .NET snippets using a REPL (read-evaluate-print-loop), without the effort of creating multiple unit testing or console projects.

Chapter 8, *Contribute Simple Functionality to Roslyn C# Compiler Open Source Code*, enables developers to add new functionality to the open source Roslyn C# compiler. You will learn how to implement new C# compiler errors, add unit tests for them, and then send a pull request for your code changes to the Roslyn repo to incorporate them in the next version of the C# compiler.

Chapter 9, *Design and Implement a New C# Language Feature*, enables developers to design a new C# language feature and implement various compiler phases for this feature in the open source Roslyn C# compiler. You will learn the following aspects of compiler design and implementation: language design, parsing, semantic analysis and binding, and code generation, with suitable code examples.

Chapter 10, *Command-Line Tools Based on Roslyn API*, enables developers to write command-line tools using the Roslyn Compiler and Workspaces API to analyze and/or edit C# code.

What you need for this book

You require Visual Studio 2017 Community/Enterprise edition to execute the recipes in this book. You can install Visual Studio 2017 from https://www.visualstudio.com/downloads/. Additionally, there are some chapters that require you to install GitHub for desktop tooling from https://desktop.github.com/.

Who this book is for

The .NET developers and architects, who are interested in taking full advantage of the Roslyn-based extensions and tools to improve the development processes, will find this book useful. Roslyn contributors, that is the producers and C# community developers, will also find this book useful.

Conventions

In this book, you will find a number of styles of text that distinguish between different kinds of information. Here are some examples of these styles, and an explanation of their meaning.

Code words in text, database table names, folder names, filenames, file extensions, pathnames, and user input are shown as follows: "Additionally, the `.editorconfig` files can be checked into the repo alongside the sources, so that the rules are enforced for every user that contributes to the repo."

A block of code is set as follows:

```
private void Method_PreferBraces(bool flag)
{
  if (flag)
  {
    Console.WriteLine(flag);
  }
}
```

Any command-line input or output is written as follows:

```
msbuild ClassLibrary.csproj /v:m
```

New terms and important words are shown in bold. Words that you see on the screen, in menus or dialog boxes for example, appear in the text like this: "Start Visual Studio, click **File** | **New** | **Project...**, create a new C# class library project, and replace the code in `Class1.cs` with code from the code sample at `ClassLibrary/Class1.cs`."

Warnings or important notes appear in a box like this.

Tips and tricks appear like this.

Reader feedback

Feedback from our readers is always welcome. Let us know what you think about this book-what you liked or disliked. Reader feedback is important for us as it helps us develop titles that you will really get the most out of.

To send us general feedback, simply e-mail `feedback@packtpub.com`, and mention the book's title in the subject of your message.

If there is a topic that you have expertise in and you are interested in either writing or contributing to a book, see our author guide at `www.packtpub.com/authors`.

Customer support

Now that you are the proud owner of a Packt book, we have a number of things to help you to get the most from your purchase.

Downloading the example code

You can download the example code files for this book from your account at `http://www.packtpub.com`. If you purchased this book elsewhere, you can visit `http://www.packtpub.com/support` and register to have the files e-mailed directly to you.

You can download the code files by following these steps:

1. Log in or register to our website using your e-mail address and password.
2. Hover the mouse pointer on the **SUPPORT** tab at the top.
3. Click on **Code Downloads & Errata**.
4. Enter the name of the book in the **Search** box.
5. Select the book for which you're looking to download the code files.
6. Choose from the drop-down menu where you purchased this book from.
7. Click on **Code Download**.

Once the file is downloaded, please make sure that you unzip or extract the folder using the latest version of:

- WinRAR / 7-Zip for Windows
- Zipeg / iZip / UnRarX for Mac
- 7-Zip / PeaZip for Linux

Preface

The code bundle for the book is also hosted on GitHub at https://github.com/PacktPublishing/Roslyn-Cookbook. We also have other code bundles from our rich catalog of books and videos available at https://github.com/PacktPublishing/. Check them out!

Downloading the color images of this book

We also provide you with a PDF file that has color images of the screenshots/diagrams used in this book. The color images will help you better understand the changes in the output. You can download this file from https://www.packtpub.com/sites/default/files/downloads/RoslynCookbook_ColorImages.pdf.

Errata

Although we have taken every care to ensure the accuracy of our content, mistakes do happen. If you find a mistake in one of our books-maybe a mistake in the text or the code-we would be grateful if you could report this to us. By doing so, you can save other readers from frustration and help us improve subsequent versions of this book. If you find any errata, please report them by visiting http://www.packtpub.com/submit-errata, selecting your book, clicking on the **Errata Submission Form** link, and entering the details of your errata. Once your errata are verified, your submission will be accepted and the errata will be uploaded to our website or added to any list of existing errata under the Errata section of that title.

To view the previously submitted errata, go to https://www.packtpub.com/books/content/support and enter the name of the book in the search field. The required information will appear under the **Errata** section.

Piracy

Piracy of copyrighted material on the Internet is an ongoing problem across all media. At Packt, we take the protection of our copyright and licenses very seriously. If you come across any illegal copies of our works in any form on the Internet, please provide us with the location address or website name immediately so that we can pursue a remedy.

Please contact us at copyright@packtpub.com with a link to the suspected pirated material.

We appreciate your help in protecting our authors and our ability to bring you valuable content.

Questions

If you have a problem with any aspect of this book, you can contact us at `questions@packtpub.com`, and we will do our best to address the problem.

Writing Diagnostic Analyzers

In this chapter, we will cover the following recipes:

- Creating, debugging, and executing an analyzer project in Visual Studio
- Creating a symbol analyzer to report issues about symbol declarations
- Creating a syntax node analyzer to report issues about language syntax
- Creating a syntax tree analyzer to analyze source file and report syntax issues
- Creating a method body analyzer to analyze whole method and report issues
- Creating a compilation analyzer to analyze whole compilation and report issues
- Writing unit tests for an analyzer project
- Publishing the NuGet package and VSIX for an analyzer project

Introduction

Diagnostic analyzers are extensions to the Roslyn C# compiler and Visual Studio IDE to analyze user code and report diagnostics. Users will see these diagnostics in the error list after building the project from Visual Studio, and even when building the project on the command line. They will also see the diagnostics live while editing the source code in the Visual Studio IDE. Analyzers can report diagnostics to enforce specific code styles, improve code quality and maintenance, recommend design guidelines, or even report very domain-specific issues which cannot be covered by the core compiler. This chapter enables C# developers to write, debug, test, and publish analyzers that perform different kinds of analyses.

If you are not familiar with the Roslyn's architecture and API layers, it is recommended that, before reading this chapter further, you read the Preface of this book to gain a basic understanding of Roslyn APIs.

Diagnostic analyzers are built on top of the Roslyn's **CodeAnalysis/Compiler layer** API. Analyzers can analyze specific code units, such as a symbol, syntax node, code block, compilation, and so on, by registering one or more analyzer actions. The compiler layer makes a callback into the analyzer whenever it compiles a code unit of interest. The analyzer can report diagnostics on code units, which are added to the list of the compiler diagnostics and reported back to the end user.

Analyzers can be broadly categorized into the following two buckets based on the kind of analysis performed:

- **Stateless analyzers**: Analyzers that report diagnostics about a specific code unit by registering one or more analyzer actions that:
  - Do not require maintaining any state across analyzer actions.
  - Independent of the order of execution of individual analyzer actions.

For example, an analyzer that looks at every single class declaration independently and reports issues about the declaration is a stateless analyzer. We will show you how to write a stateless symbol, syntax node, and syntax tree analyzer, later in this chapter.

- **Stateful analyzers**: Analyzers that report diagnostics about a specific code unit, but in the context of an enclosing code unit, such as a code block or a compilation. These are more complicated analyzers that require powerful and wider analysis, hence, need careful design to achieve efficient analyzer execution without memory leaks. These analyzers require at least one of the following kinds of state manipulation for analysis:
  - Access to immutable state objects for the enclosing code unit, such as a compilation or the code block. For example, access to certain well-known types defined in a compilation.
  - Perform analysis over the enclosing code unit, with mutable state defined and initialized in a start action for the enclosing code unit, intermediate nested actions that access and/or update this state, and an end action to report diagnostic on the individual code units.

For example, an analyzer that looks at all class declarations in a compilation, gathering and updating a common state when analyzing each class declaration, and then finally, after it has analyzed all declarations, reports issues about those declarations is a stateful analyzer. We will show you how to write a stateful method body and compilation analyzer in this chapter.

By default, analyzers can analyze and report diagnostics on source files in a project. However, we can also write an analyzer that analyzes additional files, that is, non-source text files included in the project, and also report diagnostics in additional files. Non-source files could be files, such as Web.config files in a web project, cshtml files in a Razor project, XAML files in a WPF project, and so on. You can read more about how to write and consume additional file analyzers at `https://github.com/dotnet/roslyn/blob/master/docs/analyzers/Using%20Additional%20Files.md`.

Creating, debugging, and executing an analyzer project in Visual Studio

We will show you how to install the .NET Compiler Platform SDK, create an analyzer project from a template, and then debug and execute the default analyzer.

The analyzer project that you create in this recipe can be used in the subsequent recipes in this chapter to add new analyzers and write unit tests.

Getting ready

You will need to have Visual Studio 2017 installed on your machine to execute the recipes in this chapter. You can install a free community version of Visual Studio 2017 from `https://www.visualstudio.com/thank-you-downloading-visual-studio/?sku=Community&rel=15`.

How to do it...

1. Start Visual Studio and click on **File | New | Project**.
2. Search for `Analyzer` templates in the textbox at the top right corner of the **New Project** dialog, select **Download the .NET Compiler Platform SDK**, and click on **OK**:

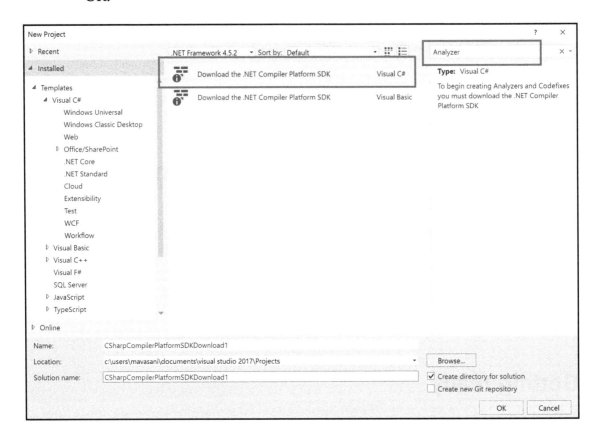

Chapter 1

3. The new project will have an `index.html` file opened by default. Click on **Download .NET Compiler Platform SDK Templates >>** button to install the analyzer SDK templates.

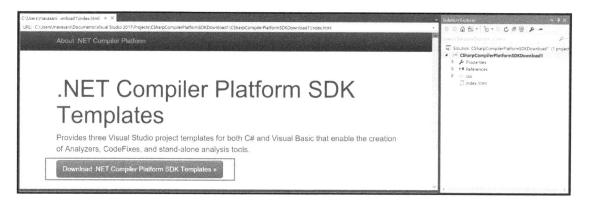

4. In the subsequent **File Download** dialog, click on **Open**.

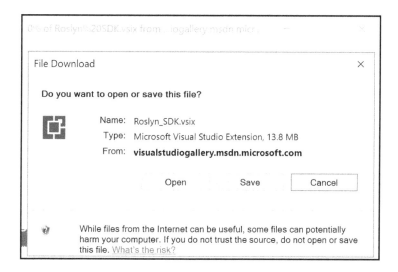

Writing Diagnostic Analyzers

5. Click **Install** on the next **VSIX Installer** dialog and **End Tasks** on the subsequent prompt to install the SDK:

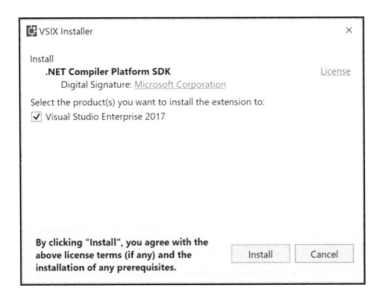

6. Start a new instance of Visual Studio and click on **File | New | Project...** to get the **New Project** dialog.
7. Change the project target framework combo box to **.NET Framework 4.6** (or above). Under **Visual C# | Extensibility**, choose **Analyzer with Code Fix (NuGet + VSIX)**, name your project CSharpAnalyzers, and click on **OK**.

Chapter 1

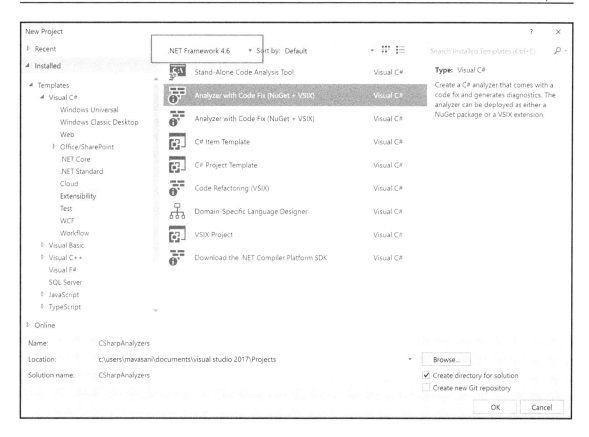

8. You should now have an analyzers solution with 3 projects: `CSharpAnalyzers (Portable)`, `CSharpAnalyzers.Test`, and `CSharpAnalyzer.Vsix`:

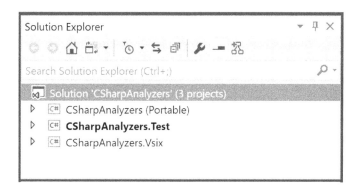

9. Open source file `DiagnosticAnalyzer.cs` in `CSharpAnalyzers` project and set breakpoints (press *F9*) at the start of the `Initialize` and `AnalyzeSymbol` methods, as shown here:

```csharp
        public override ImmutableArray<DiagnosticDescriptor> SupportedDiagnostics { get { return ImmutableArra

        public override void Initialize(AnalysisContext context)
        {
            // TODO: Consider registering other actions that act on syntax instead of or in addition to symbol
            // See https://github.com/dotnet/roslyn/blob/master/docs/analyzers/Analyzer%20Actions%20Semantics.
            context.RegisterSymbolAction(AnalyzeSymbol, SymbolKind.NamedType);
        }


        private static void AnalyzeSymbol(SymbolAnalysisContext context)
        {
            // TODO: Replace the following code with your own analysis, generating Diagnostic objects for any
            var namedTypeSymbol = (INamedTypeSymbol)context.Symbol;

            // Find just those named type symbols with names containing lowercase letters.
            if (namedTypeSymbol.Name.ToCharArray().Any(char.IsLower))
            {
                // For all such symbols, produce a diagnostic.
                var diagnostic = Diagnostic.Create(Rule, namedTypeSymbol.Locations[0], namedTypeSymbol.Name);

                context.ReportDiagnostic(diagnostic);
            }
```

10. Set `CSharpAnalyzers.Vsix` as the start-up project and click on *F5* to build the analyzer and start debugging a new instance of Visual Studio with the analyzer enabled.
11. In the new Visual Studio instance, create a new C# class library project, say `ClassLibrary`.
12. Verify that we hit both the preceding breakpoints in our analyzer code in the first VS instance. You can step through the analyzer code using *F10* or click on *F5* to continue debugging.

13. We should now see the analyzer diagnostic in the error list and a squiggle in the editor:

14. Edit the name of the class from `Class1` to `CLASS1`.
15. We should hit the breakpoint in the `AnalyzeSymbol` method again. Continue debugging with *F5* and the diagnostic and squiggle should go away immediately, demonstrating the powerful live and extensible analysis.

How it works…

.NET Compiler Platform SDK is a wrapper project that redirects us to fetch the project templates for analyzer + CodeFix projects for C# and Visual Basic. Creating a new project from these templates creates a fully functional analyzer project which has a default analyzer, unit tests, and a VSIX project:

- `CSharpAnalyzers`: Core analyzer project that contains the default analyzer implementation that reports a diagnostic for all type names that contain any lowercase letters.
- `CSharpAnalyzers.Test`: Analyzer unit test project that contains a couple of analyzer and code fixer unit tests and test helpers.
- `CSharpAnalyzers.Vsix`: The VSIX project that packages the analyzer into a VSIX. This is the start-up project in the solution.

Writing Diagnostic Analyzers

Clicking on *F5* to start debugging the solution builds and deploys the analyzer to the Visual Studio extension hive and then starts a new Visual Studio instance from this hive. Our analyzer is enabled by default for all C# projects created in this VS instance.

Let's expand a bit more on the diagnostic analyzer source code defined in `DiagnosticAnalyzers.cs`. It contains a type named `CSharpAnalyzersAnalyzer`, which derives from `DiagnosticAnalyzer`. `DiagnosticAnalyzer` is an abstract type with the following two abstract members:

- `SupportedDiagnostics` property: Analyzer must define one or more supported diagnostic descriptors. Descriptors describe the metadata for the diagnostics that an analyzer can report in analyzer actions. It contains fields such as the diagnostic ID, message format, title, description, hyperlink to documentation for the diagnostic, and so on. Can be used to create and report diagnostics:

    ```
    private static DiagnosticDescriptor Rule = new
    DiagnosticDescriptor(DiagnosticId, Title, MessageFormat,
    Category, DiagnosticSeverity.Warning, isEnabledByDefault: true,
    description: Description);

    public override ImmutableArray<DiagnosticDescriptor>
    SupportedDiagnostics { get { return
    ImmutableArray.Create(Rule); } }
    ```

- `Initialize` method: Diagnostic analyzers must implement the `Initialize` method to register analyzer action callbacks for a specific code entity kind of interest, which is named type symbols for the default analyzer. The initialize method is invoked once for the analyzer lifetime to allow analyzer initialization and registration of actions.

    ```
    public override void Initialize(AnalysisContext context)
    {
      context.RegisterSymbolAction(AnalyzeSymbol,
    SymbolKind.NamedType);
    }

    private static void AnalyzeSymbol(SymbolAnalysisContext
    context)
    {
       ...
    }
    ```

Invoke `AnalysisContext.EnableConcurrentExecution()` in the `Initialize` method if your analyzer can handle action callbacks from multiple threads simultaneously -- this enables the analyzer driver to execute the analyzer more efficiently on a machine with multiple cores. Additionally, also invoke `AnalysisContext.ConfigureGeneratedCodeAnalysis()` in the `Initialize` method to configure whether or not the analyzer wants to analyze and/or report diagnostics in generated code.

Analyzer actions are invoked for every code entity of interest in a user's source code. Additionally, as the user edits code and a new compilation is created, action callbacks are continuously invoked for entities defined in the new compilation during code editing. The error list makes sure that it only reports the diagnostics from the active compilation.

Use `http://source.roslyn.io` for rich semantic search and navigation of Roslyn source code, which is open sourced at `https://github.com/dotnet/roslyn.git`. For example, you can look at the definition and references for `DiagnosticAnalyzer` using the query URL `http://source.roslyn.io/#q=DiagnosticAnalyzer`.

Creating a symbol analyzer to report issues about symbol declarations

A symbol analyzer registers action callbacks to analyze one or more kinds of symbol declarations, such as types, methods, fields, properties, events, and so on, reports semantic issues about declarations.

In this section, we will create a symbol analyzer that extends the compiler diagnostic *CS0542* (member names cannot be the same as their enclosing type) to report a diagnostic if member names are the same as any of the outer parent type. For example, the analyzer will report a diagnostic for the innermost type `NestedClass` here:

```
public class NestedClass
{
  public class InnerClass
  {
    public class NestedClass
    {
    }
  }
}
```

Getting ready

You will need to have created and opened an analyzer project, say `CSharpAnalyzers` in Visual Studio 2017. Refer to the first recipe in this chapter to create this project.

How to do it...

1. In **Solution Explorer**, double-click on `Resources.resx` file in `CSharpAnalyzers` project to open the resource file in the resource editor.
2. Replace the existing resource strings for `AnalyzerDescription`, `AnalyzerMessageFormat` and `AnalyzerTitle` with new strings:

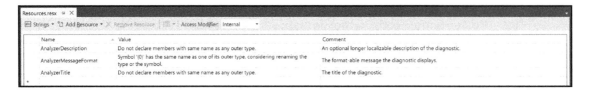

3. Replace the `Initialize` method implementation with the following:

```
public override void Initialize(AnalysisContext context)
{
  context.RegisterSymbolAction(symbolContext =>
  {
    var symbolName = symbolContext.Symbol.Name;

    // Skip the immediate containing type, CS0542 already covers this case.
    var outerType =
symbolContext.Symbol.ContainingType?.ContainingType;
    while (outerType != null)
    {
      // Check if the current outer type has the same name as the given member.
      if (symbolName.Equals(outerType.Name))
      {
        // For all such symbols, report a diagnostic.
        var diagnostic = Diagnostic.Create(Rule, symbolContext.Symbol.Locations[0], symbolContext.Symbol.Name);
        symbolContext.ReportDiagnostic(diagnostic);
        return;
      }
```

```
            outerType = outerType.ContainingType;
        }
    },
    SymbolKind.NamedType,
    SymbolKind.Method,
    SymbolKind.Field,
    SymbolKind.Event,
    SymbolKind.Property);
}
```

4. Click on *Ctrl + F5* to start a new Visual Studio instance with the analyzer enabled.
5. In the new Visual Studio instance, create a new C# class library with the following code:

```
namespace ClassLibrary
{
 public class OuterClass
 {
  public class NestedClass
  {
   public class NestedClass
   {
   }
  }
 }
}
```

6. Verify the compiler reported diagnostic *CS0542* in the error list:
   `'NestedClass': member names cannot be the same as their enclosing type.`
7. Change the class library code to following:

```
namespace ClassLibrary
{
 public class OuterClass
 {
  public class NestedClass
  {
   public class InnerClass
   {
    public class NestedClass
    {
    }
   }
  }
 }
}
```

Writing Diagnostic Analyzers

8. Verify that *CS0542* isn't reported anymore, but the error list has our analyzer diagnostic:

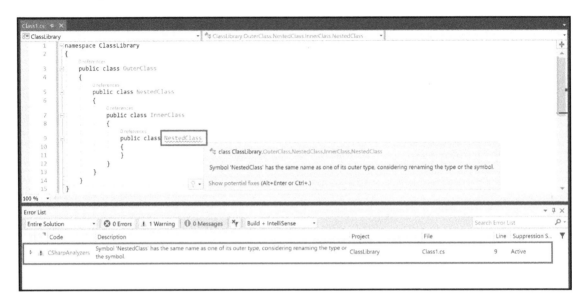

9. Replace the innermost type declaration for `NestedClass` with a field: `public int NestedClass`, and verify the same analyzer diagnostic is reported. You should get the same diagnostic for other member kinds such as method, property, and events with the same name.

How it works...

Symbol analyzers register one or more symbol action callbacks to analyze symbol kinds of interest. Note that, unlike the default implementation that registered a delegate method named `AnalyzeSymbol`, we registered a lambda callback.

We specified interest in analyzing all the top-level symbol kinds that can have an enclosing type, namely types, methods, fields, properties, and events in the `RegisterSymbolAction` invocation:

```
context.RegisterSymbolAction(symbolContext =>
{
    ...
},
SymbolKind.NamedType,
SymbolKind.Method,
```

```
SymbolKind.Field,
SymbolKind.Event,
SymbolKind.Property);
```

The analyzer driver ensures that the registered lambda is invoked for all symbols of the registered interest kinds in the compilation.

Analysis skips the immediate enclosing type, as C# compiler already reports error *CS0542*, if a member has the same name as its enclosing type.

```
// Skip the immediate containing type, CS0542 already covers this case.
var outerType = symbolContext.Symbol.ContainingType?.ContainingType;
```

Core analysis works by looping over the outer types and comparing the name of the symbol in a symbol analysis context with the relevant outer types, until it finds a match, in which case, it reports a diagnostic; if the outer type has no containing type, it doesn't report a diagnostic.

```
while (outerType != null)
{
 // Check if the current outer type has the same name as the given member.
 if (symbolName.Equals(outerType.Name))
 {
  // For all such symbols, report a diagnostic.
  ...
 }

 outerType = outerType.ContainingType;
}
```

It is recommended that symbol actions only analyze and report diagnostics about declarations, not the executable code within it. If you need to analyze executable code within a symbol, you should try to register other action kinds discussed later in this chapter.

There's more...

Trivia: The preceding implementation of the symbol analyzer does not have optimal performance. For example, if you have n levels of type nesting, and m fields in the inner innermost nested type, the analysis we implemented will be $O(m*n)$ algorithmic complexity. Can you implement an alternate implementation where the analysis can be implemented with a much superior $O(m + n)$ complexity?

See also

Our current analyzer implementation is completely stateless because it doesn't require analysis that is dependent upon more than one symbol at a time. We analyze each symbol individually and report diagnostics for it. However, if you need to do more complex analysis that requires collecting state from multiple symbols and then doing a compilation-wide analysis, you should write a stateful compilation analyzer with symbol and compilation actions. This is covered later in this chapter in the recipe *Creating a compilation analyzer to analyze a whole compilation and report issues*.

Creating a syntax node analyzer to report issues about language syntax

A syntax node analyzer registers action callbacks to analyze one or more kinds of syntax nodes, such as operators, identifiers, expressions, declarations, and so on, and reports semantic issues about syntax. These analyzers generally need to fetch semantic information about different syntax nodes being analyzed and use the compiler semantic model APIs to get this information.

In this section, we will create a syntax analyzer that analyzes `VariableDeclarationSyntax` nodes for local declarations and reports a diagnostic recommending use of the explicit type instead of an implicitly typed declaration, that is, variables defined with the keyword `var`, such as `var i = new X();`. Analyzer will not report diagnostics if there is a compiler syntax error (implicitly typed declarations cannot define more than one variable), or the right side of the assignment has an error type or special System type such as int, char, string, and so on. For example, the analyzer will not flag locals `local1`, `local2`, and `local3` here, but will flag `local4`.

```
int local1 = 0;
Class1 local2 = new Class1();
var local3 = 0;
var local4 = new Class1();
```

Getting ready

You will need to have created and opened an analyzer project, say `CSharpAnalyzers` in Visual Studio 2017. Refer to the first recipe in this chapter to create this project.

How to do it…

1. In **Solution Explorer**, double-click on `Resources.resx` file in `CSharpAnalyzers` project to open the resource file in the resource editor.
2. Replace the existing resource strings for `AnalyzerDescription`, `AnalyzerMessageFormat` and `AnalyzerTitle` with new strings:

3. Replace the `Initialize` method implementation with the following:

```
public override void Initialize(AnalysisContext context)
{
  context.RegisterSyntaxNodeAction(syntaxNodeContext =>
  {
    // Find implicitly typed variable declarations.
    // Do not flag implicitly typed declarations that declare more than one variables,
    // as the compiler already generates error CS0819 for those cases.
    var declaration = (VariableDeclarationSyntax)syntaxNodeContext.Node;
    if (!declaration.Type.IsVar || declaration.Variables.Count != 1)
    {
      return;
    }

    // Do not flag variable declarations with error type or special System types, such as int, char, string, and so on.
    var typeInfo = syntaxNodeContext.SemanticModel.GetTypeInfo(declaration.Type, syntaxNodeContext.CancellationToken);
    if (typeInfo.Type.TypeKind == TypeKind.Error || typeInfo.Type.SpecialType != SpecialType.None)
    {
      return;
    }

    // Report a diagnostic.
```

```
            var variable = declaration.Variables[0];
            var diagnostic = Diagnostic.Create(Rule,
       variable.GetLocation(), variable.Identifier.ValueText);
            syntaxNodeContext.ReportDiagnostic(diagnostic);
        },
        SyntaxKind.VariableDeclaration);
    }
```

4. Click on *Ctrl + F5* to start a new Visual Studio instance with the analyzer enabled.
5. In the new Visual Studio instance, create a new C# class library with the following code:

```
namespace ClassLibrary
{
  public class Class1
  {
    public void M(int param1, Class1 param2)
    {
      // Explicitly typed variables - do not flag.
      int local1 = param1;
      Class1 local2 = param2;
    }
  }
}
```

6. Verify the analyzer diagnostic is not reported in the error list for explicitly typed variables.
7. Now, add the following implicitly typed variable declarations to the method:

```
// Implicitly typed variable with error type - do not flag.
var local3 = UndefinedMethod();

// Implicitly typed variable with special type - do not flag.
var local4 = param1;
```

8. Verify the analyzer diagnostic is not reported in the error list for implicitly typed variables with error type or special type.
9. Add the violating implicitly typed variable declaration to the method:

```
// Implicitly typed variable with user defined type - flag.
var local5 = param2;
```

10. Verify the analyzer diagnostic is reported for this implicitly typed variable:

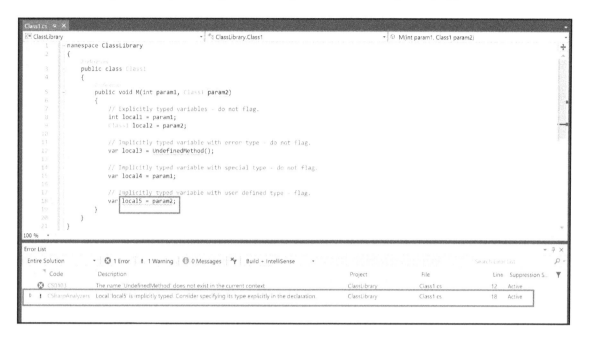

How it works…

Syntax node analyzers register one or more syntax node action callbacks to analyse syntax kinds of interest. We specified interest in analyzing `VariableDeclaration` syntax kind in the `RegisterSyntaxNodeAction` invocation.

```
context.RegisterSyntaxNodeAction(syntaxNodeContext =>
{
...
}, SyntaxKind.VariableDeclaration);
```

Analysis works by operating on the syntax node and semantic model exposed off the syntax node analysis context in the callback. We first do syntactic checks to verify that we are operating on a valid implicitly typed declaration:

```
// Do not flag implicitly typed declarations that declare more than one
variables,
// as the compiler already generates error CS0819 for those cases.
var declaration = (VariableDeclarationSyntax)syntaxNodeContext.Node;
```

```
if (!declaration.Type.IsVar || declaration.Variables.Count != 1)
{
 return;
}
```

We then perform semantic checks using the semantic model APIs to get semantic type information about the type declaration syntax node and verify it is not an error type or primitive system type:

```
// Do not flag variable declarations with error type or special System
types, such as int, char, string, and so on.
var typeInfo =
syntaxNodeContext.SemanticModel.GetTypeInfo(declaration.Type,
syntaxNodeContext.CancellationToken);
if (typeInfo.Type.TypeKind == TypeKind.Error || typeInfo.Type.SpecialType
!= SpecialType.None)
{
 return;
}
```

You can perform many powerful semantic operations on the syntax node exposed from the SyntaxNodeAnalysisContext using the public semantic model APIs, for reference see https://github.com/dotnet/roslyn/blob/master/src/Compilers/Core/Portable/Compilation/SemanticModel.cs.

If both the syntactic and semantics check succeed, then we report a diagnostic about recommending explicit type instead of var.

Creating a syntax tree analyzer to analyze the source file and report syntax issues

A syntax tree analyzer registers action callbacks to analyze the syntax/grammar for the source file and reports pure syntactic issues. For example, a missing semicolon at the end of a statement is a syntactic error, while assigning an incompatible type to a symbol with no possible type conversion is a semantic error.

In this section, we will write a syntax tree analyzer that analyzes all the statements in a source file and generates a syntax warning for any statement that is not enclosed in a block, that is curly braces { and }. For example, the following code will generate a warning for both the `if` statement and the `System.Console.WriteLine` invocation statement, but the `while` statement is not flagged:

```
void Method()
{
 while (...)
   if (...)
     System.Console.WriteLine(value);
}
```

Getting ready

You will need to have created and opened an analyzer project, say `CSharpAnalyzers` in Visual Studio 2017. Refer to the first recipe in this chapter to create this project.

How to do it...

1. In **Solution Explorer**, double-click on the `Resources.resx` file in `CSharpAnalyzers` project to open the resource file in the resource editor.
2. Replace the existing resource strings for `AnalyzerDescription`, `AnalyzerMessageFormat` and `AnalyzerTitle` with new strings.

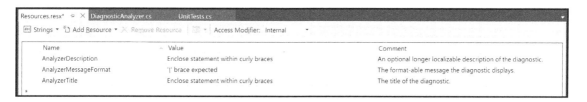

3. Replace the `Initialize` method implementation with the following:

```
public override void Initialize(AnalysisContext context)
{
   context.RegisterSyntaxTreeAction(syntaxTreeContext =>
   {
     // Iterate through all statements in the tree.
     var root =
syntaxTreeContext.Tree.GetRoot(syntaxTreeContext.CancellationTo
```

```
            ken);
            foreach (var statement in
        root.DescendantNodes().OfType<StatementSyntax>())
            {
              // Skip analyzing block statements.
              if (statement is BlockSyntax)
              {
                continue;
              }

              // Report issue for all statements that are nested
        within a statement,
              // but not a block statement.
              if (statement.Parent is StatementSyntax &&
        !(statement.Parent is BlockSyntax))
              {
                var diagnostic = Diagnostic.Create(Rule,
        statement.GetFirstToken().GetLocation());
                syntaxTreeContext.ReportDiagnostic(diagnostic);
              }
            }
          });
        }
```

4. Click on *Ctrl* + *F5* to start a new Visual Studio instance with the analyzer enabled.
5. In the new Visual Studio instance, create a new C# class library with the following code:

```
        namespace ClassLibrary
        {
          public class Class1
          {
            void Method(bool flag, int value)
            {
              while (flag)
              if (value > 0)
              System.Console.WriteLine(value);
            }
          }
        }
```

6. Verify the analyzer diagnostic is neither reported for the method block for `Method` nor the `while` statement, but is reported for the `if` statement and `System.Console.WriteLine` invocation statement:

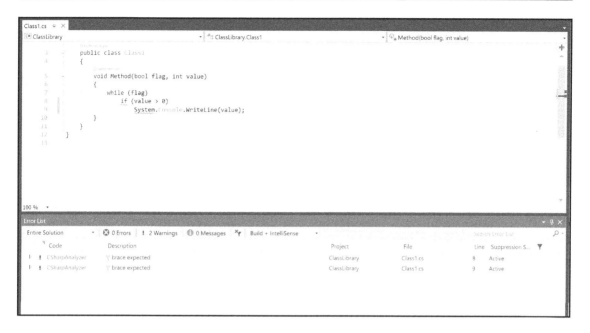

7. Now, add curly braces around the `System.Console.WriteLine` invocation statement and verify the only single warning is now reported for the `if` statement:

How it works...

Syntax tree analyzers register callbacks to analyze syntax of all source files in the compilation. Our analysis works by getting the roots of the syntax tree and then operating on all the descendant syntax nodes of the roots which are of type `StatementSyntax`. First, we note that a block statement is itself an aggregate statement, and by definition has curly braces, so we skip past these.

```
// Skip analyzing block statements.
if (statement is BlockSyntax)
{
  continue;
}
```

We then perform syntactic checks for the parent of statement syntax. If the parent of the statement is also a statement, but not a block with curly braces, then we report a diagnostic on the first syntax token of the statement recommending usage of curly braces.

```
// Report issue for all statements that are nested within a statement,
// but not a block statement.
if (statement.Parent is StatementSyntax && !(statement.Parent is BlockSyntax))
{
  var diagnostic = Diagnostic.Create(Rule,
statement.GetFirstToken().GetLocation());
  syntaxTreeContext.ReportDiagnostic(diagnostic);
}
```

`SyntaxTreeAnalysisContext` provided to syntax tree actions does not expose the semantic model for the source file, hence no semantic analysis can be performed within a syntax tree action.

Creating a method body analyzer to analyze whole method and report issues

A stateful method body or code block analyzer registers action callbacks that require whole method body analysis to report issues about the method declaration or executable code. These analyzers generally need to initialize some mutable state at the start of the analysis, which is updated while analyzing the method body, and the final state is used to report diagnostics.

Chapter 1

In this section, we will create a code block analyzer that flags unused method parameters. For example, it will not flag `param1` and `param2` as unused, but will flag `param3` and `param4`.

```
void M(int param1, ref int param2, int param3, params int[] param4)
{
 int local1 = param1;
 param2 = 0;
}
```

Getting ready

You will need to have created and opened an analyzer project, say `CSharpAnalyzers` in Visual Studio 2017. Refer to the first recipe in this chapter to create this project.

How to do it...

1. In **Solution Explorer**, double-click on `Resources.resx` file in `CSharpAnalyzers` project to open the resource file in the resource editor.
2. Replace the existing resource strings for `AnalyzerDescription`, `AnalyzerMessageFormat` and `AnalyzerTitle` with new strings.

3. Replace the `Initialize` method implementation with the code from `CSharpAnalyzers/CSharpAnalyzers/CSharpAnalyzers/DiagnosticAnalyzer.cs/` method named `Initialize`.
4. Add private class `UnusedParametersAnalyzer` from `CSharpAnalyzers/CSharpAnalyzers/CSharpAnalyzers/DiagnosticAnalyzer.cs/` type named `UnusedParametersAnalyzer` in your analyzer to perform the core method body analysis for a given method.
5. Click on *Ctrl* + *F5* to start a new Visual Studio instance with the analyzer enabled.

6. In the new Visual Studio instance, create a new C# class library with the following code:

```
namespace ClassLibrary
{
  public class Class1
  {
     void M(int param1, ref int param2, int param3, params int[] param4)
     {
        int local1 = param1;
        param2 = 0;
     }
  }
}
```

7. Verify the analyzer diagnostic is not reported for `param1` and `param2`, but is reported for `param3` and `param4`:

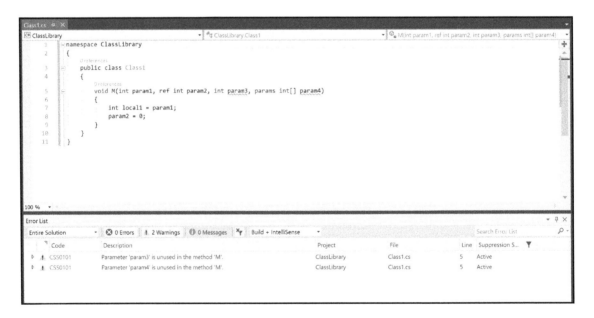

8. Now, add code to use `param3` in the local declaration statement, delete `param4`, and verify the diagnostics go away:

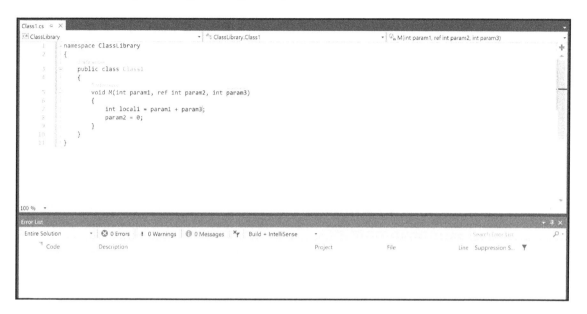

How it works…

Code block analyzers register code block actions to analyze executable code blocks in the compilation. You can register either a stateless `CodeBlockAction` or a stateful `CodeBlockStartAction` with nested actions to analyze syntax nodes within a code block. Our analyzer registers a `CodeBlockStartAction` to perform stateful analysis.

```
context.RegisterCodeBlockStartAction<SyntaxKind>(startCodeBlockContext =>
{
  ...
}
```

Analysis begins with a couple of early bail out checks: we are only interested in analyzing executable code within a method body and methods that have at least one parameter.

```
// We only care about method bodies.
if (startCodeBlockContext.OwningSymbol.Kind != SymbolKind.Method)
{
  return;
}
```

Writing Diagnostic Analyzers

```
// We only care about methods with parameters.
var method = (IMethodSymbol)startCodeBlockContext.OwningSymbol;
if (method.Parameters.IsEmpty)
{
  return;
}
```

We allocate a new `UnusedParametersAnalyzer` instance for every method to be analyzed. A constructor of this type initializes the mutable state tracked for analysis (explained later):

```
// Initialize local mutable state in the start action.
var analyzer = new UnusedParametersAnalyzer(method);
```

We then register a nested syntax node action, `UnusedParametersAnalyzer.AnalyzeSyntaxNode`, on the given code block context for the given method. We register interest in analyzing `IdentifierName` syntax nodes within the code block:

```
// Register an intermediate non-end action that accesses and modifies the
state.
startCodeBlockContext.RegisterSyntaxNodeAction(analyzer.AnalyzeSyntaxNode,
SyntaxKind.IdentifierName);
```

Finally, we register a nested `CodeBlockEndAction` to be executed on the instance of `UnusedParametersAnalyzer` at the end of the code block analysis.

```
// Register an end action to report diagnostics based on the final state.
startCodeBlockContext.RegisterCodeBlockEndAction(analyzer.CodeBlockEndActio
n);
```

Nested end actions are always guaranteed to be executed *after* all the nested non-end actions registered on the same analysis context have finished executing.

Let's now understand the working of the core `UnusedParametersAnalyzer` type to analyze a specific code block. This analyzer defines mutable state fields to track parameters (and their names) that are considered to be unused:

```
#region Per-CodeBlock mutable state
private readonly HashSet<IParameterSymbol> _unusedParameters;
private readonly HashSet<string> _unusedParameterNames;
#endregion
```

We initialize this mutable state in the constructor of the analyzer. At the start of the analysis, we filter out implicitly declared parameters and parameters with no source locations - these are never considered to be redundant. We mark the remaining parameters as unused.

```
#region State intialization
public UnusedParametersAnalyzer(IMethodSymbol method)
{
  // Initialization: Assume all parameters are unused, except for:
  //   1. Implicitly declared parameters
  //   2. Parameters with no locations (example auto-generated parameters for accessors)
  var parameters = method.Parameters.Where(p => !p.IsImplicitlyDeclared && p.Locations.Length > 0);
  _unusedParameters = new HashSet<IParameterSymbol>(parameters);
  _unusedParameterNames = new HashSet<string>(parameters.Select(p => p.Name));
}
#endregion
```

`AnalyzeSyntaxNode` has been registered as a nested syntax node action to analyze all `IdentifierName` nodes within the code block. We perform a couple of quick checks at the start of the method and bail out of analysis if (a) We have no unused parameters in our current analysis state, or (b) The identifier name doesn't match any of the unused parameter names. The latter check is done to avoid the performance hit of attempting to compute symbol info for the identifier.

```
#region Intermediate actions
public void AnalyzeSyntaxNode(SyntaxNodeAnalysisContext context)
{
  // Check if we have any pending unreferenced parameters.
  if (_unusedParameters.Count == 0)
  {
    return;
  }

  // Syntactic check to avoid invoking GetSymbolInfo for every identifier.
  var identifier = (IdentifierNameSyntax)context.Node;
  if (!_unusedParameterNames.Contains(identifier.Identifier.ValueText))
  {
    return;
  }
```

Then, we use the semantic model APIs to get semantic symbol info for the identifier name and check if it binds to one of the parameters that is currently considered unused. If so, we remove this parameter (and it's name) from the unused set.

```
    // Mark parameter as used.
    var parmeter = context.SemanticModel.GetSymbolInfo(identifier,
context.CancellationToken).Symbol as IParameterSymbol;
    if (parmeter != null && _unusedParameters.Contains(parmeter))
    {
      _unusedParameters.Remove(parmeter);
      _unusedParameterNames.Remove(parmeter.Name);
    }
  }
  #endregion
```

Finally, the registered code block end action walks through all the remaining parameters in the unused set and flags them as unused parameters.

```
    #region End action
    public void CodeBlockEndAction(CodeBlockAnalysisContext context)
    {
      // Report diagnostics for unused parameters.
      foreach (var parameter in _unusedParameters)
      {
         var diagnostic = Diagnostic.Create(Rule, parameter.Locations[0],
parameter.Name, parameter.ContainingSymbol.Name);
         context.ReportDiagnostic(diagnostic);
      }
    }
    #endregion
```

Creating a compilation analyzer to analyze whole compilation and report issues

A stateful compilation analyzer registers action callbacks that require compilation-wide analysis of symbols and/or syntax to report issues about declarations or executable code in the compilation. These analyzers generally need to initialize some mutable state at the start of the analysis, which is updated while analyzing the compilation, and the final state is used to report diagnostics.

In this section, we will create an analyzer that performs compilation-wide analysis and reports. Diagnostic secure types must not implement interfaces with insecure methods for the following scenarios:

- Assume we have an interface, say `MyNamespace.ISecureType`, which is a well-known secure interface, i.e. it is a marker for all secure types in an assembly.
- Assume we have a method attribute, say `MyNamespace.InsecureMethodAttribute`, which marks the method on which the attribute is applied as insecure. An interface which has any member with such an attribute, must be considered insecure.
- We want to report diagnostics for types implementing the well-known secure interface that also implements any insecure interfaces.

Analyzer performs compilation-wide analysis to detect such violating types and reports diagnostics for them in the compilation end action.

Getting ready

You will need to have created and opened an analyzer project, say `CSharpAnalyzers` in Visual Studio 2017. Refer to the first recipe in this chapter to create this project.

How to do it...

1. In **Solution Explorer**, double click on `Resources.resx` file in `CSharpAnalyzers` project to open the resource file in the resource editor.
2. Replace the existing resource strings for `AnalyzerDescription`, `AnalyzerMessageFormat` and `AnalyzerTitle` with new strings.

3. Replace the `Initialize` method implementation with the code from `CSharpAnalyzers/CSharpAnalyzers/CSharpAnalyzers/DiagnosticAnalyzer.cs/` method named `Initialize`.

Writing Diagnostic Analyzers

4. Add a private class `CompilationAnalyzer` from `CSharpAnalyzers/CSharpAnalyzers/CSharpAnalyzers/DiagnosticAnalyzer.cs/` type named `CompilationAnalyzer` in your analyzer to perform the core method body analysis for a given method.
5. Click on *Ctrl + F5* to start a new Visual Studio instance with the analyzer enabled.
6. In the new Visual Studio instance, enable full solution analysis for C# projects by following the steps here: https://msdn.microsoft.com/en-us/library/mt709421.aspx

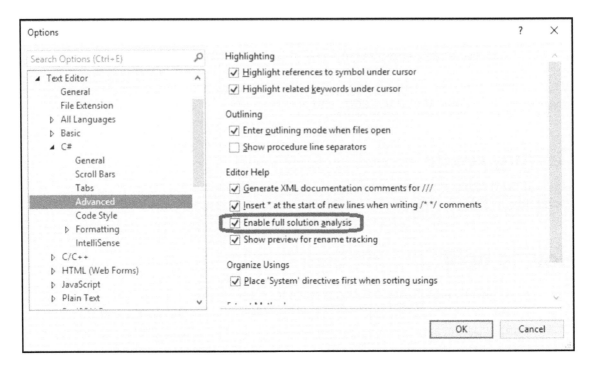

7. In the new Visual Studio instance, create a new C# class library with the following code:

```
namespace MyNamespace
{
  public class InsecureMethodAttribute : System.Attribute { }

  public interface ISecureType { }

  public interface IInsecureInterface
  {
    [InsecureMethodAttribute]
```

```
            void F();
        }

        class MyInterfaceImpl1 : IInsecureInterface
        {
            public void F() { }
        }

        class MyInterfaceImpl2 : IInsecureInterface, ISecureType
        {
            public void F() { }
        }

        class MyInterfaceImpl3 : ISecureType
        {
            public void F() { }
        }
    }
```

8. Verify the analyzer diagnostic is not reported for MyInterfaceImpl1 and MyInterfaceImpl3, but is reported for MyInterfaceImpl2:

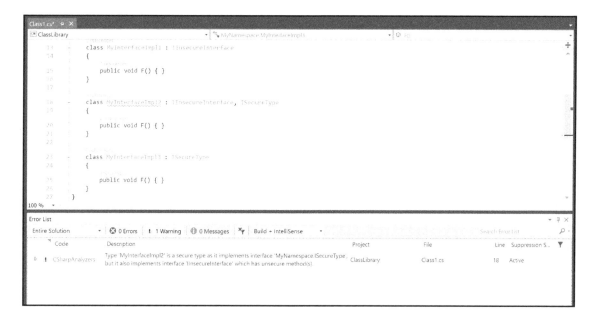

9. Now, change `MyInterfaceImpl2` so that it no longer implements `IInsecureInterface` and verify that the diagnostic is no longer reported.

```
class MyInterfaceImpl2 : ISecureType
{
  public void F() {}
}
```

How it works…

Compilation analyzers register compilation actions to analyze symbols and/or syntax nodes in the compilation. You can register either a stateless `CompilationAction` or a stateful `CompilationStartAction` with nested actions to analyze symbols and/or syntax nodes within a compilation. Our analyzer registers a `CompilationStartAction` to perform stateful analysis.

```
context.RegisterCompilationStartAction(compilationContext =>
{
  ...
}
```

Analysis begins with a couple of early bail out checks: we are only interested in analyzing compilations which have source or metadata types by name `MyNamespace.ISecureType` and `MyNamespace.InsecureMethodAttribute`.

```
 // Check if the attribute type marking insecure methods is defined.
 var insecureMethodAttributeType =
compilationContext.Compilation.GetTypeByMetadataName("MyNamespace.InsecureM
ethodAttribute");
 if (insecureMethodAttributeType == null)
 {
   return;
 }

 // Check if the interface type marking secure types is defined.
 var secureTypeInterfaceType =
compilationContext.Compilation.GetTypeByMetadataName("MyNamespace.ISecureTy
pe");
 if (secureTypeInterfaceType == null)
 {
   return;
 }
```

We allocate a new `CompilationAnalyzer` instance for compilations to be analyzed. A constructor of this type initializes the mutable and immutable state tracked for analysis (explained later).

```
// Initialize state in the start action.
var analyzer = new CompilationAnalyzer(insecureMethodAttributeType,
secureTypeInterfaceType);
```

We then register a nested symbol action, `CompilationAnalyzer.AnalyzeSymbol`, on the given compilation start context for the given compilation. We register interest in analyzing type and method symbols within the compilation.

```
// Register an intermediate non-end action that accesses and modifies the
state. compilationContext.RegisterSymbolAction(analyzer.AnalyzeSymbol,
SymbolKind.NamedType, SymbolKind.Method);
```

Finally, we register a nested `CompilationEndAction` to be executed on the instance of `CompilationAnalyzer` at the end of the compilation analysis.

```
// Register an end action to report diagnostics based on the final state.
compilationContext.RegisterCompilationEndAction(analyzer.CompilationEndActi
on);
```

Nested compilation end actions are always guaranteed to be executed *after* all the nested non-end actions registered on the same analysis context have finished executing.

Let's now understand the working of the core `CompilationAnalyzer` type to analyze a specific compilation. This analyzer defines an immutable state for type symbols corresponding to the secure interface and insecure method attribute. It also defines mutable state fields to track the set of types defined in the compilation that implement the secure interface and a set of interfaces defined in the compilation that have methods with an insecure method attribute.

```
#region Per-Compilation immutable state
 private readonly INamedTypeSymbol _insecureMethodAttributeType;
 private readonly INamedTypeSymbol _secureTypeInterfaceType;
#endregion

#region Per-Compilation mutable state
 /// <summary>
 /// List of secure types in the compilation implementing secure interface.
 /// </summary>
 private List<INamedTypeSymbol> _secureTypes;
```

```
/// <summary>
/// Set of insecure interface types in the compilation that have methods
with an insecure method attribute.
/// </summary>
private HashSet<INamedTypeSymbol> _interfacesWithInsecureMethods;
#endregion
```

At the start of the analysis, we initialize the set of secure types and interfaces with insecure methods to be empty.

```
#region State intialization
 public CompilationAnalyzer(INamedTypeSymbol insecureMethodAttributeType,
INamedTypeSymbol secureTypeInterfaceType)
{
  _insecureMethodAttributeType = insecureMethodAttributeType;
  _secureTypeInterfaceType = secureTypeInterfaceType;

  _secureTypes = null;
  _interfacesWithInsecureMethods = null;
 }
#endregion
```

`AnalyzeSymbol` is registered as a nested symbol action to analyze all types and methods within the compilation. For every type declaration in the compilation, we check whether it implements the secure interface, and if so, add it to our set of secure types. For every method declaration in the compilation, we check whether its containing type is an interface and the method has the insecure method attribute, and if so, add the containing interface type to our set of interface types with insecure methods.

```
#region Intermediate actions
public void AnalyzeSymbol(SymbolAnalysisContext context)
{
  switch (context.Symbol.Kind)
  {
    case SymbolKind.NamedType:
    // Check if the symbol implements "_secureTypeInterfaceType".
    var namedType = (INamedTypeSymbol)context.Symbol;
    if (namedType.AllInterfaces.Contains(_secureTypeInterfaceType))
    {
      _secureTypes = _secureTypes ?? new List<INamedTypeSymbol>();
      _secureTypes.Add(namedType);
    }

    break;

    case SymbolKind.Method:
    // Check if this is an interface method with
```

```
      "_insecureMethodAttributeType" attribute.
      var method = (IMethodSymbol)context.Symbol;
      if (method.ContainingType.TypeKind == TypeKind.Interface &&
method.GetAttributes().Any(a =>
a.AttributeClass.Equals(_insecureMethodAttributeType)))
      {
          _interfacesWithInsecureMethods = _interfacesWithInsecureMethods ??
new HashSet<INamedTypeSymbol>();
          _interfacesWithInsecureMethods.Add(method.ContainingType);
      }

      break;
    }
  }
  #endregion
```

Finally, the registered the compilation end action uses the final state at the end of compilation analysis to report diagnostics. Analysis in this action starts by bailing out early if we either have no secure types or no interfaces with insecure methods. Then, we walk through all secure types and all interfaces with insecure methods, and for every pair. check whether the secure type or any of its base types implements the insecure interface. If so, we report a diagnostic on the secure type.

```
      #region End action
      public void CompilationEndAction(CompilationAnalysisContext context)
      {
        if (_interfacesWithInsecureMethods == null || _secureTypes == null)
        {
          // No violating types.
          return;
        }

        // Report diagnostic for violating named types.
        foreach (var secureType in _secureTypes)
        {
          foreach (var insecureInterface in _interfacesWithInsecureMethods)
          {
            if (secureType.AllInterfaces.Contains(insecureInterface))
            {
              var diagnostic = Diagnostic.Create(Rule,
secureType.Locations[0], secureType.Name, "MyNamespace.ISecureType",
insecureInterface.Name);
              context.ReportDiagnostic(diagnostic);

              break;
            }
          }
```

Writing Diagnostic Analyzers

```
        }
    }
#endregion
```

Writing unit tests for an analyzer project

In this section, we will show you how to write and execute unit tests for an analyzer project.

Getting ready

You will need to have created and opened an analyzer project, say `CSharpAnalyzers` in Visual Studio 2017. Refer to the first recipe in this chapter to create this project.

How to do it...

1. Open UnitTests.cs in the `CSharpAnalyzers.Test` project in the **Solution Explorer** solution to view the default unit tests created for the default symbol analyzer (type names should not contain lowercase letters) for the template analyzer project.

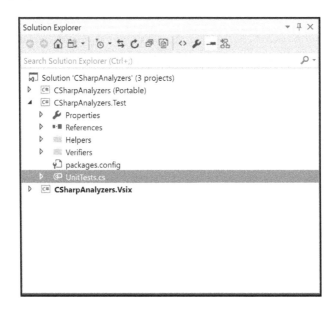

Chapter 1

2. Navigate to **Test | Windows | Test Window** to open the **Test Explorer** window to view the unit tests in the project. Default analyzer project has two unit tests:
    - `TestMethod1`: This tests the scenario where analyzer diagnostic does not fire on the test code and
    - `TestMethod2`: This tests the scenario where analyzer diagnostic does fire on the test code.

Note that the unit test project contains unit tests for both the DiagnosticAnalyzer and CodeFixProvider. This chapter deals with analyzer testing only. We will expand on the unit tests for the CodeFixProvider later in this book.

3. Run all the unit tests for the project by right-clicking **Not Run tests** node in the **Test Explorer**, executing the **Run selected tests** context menu command, and verify that the tests pass.

[47]

Writing Diagnostic Analyzers

4. Edit `TestMethod1` so that the test code now has a type with lower-case letters:

   ```
   [TestMethod]
   public void TestMethod1()
   {
     var test = @"class Class1 { }";

     VerifyCSharpDiagnostic(test);
   }
   ```

5. Right-click on `TestMethod1` in the editor, execute the **Run tests** context menu command, and verify that the test now fails with the diagnostic mismatch assert - expected `"0"` actual `"1"`:

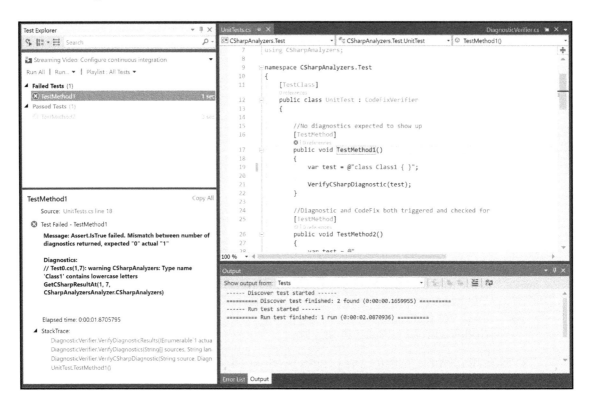

6. Edit `TestMethod1` to now add an excepted diagnostic for the new test code:

   ```
   var expected = new DiagnosticResult
   {
     Id = "CSharpAnalyzers",
     Message = String.Format("Type name '{0}' contains lowercase
   ```

```
        letters", "Class1"),
          Severity = DiagnosticSeverity.Warning,
          Locations = new[] {
            new DiagnosticResultLocation("Test0.cs", 11, 15)
          }
        };

        VerifyCSharpDiagnostic(test, expected);
```

7. Run the unit test again and note that the test still fails, but now it fails due to a difference in the location (column number) at which the diagnostic was reported.

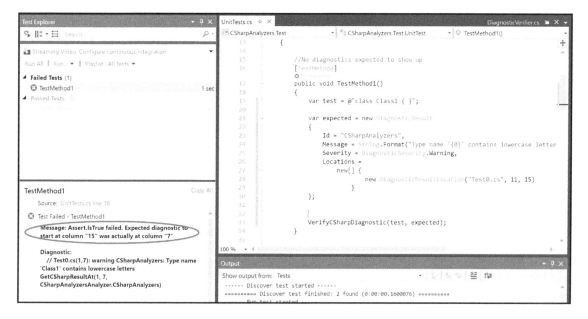

8. Edit the diagnostic location to use the correct expected column number and rerun the test - verify that the test passes now.

```
        new DiagnosticResultLocation("Test0.cs", 11, 7)
```

9. Edit `TestMethod1` and change the test code to rename `Class1` to `CLASS1`:

```
        var test = @"class CLASS1 { }";
```

Writing Diagnostic Analyzers

10. Run the unit test again and verify that the test fails now due to a diagnostic mismatch assert - `expected "1" actual "0"`.

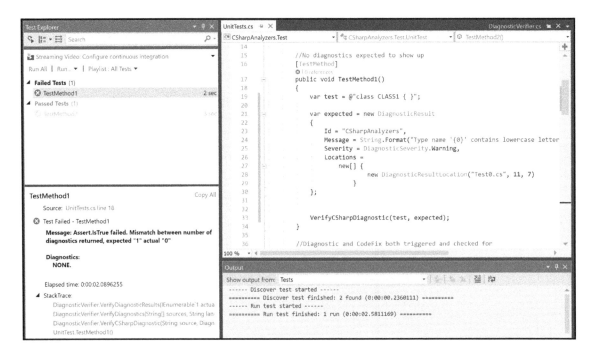

11. Edit `TestMethod1` to remove the expected diagnostic and verify the test passes:

    ```
    var test = @"class CLASS1 { }";

    VerifyCSharpDiagnostic(test);
    ```

How it works...

The analyzer unit test project allows us to write unit tests for the execution of our analyzer on different code samples. Each unit test is marked with a `TestMethod` attribute and defines sample test code, expected diagnostic(s) reported by the analyzer on that code (if any), and invocation of test helper method(s), here `VerifyCSharpDiagnostic`, to verify diagnostics.

```
//No diagnostics expected to show up
[TestMethod]
public void TestMethod1()
{
```

```
            var test = @"";

            VerifyCSharpDiagnostic(test);
        }
```

Unit tests can define expected diagnostics using the `DiagnosticResult` type, which must specify the diagnostic `Id`, `Message`, `Severity` and `Locations` for the diagnostic:

```
var expected = new DiagnosticResult
{
  Id = "CSharpAnalyzers",
  Message = String.Format("Type name '{0}' contains lowercase letters", "Class1"),
  Severity = DiagnosticSeverity.Warning,
  Locations = new[] { new DiagnosticResultLocation("Test0.cs", 11, 15) }
};

VerifyCSharpDiagnostic(test, expected);
```

Computing the correct line number and column number for an expected diagnostic, for example (11, 15), can be a bit tricky. The approach that normally works is to start with a default location of (0, 0), execute the test once, and look at the failure text in the Test Explorer window to get the expected and actual line number. Then, replace the expected line number in the test code with the actual line number. Re-execute the test and repeat the process to get the correct column number.

`UnitTest` type containing all the unit tests also overrides the following methods to return the `DiagnosticAnalyzer` (and optionally a `CodeFixProvider`) to be tested:

```
    protected override CodeFixProvider GetCSharpCodeFixProvider()
    {
       return new CSharpAnalyzersCodeFixProvider();
    }

    protected override DiagnosticAnalyzer GetCSharpDiagnosticAnalyzer()
    {
       return new CSharpAnalyzersAnalyzer();
    }
```

Writing Diagnostic Analyzers

Now, let us expand a bit more on the test framework helpers for the unit tests. The analyzer unit test project contains two primary helper abstract types to write unit tests for analyzers and code fixes:

- `DiagnosticVerifier`: Contains helper methods to run `DiagnosticAnalyzer` unit tests that verify the analyzer diagnostics for a given set of test sources.
- `CodeFixVerifier`: Contains helper methods to run `DiagnosticAnalyzer` and `CodeFixProvider` unit tests that verify the analyzer diagnostics for a given set of test sources before and after applying a code fix. This type derives from `DiagnosticVerifier`.

In the default analyzer project, `UnitTest` type derives from `CodeFixVerifier`, but could also be changed to derive from `DiagnosticVerifier`, if you are only interested in writing analyzer unit tests. We will just focus on the `DiagnosticVerifier` here; `CodeFixVerifier` is covered later in chapter.

`DiagnosticVerifier` type is split into 2 source files `DiagnosticVerifier.cs` and `DiagnosticVerifier.Helper.cs`.

- `DiagnosticVerifier.Helper.cs` contains the following core functionality:
    - Helper methods to create a compilation with source files based on given C# or VisualBasic source code (**Set up compilation and documents** region in the preceding screenshot).
    - Helper methods to invoke the preceding functionality to create a compilation with the given C# or VisualBasic source code, and execute the given `DiagnosticAnalyzer` on the compilation to produce analyzer diagnostics and return sorted diagnostics for verification (**Get Diagnostics** region in the preceding screenshot).
- `DiagnosticVerifier.cs` contains the following core functionality:
    - Method(s) to get the `DiagnosticAnalyzer` type to be tested (**To be implemented by Test classes** region in the preceding screenshot).
    - Private helpers to perform actual diagnostic comparison and verification and formatting of diagnostics to get a string representation of actual/expected diagnostics when a unit test fails (**Actual comparisons and verifications** region and **Formatting Diagnostics** region in the preceding screenshot).
    - Diagnostic verification methods `VerifyCSharpDiagnostic` and `VerifyBasicDiagnostic` that can be invoked by the unit tests to verify analyzer diagnostics generated on the given C# or Visual Basic source code (**Verifier wrappers** section in the preceding screenshot). These methods invoke the **Get Diagnostics** helpers to create a compilation and get sorted analyzer diagnostics and then invoke the preceding private helpers to compare and verify diagnostics.

See also

Live Unit testing is a new feature in *Visual Studio 2017* Enterprise Edition, which automatically runs the impacted unit tests in the background as you edit code, and visualizes the results and code coverage live, in the editor, in real-time. Refer to `Chapter 6`, *Live Unit Testing in Visual Studio Enterprise*, to enable live unit testing for the project and visualize unit tests automatically executing after you edit the code in the steps in this recipe.

Publishing NuGet package and VSIX for an analyzer project

We will show you how to configure, build, and publish a NuGet package and a VSIX package for an analyzer project created in Visual Studio 2017 using the .NET Compiler platform SDK.

Before we start digging into these topics, let's understand the difference between NuGet-based analyzer packages and VSIX-based analyzer packages. NuGet and VSIX are basically two different packaging schemes for the Microsoft development platform to package files such as assemblies, resources, build targets, tools, and so on, into a single installable package.

- NuGet is a more generic packaging scheme. NuGet packages (`.nupkg` files) can be directly referenced in .NET projects and installed to a specific project or solution using the NuGet package manager in Visual Studio. Analyzer NuGet packages based on the analyzer template project get installed as AnalyzerReferences in the project file, and then get passed onto the compiler command line to be executed during build. Additionally, AnalyzerReferences are resolved at design time by the Visual Studio IDE and executed while code editing to generate live diagnostics.
- A VSIX package is a `.vsix` file that contains one or more Visual Studio extensions, together with the metadata Visual Studio uses to classify and install the extensions. An analyzer VSIX package can be installed machine-wide or to a specific extension hive, and is enabled for all projects/solutions opened from the Visual Studio hive. Unlike a `NuGet` package, it cannot be installed specifically to a project/solution and does not travel along with the project sources.

As of Visual Studio 2017, analyzers installed as `AnalyzerReferences` via NuGet packages execute during both: command line builds and live code editing in Visual Studio. Analyzers installed via Analyzer VSIX packages execute only during live code editing in Visual Studio and not during project build. Hence, only analyzer NuGet packages can be configured to execute in continuous integration (CI) build systems and break the build.

Getting ready

You will need to have created and opened an analyzer project, say `CSharpAnalyzers` in Visual Studio 2017. Refer to the first recipe in this chapter to create this project.

How to do it…

1. Build `CSharpAnalyzers` solution in Visual Studio by executing the **Build | Build Solution** command.
2. Open the binary output folder for the `CSharpAnalyzers` project (`<%SolutionFolder%>\CSharpAnalyzers\bin\debug`) in Windows Explorer and verify that the NuGet package for the analyzer named, `CSharpAnalyzers.1.0.X.Y.nupkg`, is generated in the folder.
3. Double-click on the `Diagnostic.nuspec` file in the `CSharpAnalyzers` project in **Solution Explorer** to view and configure the properties of the nupkg.

```xml
<?xml version="1.0"?>
<package xmlns="http://schemas.microsoft.com/packaging/2011/08/nuspec.xsd">
    <metadata>
        <id>CSharpAnalyzers</id>
        <version>1.0.0.0</version>
        <title>CSharpAnalyzers</title>
        <authors>mavasani</authors>
        <owners>mavasani</owners>
        <licenseUrl>http://LICENSE_URL_HERE_OR_DELETE_THIS_LINE</licenseUrl>
        <projectUrl>http://PROJECT_URL_HERE_OR_DELETE_THIS_LINE</projectUrl>
        <iconUrl>http://ICON_URL_HERE_OR_DELETE_THIS_LINE</iconUrl>
        <requireLicenseAcceptance>false</requireLicenseAcceptance>
        <description>CSharpAnalyzers</description>
        <releaseNotes>Summary of changes made in this release of the package.</releaseNotes>
        <copyright>Copyright</copyright>
        <tags>CSharpAnalyzers, analyzers</tags>
        <frameworkAssemblies>
            <frameworkAssembly assemblyName="System" targetFramework="" />
        </frameworkAssemblies>
        <developmentDependency>true</developmentDependency>
    </metadata>
    <!-- The convention for analyzers is to put language agnostic dlls in analyzers\portable50 and language specific analyzers in eit
    <files>
        <file src="*.dll" target="analyzers\dotnet\cs" exclude="**\Microsoft.CodeAnalysis.*;**\System.Collections.Immutable.*;**\System
        <file src="tools\*.ps1" target="tools\" />
    </files>
</package>
```

4. Rebuild the project to regenerate the nupkg with new properties.
5. Publish the nupkg as a public or private package by following the steps listed here: `https://docs.microsoft.com/en-us/nuget/create-packages/publish-a-package`.

6. Open the binary output folder for the `CSharpAnalyzers.Vsix` project (`<%SolutionFolder%\CSharpAnalyzers.Vsix\bin\debug`) in Windows Explorer and verify that VSIX for the analyzer named, `CSharpAnalyzers.Vsix.vsix`, is present in the folder.
7. Double-click on the `source.extension.vsixmanifest` file in the `CSharpAnalyzers.Vsix` project in the **Solution Explorer** to view and configure the properties of the VSIX package.

8. Rebuild the VSIX project to regerate the VSIX.
9. Publish it to the Visual Studio Extension Gallery by following the steps listed here: https://msdn.microsoft.com/en-us/library/ff728613.aspx.

2
Consuming Diagnostic Analyzers in .NET Projects

In the previous chapter, we showed you how to write diagnostic analyzers to analyze and report issues about the .NET source code and contribute them to the .NET developer community. In this chapter, we will show you how to search, install, view, and configure the analyzers that have already been published by various analyzer authors on NuGet and the VS extension gallery. We will cover the following recipes:

- Searching and installing analyzers through the NuGet package manager
- Searching and installing VSIX analyzers through the VS extension gallery
- Viewing and configuring analyzers in the solution explorer in Visual Studio
- Using the ruleset file and Rule Set editor to configure analyzers

Introduction

Diagnostic analyzers are extensions to the Roslyn C# compiler and Visual Studio IDE to analyze user code and report diagnostics. The user will see these diagnostics in the error list after building the project from Visual Studio and even when building the project on the command line. They will also see the diagnostics live while editing the source code in the Visual Studio IDE. Analyzers can report diagnostics to enforce specific code styles, improve code quality and maintenance, recommend design guidelines, or even report very domain-specific issues, which cannot be covered by the core compiler.

Analyzers can be installed in a .NET project either as a NuGet package or as a VSIX. To get a better understanding of these packaging schemes and learn about the differences in the analyzer experience when installed as a NuGet package versus a VSIX, it is recommended that you read the introduction part of the recipe *Publishing NuGet package and VSIX for an analyzer project* in `Chapter 1`, *Writing Diagnostic Analyzers*.

Analyzers are supported on various different flavors of .NET Standard, .NET Core, and .NET Framework projects, for example, class library, console app, and so on.

Searching and installing analyzers through the NuGet package manager

In this recipe, we will show you how to search and install analyzer NuGet packages in the NuGet package manager in Visual Studio, and see the analyzer diagnostics from an installed NuGet package shown in project build and as live diagnostics during code editing in Visual Studio.

Getting ready

You will need to have Visual Studio 2017 installed on your machine for this recipe. You can install a free community version of Visual Studio 2017 from `https://www.visualstudio.com/thank-you-downloading-visual-studio/?sku=Community&rel=15`.

How to do it…

1. Create a C# class library project, say `ClassLibrary`, in Visual Studio 2017.
2. In solution explorer, right-click on the solution or project node and execute the **Manage NuGet Packages** command:

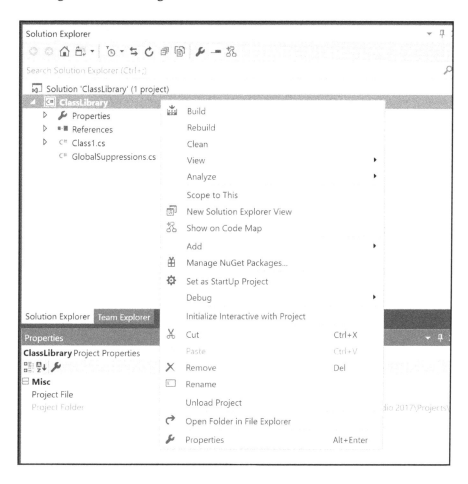

3. This brings up the **NuGet Package Manager**, which can be used to search and install NuGet packages to the solution or project:

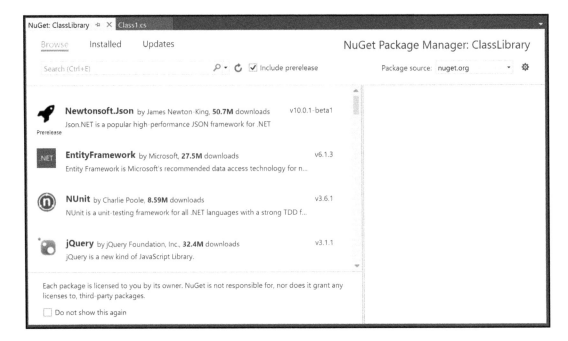

4. In the search bar, type the following text to find NuGet packages tagged as analyzers : `Tags:"analyzers"`.

> Note that some of the well-known packages are tagged as `analyzer`, so you may also want to search for `Tags:"analyzer"`.

5. Check or uncheck the **Include prerelease** checkbox to the right of the search bar to search or hide the pre-release analyzer packages, respectively. The packages are listed based on the number of downloads, with the highest downloaded package at the top:

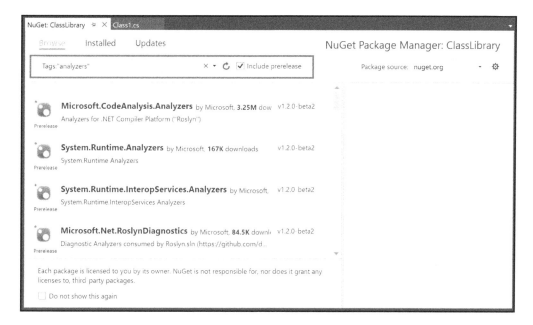

Consuming Diagnostic Analyzers in .NET Projects

6. Select a package to install, say System.Runtime.Analyzers, and pick a specific version, say *1.1.0*, and click on **Install:**

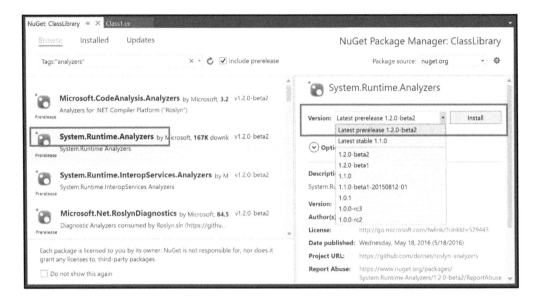

7. Click on the **I Accept** button on the **License Acceptance** dialog to install the NuGet package.

8. Verify the installed analyzer(s) that shows up under the **Analyzers** node in the solution explorer:

9. Verify that the project file has a new `ItemGroup` with the following analyzer references from the installed analyzer package:

```
<ItemGroup>
 <Analyzer
Include="..\packages\System.Runtime.Analyzers.1.1.0\analyzers\d
otnet\cs\System.Runtime.Analyzers.dll" />
 <Analyzer
Include="..\packages\System.Runtime.Analyzers.1.1.0\analyzers\d
otnet\cs\System.Runtime.CSharp.Analyzers.dll" />
 </ItemGroup>
```

10. Add the following code to your C# project:

```
namespace ClassLibrary
{
    public class MyAttribute : System.Attribute
    {
    }
}
```

11. Verify the analyzer diagnostic from the installed analyzer that is shown in the error list:

12. Open **Developer Command Prompt for VS 2017** and build the project to verify that the analyzer is executed on the command-line build and that the analyzer diagnostic is reported:

13. Create a new C# project in VS 2017 and add the same code to it as step 10. Verify that no analyzer diagnostic shows up in the error list or command line, confirming that the analyzer package was only installed to the selected project in steps 1-6.

> Note that **CA1018** (*the custom attribute should have AttributeUsage defined*) has been moved to a separate analyzer assembly in future versions of the FxCop/System.Runtime.Analyzers package. It is recommended that you install the Microsoft.CodeAnalysis.FxCopAnalyzers NuGet package from (https://www.nuget.org/packages/Microsoft.CodeAnalysis.FxCopAnalyzers)to get the latest group of Microsoft-recommended analyzers.

Searching and installing VSIX analyzers through the VS extension gallery

In this recipe, we will show you how to search and install analyzer VSIX packages in the Visual Studio extension manager and see how the analyzer diagnostics from an installed VSIX light up as live diagnostics during code editing in Visual Studio.

Getting ready

You will need to have Visual Studio 2017 installed on your machine to follow this recipe. You can install a free community version of Visual Studio 2017 from `https://www.visualstudio.com/thank-you-downloading-visual-studio/?sku=Community&rel=15`.

How to do it...

1. Create a C# class library project, say `ClassLibrary`, in Visual Studio 2017.
2. From the top-level menu, navigate to **Tools | Extensions and Updates.**
3. Navigate to **Online | Visual Studio Marketplace** on the left tab of the dialog to view the available VSIXes in the Visual Studio extension gallery/marketplace:

4. Search `analyzers` in the search textbox in the upper-right corner of the dialog and download an analyzer VSIX, say `Refactoring Essentials for Visual Studio`:

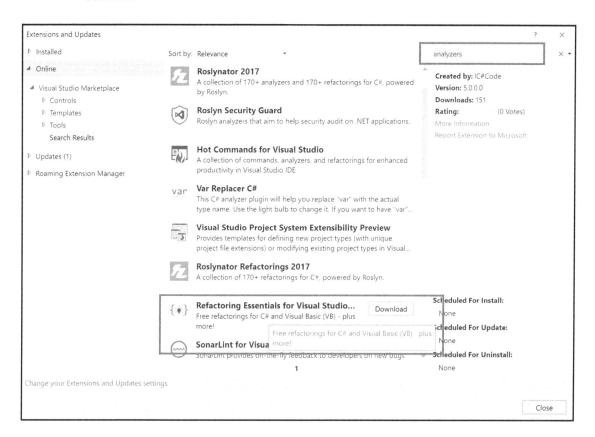

Consuming Diagnostic Analyzers in .NET Projects

5. Once the download completes, you will get a message at the bottom of the dialog saying that the install will be scheduled to execute once Visual Studio and related windows are closed:

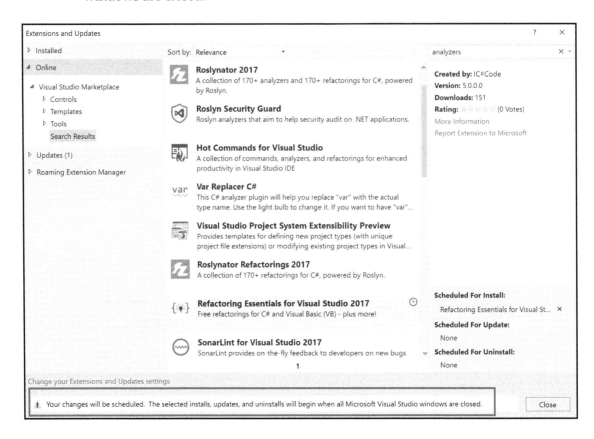

6. Close the dialog and then close the Visual Studio instance to start the install.
7. In the **VSIX Installer** dialog, click on **Modify** to start installation:

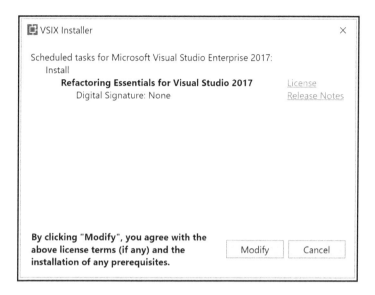

8. The subsequent message prompts you to kill all the active Visual Studio and satellite processes. Save all your relevant work in all the open Visual Studio instances and click on **End Tasks** to kill these processes and install the VSIX:

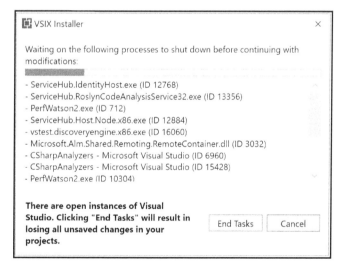

9. After installation, restart VS, click on **Tools | Extensions And Updates**, and verify that `Refactoring Essentials VSIX` is installed:

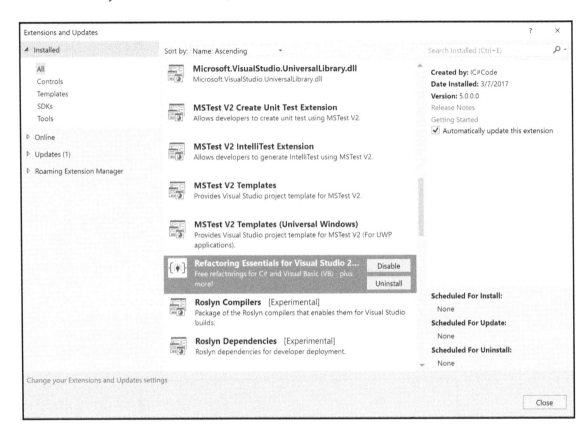

10. Create a new C# project with the following source code and verify analyzer diagnostic *RECS0085* (*Redundant array creation expression*) in the error list:

```
namespace ClassLibrary
{
  public class Class1
  {
    void Method()
    {
      int[] values = new int[] { 1, 2, 3 };
    }
  }
}
```

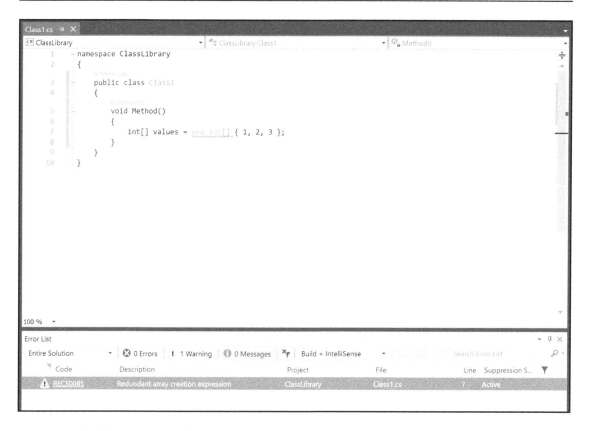

11. Build the project from Visual Studio 2017 or the command line and confirm that no analyzer diagnostic shows up in the output window or the command line, respectively, confirming that the VSIX analyzer did not execute as a part of the build.

Viewing and configuring analyzers in solution explorer in Visual Studio

In this recipe, we will show you how to use the Solution explorer in Visual Studio 2017 to view the different analyzers installed in a project, view the implemented analyzer rules in these assemblies, as well as the rule properties (or the descriptor metadata), and configure the rule severity and persist the new severity settings.

Getting ready

You will need to have created and opened a .NET project in Visual Studio 2017 with NuGet-based analyzers installed in the project. Refer to the first recipe in this chapter for installing analyzers in a .NET project.

How to do it...

1. Open a C# project, say `ClassLibrary`, with the analyzer NuGet package `System.Runtime.Analyzers.nupkg` pre-release version *1.2.0-beta2* installed in it.
2. In the solution explorer, expand **References** | **Analyzers** nodes to view the analyzer assemblies installed through the analyzer NuGet package(s). We should see two analyzer assemblies, `System.Runtime.Analyzers` and `System.Runtime.CSharp.Analyzers`:

3. Expand the **System.Runtime.Analyzers** node to view all the *CAXXXX* rules implemented in the assembly and click on a specific rule, say **CA1813: Avoid unsealed attributes**, to view the rule properties, such as **ID**, **Message**, **Title**, **Description**, **Category**, **Effective severity**, **Enabled by default,** and so on, in the **Properties Window:**

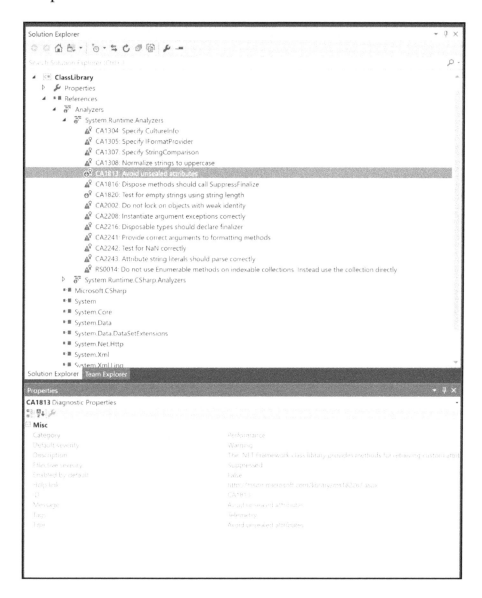

4. Note that the *CA1813* rule's **Enabled by default** is **False**, which means that the rule is turned off by default. We can confirm this by adding the following source code that violates this rule because we declared a public unsealed attribute, but *CA1813* is not reported for the violation:

   ```
   using System;
   
   namespace ClassLibrary
   {
       [AttributeUsage(AttributeTargets.All)]
       public class MyAttribute: Attribute
       {
       }
   }
   ```

5. Right-click on the rule node, click on **Set Rule Set Severity**, and change the severity from **Default** to **Warning**:

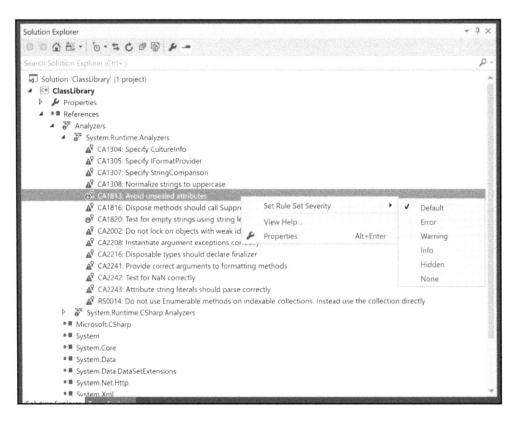

6. Confirm that *CA1813* is now reported for the preceding code:

```
Class1.cs
C# ClassLibrary                                          ClassLibrary.MyAttribute
    1     using System;
    2
    3   ┌ namespace ClassLibrary
    4   │ {
    5   │     [AttributeUsage(AttributeTargets.All)]
    6   │     public class MyAttribute: Attribute
    7   │     {                    class ClassLibrary.MyAttribute
    8   │     }
    9   │ }                        Avoid unsealed attributes

                                   ▼  Show potential fixes (Alt+Enter or Ctrl+.)
```

7. Save the current project and then close and re-open the solution.
8. Verify that the warning CA1813 still shows up for the preceding source code, confirming that the rule set severity change was persisted for the project.

How it works…

The analyzers node in solution explorer gives a visual representation of the analyzer items defined in the project file, which correspond to analyzer assemblies added manually to the project or added via analyzer NuGet package(s). The rules in the assembly come from each type in the assembly that implements the `DiagnosticAnalyzer` type and has a `DiagnosticAnalyzerAttribute` applied to it. The rule properties shown in the properties window come from instantiating the analyzer types and requesting them for it's `SupportedDiagnostics`.

Changing the rule severity in solution explorer and then persisting it for the project happens through an automatically generated ruleset file, which gets added to the project. Refer to the next recipe to get more details on ruleset-based analyzer configuration.

Using the ruleset file and Rule Set editor to configure analyzers

In this recipe, we will show you how to use the `ruleset` file and the Rule Set editor in Visual Studio to configure the per-project severity of analyzer rules, and illustrate how the severity changes are reflected in the live diagnostics in Visual Studio, as well as command-line builds.

Getting ready

You will need to have created and opened a .NET project in Visual Studio 2017 with NuGet-based analyzers installed in the project. Refer to the first recipe in this chapter for installing analyzers in a .NET project.

How to do it...

1. Open a C# project, say `ClassLibrary`, with the analyzer NuGet package `System.Runtime.Analyzers.nupkg` prerelease version *1.2.0-beta2* installed in it.
2. Add the following source code to the project and verify that no **CA1813: Avoid unsealed attributes** is fired:

   ```
   using System;

   namespace ClassLibrary
   {
     [AttributeUsage(AttributeTargets.All)]
     public class MyAttribute: Attribute
     {
     }
   }
   ```

Chapter 2

3. In the solution explorer, navigate to **ClassLibary** | **References** | **Analyzers**, right-click on the **Analyzers** node and execute the context menu command **Open Active Rule Set**:

4. In the Rule Set editor, search *CA1813* in the textbox in the top-right corner.
5. For the *CA1813*, search the result listed under **System.Runtime.Analyzers**, change the **Action** from **None** to **Warning**, and hit save:

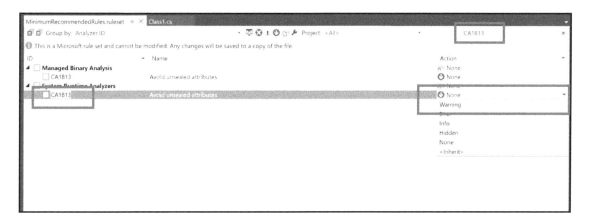

6. We should now see a *CA1813* warning being reported on our attribute definition in the source code.
7. In the solution explorer, verify that the project now contains that a new `ClassLibrary.ruleset` item, and a new `CodeAnalysisRuleset` property was added to the project file:

*<CodeAnalysisRuleSet>***ClassLibrary.ruleset***</CodeAnalysisRuleSet>*

[77]

8. Open `ClassLibrary.ruleset` in a text editor outside of Visual Studio and verify that it has the following rule action specification for *CA1813*:

    ```
    <Rules AnalyzerId="System.Runtime.Analyzers"
    RuleNamespace="System.Runtime.Analyzers">
        <Rule Id="CA1813" Action="Warning" />
    </Rules>
    ```

9. Edit the ruleset file to change the `ruleset` **Action** for *CA1813* from **Warning** to **Error** and save the file.
10. Switch back to Visual Studio and confirm that the source code editor now shows a red squiggle and that the error list also reports an error for *CA1813*:

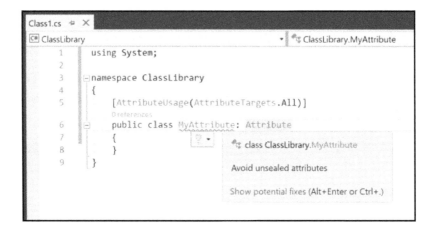

11. Double-click on *ClassLibrary.ruleset* in the solution explorer to open it with the Rule Set editor and verify that the rule severity entry for *CA1813* is now showing as **Error**.
12. Build the project and verify that the error *CA1813* is reported, confirming that the `ruleset` setting is preserved for command-line builds as well.

How it works…

The `ruleset` file is essentially a grouping of a set of code-analysis rules that you can apply to a project to configure it's analysis. It is specified in an XML format and is based on an XML schema that ships with Visual Studio. It is also open sourced, and can be found at https://github.com/dotnet/roslyn/blob/version-2.0.0/src/Compilers/Core/Portable/RuleSet/RuleSetSchema.xsd. A `ruleset` can be specified for a project using the `CodeAnalysisRuleset` property in the project file. Each **Rules** node contains a collection of rule specifications with a common analyzer ID and namespace. Each **Rule** specification has the rule **ID** and the effective **Action** or the severity. The rule Action can take one of the following five values: **None** (suppressed), **Hidden** (non-visible in the IDE, primarily a code fix trigger), **Info** (informational message), **Warning,** and **Error**. These rule actions get converted into compilation options for the compiler and override the default severity of the diagnostic ID.

The Rule Set editor is a powerful graphical user interface to search, filter, and bulk-edit rule configurations.

Refer to https://msdn.microsoft.com/en-us/library/dd264996.aspx for a more detailed walk through, and for documentation for `ruleset` file schema and the Rule Set editor in Visual Studio.

There's more…

In Visual Studio 2017, built-in IDE analyzers for coding style rules can also be configured via the new *.editorconfig* format, which applies rule configurations at folder level. See the documentation at (https://docs.microsoft.com/en-us/visualstudio/ide/editorconfig-code-style-settings-reference) for further details.

3
Writing IDE Code Fixes, Refactorings, and Intellisense Completion Providers

In this chapter, we will cover the following recipes:

- Creating, debugging, and executing a `CodeFixProvider` to fix a compiler warning
- Applying batch code fixes (FixAll) across different scopes: document, project, and solution
- Creating a custom `FixAllProvider` to fix all occurrences of an issue across a scope
- Creating a `CodeRefactoringProvider` to refactor source code to recommend using C# 7.0 tuples
- Creating a `CompletionProvider` to provide additional intellisense items while editing code
- Writing unit tests for a `CodeFixProvider`

Introduction

Code fix providers and code refactoring providers are extensions to the Visual Studio IDE to edit the user source code to fix issues and refactor it without introducing functional changes respectively. Users see a light bulb in the code editor to invoke the code action (fix/refactoring) to automatically edit their code. Additionally, code fixes can provide FixAll support, which allows fixing multiple similar issues across a document, project, or solution with a single code action.

Completion providers are extensions to the Visual Studio IDE to show additional completion items in the intellisense completion list when a user is editing source code, and to auto-generate code when a user commits a specific completion item.

This chapter enables C# developers to write, debug, execute, and test these IDE extensions.

Creating, debugging, and executing a CodeFixProvider to fix a compiler warning

Code fix providers are IDE extensions to fix diagnostics in source code, which are reported by compilers and/or analyzers. These are built on top of Roslyn's Workspaces layer and operate on the current document being edited. When the user invokes a command such as *Ctrl* + dot in Visual Studio editor, the IDE code fix engine computes all the diagnostics in the current line span and identifies all the code fix providers that have registered to fix one or more of the reported diagnostics. Each of these code fix providers are then invoked with a code fix context containing the current document, diagnostics, and span. Fixers operate on the underlying syntax tree associated with the document by adding, removing, or editing the syntax nodes within the tree, and returning the new document with the fixed code. They might also alter the contents of the containing project or solution to fix the diagnostic. When the user commits the fix by pressing the *Enter* key, the code fix engine applies this code fix to the user code.

In this section, we will write a `CodeFixProvider` to fix the compiler warning *CS0219* (https://docs.microsoft.com/en-us/dotnet/csharp/misc/cs0219) (the variable `variable` is assigned but its value is never used). For example, the following code sample contains two unused variables `a` and `b` and the code fix will remove the local declaration statement with unused variable `a` and remove the declaration `b = 1` in the next declaration statement:

```
public class MyClass
{
    public static void Main()
    {
        int a = 0;     // CS0219 for 'a'
        int b = 1, c = 2; // CS0219 for 'b'
        System.Console.WriteLine(c);
    }
}
```

Getting ready

You will need to have Visual Studio 2017 installed on your machine to execute the recipes in this chapter. You can install a free community version of Visual Studio 2017 from https://www.visualstudio.com/thank-you-downloading-visual-studio/?sku=Community&rel=15.

Additionally, you can refer to the recipe, *Creating, debugging, and executing an analyzer project in Visual Studio,* from `Chapter 1`, *Writing Diagnostic Analyzers,* to install the analyzer + code fix project templates and create a default project from the template, say `CSharpAnalyzers`.

How to do it...

1. Open `CSharpAnalyzers.sln` in Visual Studio and open source file `CodeFixProvider.cs` in the project `CSharpAnalyzers`.
2. Change the `title` of the code fix provider from `"Make Uppercase"` to `"Remove unused local"` and change **FixableDiagnosticIds** property to return `"CS0219"` instead of `CSharpAnalyzersAnalyzer.DiagnosticId`:

```
using Microsoft.CodeAnalysis.CodeActions;
using Microsoft.CodeAnalysis.CSharp;
using Microsoft.CodeAnalysis.CSharp.Syntax;
using Microsoft.CodeAnalysis.Rename;
using Microsoft.CodeAnalysis.Text;

namespace CSharpAnalyzers
{
    [ExportCodeFixProvider(LanguageNames.CSharp, Name = nameof(CSharpAnalyzersCodeFixProvider)), Shared]
    public class CSharpAnalyzersCodeFixProvider : CodeFixProvider
    {
        private const string title = "Remove unused local";

        public sealed override ImmutableArray<string> FixableDiagnosticIds
        {
            get { return ImmutableArray.Create("CS0219"); }
        }

        public sealed override FixAllProvider GetFixAllProvider()
        {
            // See https://github.com/dotnet/roslyn/blob/master/docs/analyzers/FixAllProvider.md for more informat
            return WellKnownFixAllProviders.BatchFixer;
        }
```

3. Replace the implementation of the `RegisterCodeFixesAsync` method with the code from `CSharpAnalyzers/CSharpAnalyzers/CSharpAnalyzers/CodeFixProvider.cs/Method` named `RegisterCodeFixesAsync`.
4. Add the helper methods `GetSyntaxNodeToRemoveAsync` and `RemoveDeclarationAsync` to the source file with the code from `CSharpAnalyzers/CSharpAnalyzers/CSharpAnalyzers/CodeFixProvider.cs`.

5. Set breakpoints at the first line of the newly added methods `RegisterCodeFixesAsync` and `RemoveDeclarationAsync`.
6. Set `CSharpAnalyzers.Vsix` as the startup project and press *F5* to start a new VS instance with the code fix provider enabled.
7. In the new VS instance, create a new C# class library project, say `ClassLibrary`, and replace the existing code with the following:

```
public class Class1
{
  public void Method1()
  {
    // Local declaration statement with unused local ('a')
    int a = 0;

    // Local declaration statement with a used ('c') and ununused local ('b').
    int b = 1, c = 2;
    System.Console.WriteLine(c);

    // Local declaration statement where unused local ('d') initializer is non-constant.
    int d = c;

    // Local declaration statement with errors ('e').
    if (true)
      var e = 1;
  }
}
```

8. Put the cursor on the line `int a = 0;` and verify the breakpoint in `RegisterCodeFixesAsync` is hit. Remove this breakpoint and then you can either step through the method with *F10* or hit *F5* to continue execution.

Writing IDE Code Fixes, Refactorings, and Intellisense Completion Providers

9. Verify that the light bulb shows up with a hyperlink to `Show potential fixes` under the source line:

![Screenshot showing Class1.cs with light bulb tooltip displaying "The variable 'a' is assigned but its value is never used" and "Show potential fixes (Alt+Enter or Ctrl+.)"]

10. Click on the light bulb and verify the breakpoint in `RemoveDeclarationAsync` is hit. Remove this breakpoint and then you can either step through the method with *F10* or hit *F5* to continue execution.

11. Click on the light bulb again and verify the **Remove unused local** code fix is offered with a preview of code change by the fix:

![Screenshot showing the Remove unused local code fix preview with CS0219 warning and Preview changes / Fix all occurrences options]

[86]

12. Hit enter to apply the code fix and verify that the unused local declaration statement is removed.
13. Move the cursor to unused local `b` and press keys *Ctrl* + dot and verify the same code fix is offered, and applying the fix removes the declaration `b = 1`, but retains the local declaration for `c`:

```
 3         public void Method1()
 4         {
 5
 6             // Local declaration statement with a used ('c') and ununused local ('b').
 7             int b = 1, c = 2;
 8
   Remove unused local      ! CS0219 The variable 'b' is assigned but its value is never
10 Suppress CS0219                                                        zer is non-constant.
11             int d    statement with a used ('c') and ununused local ('b').
                     = int b = 1, c = 2;
12                     int c = 2;
13             // Loca System.Console.WriteLine(c);
14             if (tru ...
15                 var  Preview changes
16         }
17     }         Fix all occurrences in: Document | Project | Solution
```

14. Verify that no code fixes are offered for a local `d` with a non-constant initializer and local `e` with a different compiler error.

How it works…

Code fix providers are VS IDE extensions that can register code actions for fixing compiler or analyzer diagnostics of specified diagnostic IDs. The primary APIs on `CodeFixProvider` are:

- `FixableDiagnosticIds` property (abstract): An immutable array of diagnostics IDs that the code fix provider can fix. Any compiler or analyzer diagnostic that is reported with one of the specified diagnostic IDs is a candidate for a code fix from the provider, and `RegisterCodeFixesAsync` is called with each such diagnostic.

- `RegisterCodeFixesAsync` method (abstract): This is the method to register code actions for fixable diagnostics. This method is invoked by the code fix engine whenever it needs to compute the code actions for diagnostics reported on a current source line in the VS IDE. This method takes a `CodeFixContext` argument, which contains a set of one or more diagnostics to be fixed for a given diagnostic span and document. All the diagnostics in the context have a fixable diagnostic ID. The `CodeFixProvider` can map the diagnostic span to the syntax node in the document and analyze it to register one or more code actions to fix one or more diagnostics in the context. `CodeAction` contains the following primary members:
  - `Title` property: This is the string that shows up with the light bulb when the code fix is offered.
  - `Callback` method: This is the delegate to be called back when the user applies a registered code action. This method returns the changed document or solution and the code fix engine applies the changes to the workspace.
  - `EquivalenceKey` property: This is the string representing the equivalence class of code actions that this code action belongs to. If the code fix provider supports `FixAllProvider`, then a FixAll code fix batches all code actions in the equivalence class of the invoked code action and fixes all of them simultaneously.
  - `GetFixAllProviderAsync` method (virtual): Code fix providers can optionally override this method and return a non-null `FixAllProvider` if they want FixAll support for their code actions. We will discuss this in more detail in the next recipe.

`CodeFixProvider` implemented in this recipe has a single fixable diagnostic ID: CS0219, a compiler diagnostic flagging unused local variable declarations. Let's expand on the implementation details of `RegisterCodeFixesAsync` override and its helpers.

The first part of `RegisterCodeFixesAsync` computes a syntax node to remove for the variable that was flagged by invoking `GetNodeToRemoveAsync`, and bails out if we get a null node:

```
public sealed override async Task RegisterCodeFixesAsync(CodeFixContext context)
{
    var diagnostic = context.Diagnostics.First();

    // Get syntax node to remove for the unused local.
    var nodeToRemove = await GetNodeToRemoveAsync(context.Document,
```

```
     diagnostic, context.CancellationToken).ConfigureAwait(false);
       if (nodeToRemove == null)
       {
         return;
       }
```

The initial part of `GetNodeToRemoveAsync` computes the syntax node that was flagged by the diagnostic:

```
  private async Task<SyntaxNode> GetNodeToRemoveAsync(Document document,
  Diagnostic diagnostic, CancellationToken cancellationToken)
  {
    var root = await
  document.GetSyntaxRootAsync(cancellationToken).ConfigureAwait(false);
    var diagnosticSpan = diagnostic.Location.SourceSpan;

    // Find the variable declarator identified by the diagnostic.
    var variableDeclarator =
  root.FindToken(diagnosticSpan.Start).Parent.AncestorsAndSelf().OfType<Varia
  bleDeclaratorSyntax>().First();
```

We first get the syntax root of the document being fixed. We then find the syntax token in the root at the start of the diagnostic span and find the first ancestor node of type `VariableDeclaratorSyntax`. For example, consider the following local declaration statement:

```
  int b = 1, c = 2;
```

The entire statement is a `LocalDeclarationStatementSyntax` node. It has a child syntax node `VariableDeclarationSyntax`, which represents `int b = 1, c = 2`, and the syntax token for the semicolon. The variable declaration syntax node contains two variable declarator nodes, each of type `VariableDeclaratorSyntax`, and text `b = 1` and `c = 2`, respectively. The `VariableDeclaratorSyntax` node contains a token for the `IdentifierName` and a syntax node for the initializer of type `EqualsValueClauseSyntax`. `CS0219` is reported on the `IdentifierName` token for the unused variable declarator.

Writing IDE Code Fixes, Refactorings, and Intellisense Completion Providers

 Use the Roslyn `SyntaxVisualizer` to understand the parsed syntax node/tokens for a given C# or VB source code:

The next part of `GetNodeToRemoveAsync` implements certain defensive checks to bail out early without registering any code action as shown in the following code snippet:

```
    if (variableDeclarator == null)
    {
      return null;
    }

    // Bail out if the initializer is non-constant (could have side effects if removed).
    if (variableDeclarator.Initializer != null)
    {
      var semanticModel = await document.GetSemanticModelAsync(cancellationToken).ConfigureAwait(false);
      if (!semanticModel.GetConstantValue(variableDeclarator.Initializer.Value).HasValue)
      {
        return null;
      }
    }

    // Bail out for code with syntax errors - parent of a declaration is not a local declaration statement.
    var variableDeclaration = variableDeclarator.Parent as VariableDeclarationSyntax;
```

```
    var localDeclaration = variableDeclaration?.Parent as
  LocalDeclarationStatementSyntax;
    if (localDeclaration == null)
    {
     return null;
    }
```

We first bail out if the diagnostic was reported on a token which does not have a `VariableDeclaratorSyntax` ancestor. We also bail out if the variable initializer is a non-constant, as removing it with the code fix can cause functional change by not executing the initializer code. Finally, we check if the variable declarator has a `VariableDeclarationSyntax` parent, which has a `LocalDeclarationStatementSyntax` parent.

Defensive checks in the code fix provider are very important checks to protect us against an unexpected third-party analyzer reporting diagnostic with same diagnostic ID, but on a different syntax node kind to what our fixer expects. We should ensure that we gracefully bail out instead of crashing unexpectedly or registering an incorrect code fix.

Finally, the method computes and returns the syntax node to be removed by the code fix:

```
    // If the statement declares a single variable, the code fix should
  remove the whole statement.
    // Otherwise, the code fix should remove only this variable declaration.
    SyntaxNode nodeToRemove;
    if (variableDeclaration.Variables.Count == 1)
    {
     if (!(localDeclaration.Parent is BlockSyntax))
     {
      // Bail out for error case where local declaration is not embedded in a
  block.
      // Compiler generates errors CS1023 (Embedded statement cannot be a
  declaration or labeled statement)
       return null;
     }

     nodeToRemove = localDeclaration;
    }
    else
    {
     nodeToRemove = variableDeclarator;
    }

    return nodeToRemove;
    }
```

Writing IDE Code Fixes, Refactorings, and Intellisense Completion Providers

We have two cases to cover:

- If the local declaration statement declares only a single variable, then we can remove the entire statement. We also cover an additional bail out case where a local declaration is not parented by a block statement, in which case, removing the local declaration statement will cause a syntax error. Given that the compiler already reports a diagnostic *CS1023* (embedded statement cannot be a declaration or labeled statement) for this case, we just bail out.
- Otherwise, if the local declaration statement declares multiple variables, we can remove just the variable declarator.

Once we have a non-null syntax node to remove, we register a code fix to remove the declaration node:

```
    // Register a code action that will invoke the fix.
    var root = await
context.Document.GetSyntaxRootAsync(context.CancellationToken).ConfigureAwait(false);
    context.RegisterCodeFix(
      CodeAction.Create(
        title: title,
        createChangedDocument: c => RemoveDeclarationAsync(context.Document, root, nodeToRemove, c),
        equivalenceKey: title),
      diagnostic);
  }
```

We create a standard CodeAction, using the `CodeAction.Create` API, with the title `Remove unused local`, and use the same equivalance key. We register `RemoveDeclarationAsync` as the callback method to be invoked when the user applies the code fix:

```
    private Task<Document> RemoveDeclarationAsync(Document document,
    SyntaxNode root, SyntaxNode declaration, CancellationToken
    cancellationToken)
    {
      var syntaxGenerator = SyntaxGenerator.GetGenerator(document);
      var newRoot = syntaxGenerator.RemoveNode(root, declaration);
      return Task.FromResult(document.WithSyntaxRoot(newRoot));
    }
```

This method uses the `SyntaxGenerator` helper utility to remove the declaration node from the original syntax root and returns the new document created with the new syntax root.

`SyntaxGenerator` is a powerful syntax factory with APIs to add, remove, or edit syntax nodes in a language agnostic way. It works for both VB and C# syntax nodes, and enables writing code fix providers that fix issues across both languages, without requiring language-specific implementations. See http://source.roslyn.io/#q=SyntaxGenerator for `SyntaxGenerator` reference source.

Applying batch code fixes (FixAll) across different scopes: document, project, and solution

In this section, you will learn how to apply batch code fixes to fix multiple instances of similar diagnostics across different scopes. We will apply the FixAll code fix for the **Make uppercase** code fix in the default analyzer + code fix template project and fix multiple type names across the document, project, and solution scopes so they all contain upper case letters only. We will show you how to invoke a FixAll code fix from the editor light bulb, and then use the FixAll preview changes dialog to selectively choose the fixes to apply to your solution.

Getting ready

You will need to have Visual Studio 2017 installed on your machine to execute the recipes in this chapter. You can install a free community version of Visual Studio 2017 from https://www.visualstudio.com/thank-you-downloading-visual-studio/?sku=Community&rel=15.

Additionally, you should execute the recipe *Creating, debugging, and executing an analyzer project in Visual Studio*, from the first `chapter 1`, *Writing Diagnostic Analyzers* to install the Analyzer + Code fix project templates and create a default project from the template, say `CSharpAnalyzers`.

How to do it…

1. Open `CSharpAnalyzers.sln` in Visual Studio. Set `CSharpAnalyzers.Vsix` as the start-up project and press *F5* to start a new VS instance with the code fix provider enabled.
2. In the new VS instance, create a new C# class library project, say `ClassLibrary`, and replace the existing code with the following:

   ```
   public class Class1
   {
    public class Class2
    {
    }
   }

   public class Class3
   {
   }
   ```

3. Add a new source file, say `Class4.cs`, to the project with the following code:

   ```
   public class Class4
   {
   }
   ```

4. Add a new C# class library project to the solution, say `ClassLibrary2.csproj`, rename the source file to `Class5.cs`, and replace its source with the following:

   ```
   public class Class5
   {
   }
   ```

5. Verify five diagnostics in the error list, one for each class: Type name 'XXX' contains lower case letters.
6. Place the cursor on `Class1`, and hit *Ctrl* + dot to bring up the light bulb for code fix **Make uppercase**.

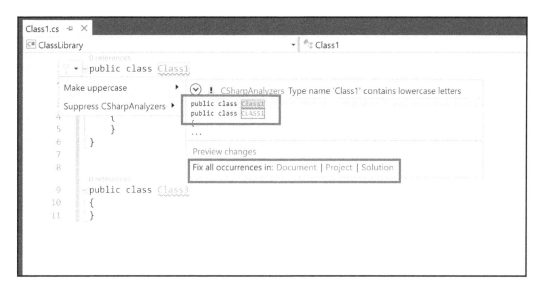

7. Click on the hyperlink **Fix all occurrences** in **Document** to bring up the **Preview Changes - Fix All Occurrences** dialog. Click on the **Apply** button to apply the **Make uppercase** fix to all types in `Class1.cs`:

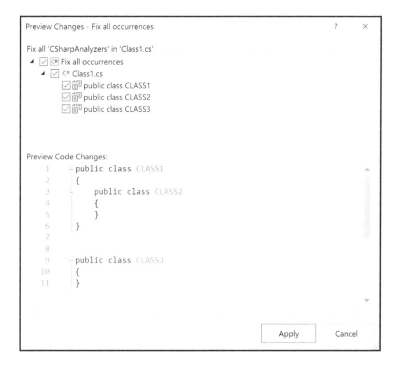

8. Verify that Class1, Class2, and Class3 are changed to CLASS1, CLASS2 and CLASS3, respectively, but Class4 and Class5 are unchanged.
9. Press *Ctrl + Z* to undo the batch code fix and verify the solution returns to the same state as before applying the fix all code fix.
10. Again press *Ctrl + dot*, but this time click on **Fix all occurrences in Project**.
11. Uncheck the checkbox next to public class CLASS2 and verify that CLASS2 is switched back to Class2 in the preview changes dialog:

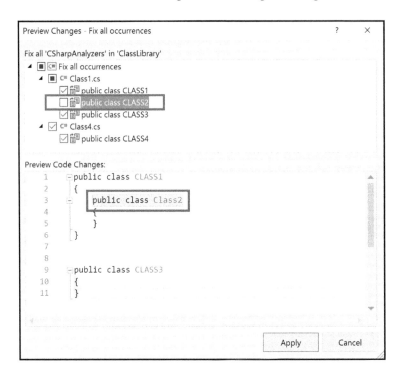

12. Apply the fix and verify that Class1, Class3, and Class4 are changed to CLASS1, CLASS3, and CLASS4, respectively, but Class2 and Class5 are unchanged.
13. Press *Ctrl + Z* to undo the project level code fix and verify changes to both source files Class1.cs and Class4.cs are reverted.
14. Again press *Ctrl + dot*, and this time click on **Fix all occurrences in Solution**.
15. Apply the code fix and verify all five classes are changed to upper case, and *Ctrl + Z* reverts the changes to all types in the solution.

Creating a custom FixAllProvider to fix all occurrences of an issue across a scope

In this section, we will show you how to a write a custom FixAll code fix provider to batch fix diagnostics. We will use the code fix implemented in the first recipe of this chapter to `Remove unused local`. As shown in that recipe, removal of an unused local might have different code fixes based on whether the enclosing local declaration statement declares a single or multiple variables. Additionally, we might have multiple unused locals declared in the single statement, and if all the locals declared in a statement are unused, the batch fix should remove the entire statement. Hence, we cannot use the well-known batch fixer. For example, for the following code, the batch fix should delete the entire first two local declaration statements, but only the declarator for `d` in the third declaration statement:

```
public class MyClass
{
    public static void M()
    {
        int a = 0;    // CS0219 for 'a'
        int b = 1, c = 2; // CS0219 for 'b' and 'c'
        int d = 3, e = 4; // CS0219 for 'd'
        System.Console.WriteLine(e);
    }
}
```

The default well-known `BatchFixer` used by code fixers only works well for simple code fixes. For other scenarios, we need to write a custom fix all provider. See (`https://github.com/dotnet/roslyn/blob/master/docs/analyzers/FixAllProvider.md`) for documentation on FixAll providers and limitations of the well-known BatchFixer.

Getting ready

You should execute the first recipe in this chapter, *Creating, debugging and executing a code fix provider to fix a compiler warning* to implement a code fix provider to `Remove unused local`.

How to do it...

1. Open `CSharpAnalyzers.sln` in Visual Studio and add two new source files to the project `CSharpAnalyzers`:
   - `CustomFixAllProvider.cs`
   - `CustomFixAllCodeAction.cs`
2. Add code to `CustomFixAllProvider.cs` to implement a custom fix all provider from `CSharpAnalyzers/CSharpAnalyzers/CSharpAnalyzers/CustomFixAllProvider.cs`.
3. Add code to `CustomFixAllCodeAction.cs` from `CSharpAnalyzers/CSharpAnalyzers/CSharpAnalyzers/CustomFixAllCodeAction.cs` to implement a custom `CodeAction`, which is returned by `CustomFixAllProvider.GetFixAsync`.
4. Make the following edits to `CodeFixProvider.cs`:
   - Change `GetNodeToRemoveAsync` to be an internal static method
   - Change `GetFixAllProviderAsync` to return a `new CustomFixAllProvider()`
5. Set `CSharpAnalyzers.Vsix` as the start-up project and press *F5* to start a new VS instance with the code fix provider enabled.
6. In the new VS instance, create a new C# class library project, say `ClassLibrary`, and replace the existing code with the following:

```
public class Class1
{
 public static void M()
 {
  int a = 0; // CS0219 for 'a'
  int b = 1, c = 2; // CS0219 for 'b' and 'c'
  int d = 3, e = 4; // CS0219 for 'd'
  System.Console.WriteLine(e);
 }
}
```

Chapter 3

7. Add a new source file, say `Class2.cs` to the project with the following code:

```
public class Class2
{
 public static void M()
 {
   int a = 0; // CS0219 for 'a'
   int b = 1, c = 2; // CS0219 for 'b' and 'c'
   int d = 3, e = 4; // CS0219 for 'd'
   System.Console.WriteLine(e);
 }
}
```

8. Add a new C# class library project to the solution, say `ClassLibrary2.csproj`, rename the source file to `Class3.cs`, and replace its source with the following:

```
public class Class3
{
 public static void M()
 {
   int a = 0; // CS0219 for 'a'
   int b = 1, c = 2; // CS0219 for 'b' and 'c'
   int d = 3, e = 4; // CS0219 for 'd'
   System.Console.WriteLine(e);
 }
}
```

9. Verify 12 diagnostics in the error list, one for each unused variable across the three classes.
10. Place the cursor on local *'a'* in `Class1.cs`, and hit *Ctrl* + dot to bring up the light bulb for code fix `Remove unused local`.

[99]

Writing IDE Code Fixes, Refactorings, and Intellisense Completion Providers

11. Click on the hyperlink **Fix all occurrences in Document** to bring up the **Preview Changes - Fix All Occurrences** dialog. Click on the **Apply** button to apply the **Remove unused local** to remove all four unused locals ('a', 'b', 'c' and 'd') in the `Class1.cs`:

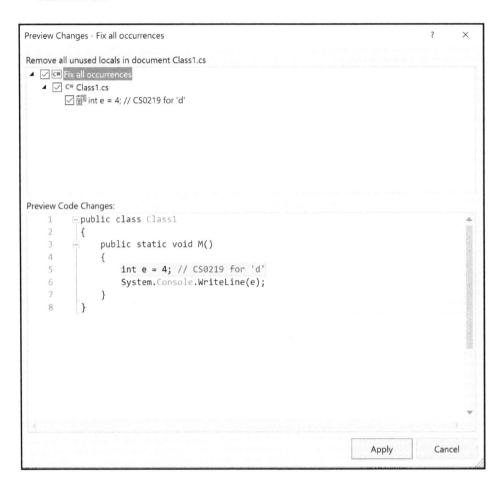

12. Switch to unused local declarations in `Class2.cs` and attempt to **Fix All Occurences** in the solution/project scope and verify all unused locals are remove in the selected scope.

How it works...

FixAll providers are VS IDE extensions that register code actions for batch fixes corresponding to code actions registered by a specific code fix provider. The primary APIs on `FixAllProvider` are:

- `GetSupportedFixAllScopes` property (virtual): This gets the supported scopes for fixing all occurrences of a diagnostic. By default, it returns document, project, and solution scopes.
- `GetSupportedFixAllDiagnosticIds` method (virtual): This gets the diagnostic IDs for which fix all occurrences is supported. By default, it returns the `FixableDiagnosticIds` of the corresponding code fix provider.
- `GetFixAsync` method (abstract): This is the primary method that takes a `FixAllContext` argument and returns a code action for a batch fix corresponding to `FixAllContext` parameters: `CodeFixProvider`, `DiagnosticIds` to fix, `FixAllScope` and `EquivalenceKey` for the origin code action.

The code fix engine invokes the `CodeFixProvider.GetFixAllProviderAsync` method to get the optional FixAll provider supported by the code fixer. In our implementation, we ensure that we return `CustomFixAllProvider` for this method. Let's expand on the implementation details of `CustomFixAllProvider`.

`CustomFixAllProvider` only overrides the `GetFixAsync` method. The first part of `GetFixAsync` computes fix title and the documents to fix for the current `FixAllScope`:

```
  public override async Task<CodeAction> GetFixAsync(FixAllContext fixAllContext)
  {
    var diagnosticsToFix = new List<KeyValuePair<Document, ImmutableArray<Diagnostic>>>();
    string titleFormat = "Remove all unused locals in {0} {1}";
    string title = null;
    var documentsToFix = ImmutableArray<Document>.Empty;

    switch (fixAllContext.Scope)
    {
     case FixAllScope.Document:
     {
      documentsToFix = ImmutableArray.Create(fixAllContext.Document);
      title = string.Format(titleFormat, "document", fixAllContext.Document.Name);
      break;
     }
```

```
    case FixAllScope.Project:
    {
      documentsToFix = fixAllContext.Project.Documents.ToImmutableArray();
      title = string.Format(titleFormat, "project",
fixAllContext.Project.Name);
      break;
    }

    case FixAllScope.Solution:
    {
      foreach (Project project in fixAllContext.Solution.Projects)
      {
        documentsToFix = documentsToFix.AddRange(project.Documents);
      }

      title = "Add all items in the solution to the public API";
      break;
    }

    case FixAllScope.Custom:
      return null;
    default:
      break;
  }
```

Then, we iterate through all the computed documents and compute the diagnostics to fix for each document and store them in a map. We return our `CustomFixAllCodeAction` with the computed title and diagnostics:

```
  foreach (Document document in documentsToFix)
  {
    ImmutableArray<Diagnostic> diagnostics = await
fixAllContext.GetDocumentDiagnosticsAsync(document).ConfigureAwait(false);
    diagnosticsToFix.Add(new KeyValuePair<Document,
ImmutableArray<Diagnostic>>(document, diagnostics));
  }

  return new CustomFixAllCodeAction(title, fixAllContext.Solution,
diagnosticsToFix);
```

Let's go through the implementation details for `CustomFixAllCodeAction`. The primary method that the custom code action overrides is `GetChangedSolutionAsync`. This method gets the new solution with edits from the batch fix. The code fix engine invokes this method when the user attempts to apply the batch fix.

The initial part of `GetChangedSolutionAsync` computes all local declaration and variable declarator syntax nodes to remove for each document, in a map named `nodesToRemove`, carrying out very basic batching of syntax nodes to fix:

```
    protected override async Task<Solution> 
GetChangedSolutionAsync(CancellationToken cancellationToken)
    {
      var nodesToRemoveMap = new Dictionary<Document, HashSet<SyntaxNode>>();
      foreach (KeyValuePair<Document, ImmutableArray<Diagnostic>> pair in 
_diagnosticsToFix)
      {
        Document document = pair.Key;
        ImmutableArray<Diagnostic> diagnostics = pair.Value;
        var nodesToRemove = new HashSet<SyntaxNode>();
        foreach (var diagnostic in diagnostics)
        {
          var nodeToRemove = await 
CSharpAnalyzersCodeFixProvider.GetNodeToRemoveAsync(document, diagnostic, 
cancellationToken).ConfigureAwait(false);
          if (nodeToRemove != null)
          {
            nodesToRemove.Add(nodeToRemove);
          }
        }
```

The second part tries to identify local declaration statements with multiple variable declarations, where all the declared locals are unused, and hence the entire statement can be removed. For such cases, we add the local declaration statement to `nodesToRemove` and remove all the individual unused variable declarators in the local declaration statement from `nodeToRemove` map:

```
        var candidateLocalDeclarationsToRemove = new 
HashSet<LocalDeclarationStatementSyntax>();
        foreach (var variableDeclarator in 
nodesToRemove.OfType<VariableDeclaratorSyntax>())
        {
          var localDeclaration = 
(LocalDeclarationStatementSyntax)variableDeclarator.Parent.Parent;
          candidateLocalDeclarationsToRemove.Add(localDeclaration);
        }

        foreach (var candidate in candidateLocalDeclarationsToRemove)
        {
          var hasUsedLocal = false;
          foreach (var variable in candidate.Declaration.Variables)
          {
            if (!nodesToRemove.Contains(variable))
```

```
    {
      hasUsedLocal = true;
      break;
    }
  }

  if (!hasUsedLocal)
  {
    nodesToRemove.Add(candidate);
    foreach (var variable in candidate.Declaration.Variables)
    {
      nodesToRemove.Remove(variable);
    }
  }
}
```

Finally, we iterate through all the `{Document, HashSet<SyntaxNode>}` pairs and for each document compute the new root with all the unused locals removed from the entire tree. We create a new document with the new root and apply the document change to the latest solution, which is tracked as `newSolution`. At the end of the loop, `newSolution` represents the current solution with all document changes applied, and is returned by the method:

```
Solution newSolution = _solution;

foreach (KeyValuePair<Document, HashSet<SyntaxNode>> pair in nodesToRemoveMap)
{
  var document = pair.Key;
  var root = await document.GetSyntaxRootAsync(cancellationToken).ConfigureAwait(false);
  var syntaxGenerator = SyntaxGenerator.GetGenerator(document);
  var newRoot = syntaxGenerator.RemoveNodes(root, pair.Value);
  newSolution = newSolution.WithDocumentSyntaxRoot(document.Id, newRoot);
}

return newSolution;
```

Creating a CodeRefactoringProvider to refactor source code to recommend using C# 7.0 tuples

Code refactoring providers are IDE extensions to refactor source code for better code structuring, without affecting the functional or semantic behavior of the code. These are built on top of Roslyn's Workspaces layer and operate on the current document being edited. When a user invokes a command such as *Ctrl* + dot in Visual Studio editor, the IDE code refactoring engine computes all the refactorings that can refactor the code in the currently selected text span in the editor. Each of these providers are then invoked with a code refactoring context containing the current document and span. Refactorings operate on the underlying syntax tree associated with the document by adding, removing, or editing the syntax nodes within the tree and returning the new document with the refactored code. They might also alter the contents of the containing project or solution. When the user commits the refactoring by pressing the *Enter* key, the code refactoring engine applies this refactoring to the user code.

In this section, we will write a `CodeRefactoringProvider` to propose the usage of tuple expressions, a C# 7.0 feature, in methods returning more than one value. Prior to C# 7.0, methods that wanted to return more than one value had the following possible implementations:

1. Declare a non-void return type of one of the return values and `out` parameters for the remaining returned values.
2. Declare a void return type and *out* parameters for each of the returned values.
3. Declare a new type wrapping these values as fields, and return an instance of that type.

With C# 7.0, the recommended implementation is to declare a tuple return type with elements defined for types of each of the returned values and have no out parameters. We will write a refactoring to identify the existing code with pattern 1 earlier and recommend a refactoring to use tuples. For example, consider the following methods returning multiple return values:

```
private int MethodReturningTwoValues(out int x)
{
  x = 0;
  return 0;
}

private int MethodReturningThreeValues(out int x, int y, out int z)
```

```
{
  x = 0;
  z = 1;
  return y;
}
```

Our code refactoring will offer to convert these methods to:

```
private (int, int) MethodReturningTwoValues()
{
  int x;
  x = 0;
  return (0, x);
}

private (int, int, int) MethodReturningThreeValues(int y)
{
  int x;
  int z;
  x = 0;
  z = 1;
  return (y, x, z);
}
```

Getting ready

You will need to have Visual Studio 2017 installed on your machine to execute the recipes in this chapter. You can install a free community version of Visual Studio 2017 from https://www.visualstudio.com/thank-you-downloading-visual-studio/?sku=Community&rel=15.

Additionally, you should have installed the .NET Compiler Platform SDK to get the `CodeRefactoring` project template. For reference, see the recipe, *Creating, debugging, and executing an analyzer project in Visual Studio,* in Chapter 1, *Writing Diagnostic Analyzers*.

By default, the `CodeRefactoring` project template targets *.NET Portable v4.5* and references version *1.0.1* of `Microsoft.CodeAnalysis` packages. As we intend to use the C# 7.0 syntax, we need to upgrade the `CodeAnalysis` packages to version 2.0.0 or later, which are based on .NET Standard and hence require the referencing project to be based on .NET standard templates or target .NET Framework v4.6 or higher. For this recipe, we change the project to target .NET Framework v4.6.

How to do it...

1. Start Visual Studio and click on **File** | **New** | **Project...**
2. Change the project target framework combo box to the .NET Framework 4.6 (or above). Under **Visual C#** | **Extensibility**, choose **Code Refactoring (VSIX)**, name your project `CodeRefactoring`, and click on **OK**:

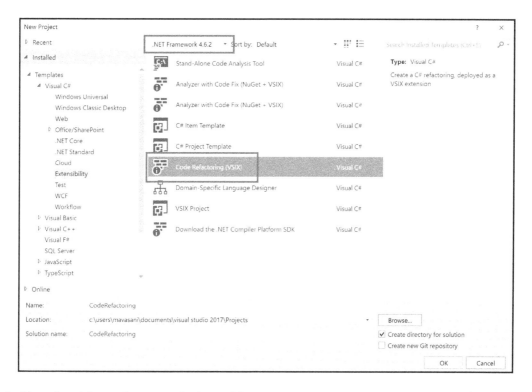

3. You should now have a solution with two projects: `CodeRefactoring` and `CodeRefactoring.Vsix`.
4. Change the `CodeRefactoring` project to target *.NET Framework v4.6* using the following steps:
   - Unload the project and edit `csproj` in Visual Studio
   - Remove the properties `ProjectTypeGuids` and `TargetFrameworkProfile`

Writing IDE Code Fixes, Refactorings, and Intellisense Completion Providers

- Change the property `TargetFrameworkVersion` from *v4.5* to *v4.6*.
- Replace the last **Imports** element in the file from portable targets to non-portable targets, that is, replace the line `<Import Project="$(MSBuildExtensionsPath32)\Microsoft\Portable\$(TargetFrameworkVersion)\Microsoft.Portable.CSharp.targets" />` with `<Import Project="$(MSBuildToolsPath)\Microsoft.CSharp.targets" />`
- Save changes and reload the project

5. Right-click on project in solution explorer, click on Manage NuGet Packages, and update `Microsoft.CodeAnalysis.CSharp.Workspaces` to *2.0.0*:

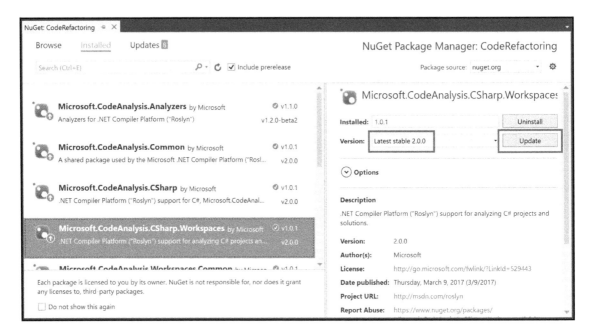

6. Open `CodeRefactoringProvider.cs` in the `CodeRefactoringProvider` project and replace the existing implementation of the `ComputeRefactoringAsync` method with the code at `CodeRefactoring/CodeRefactoring/CodeRefactoringProvider.cs/` Method named `ComputeRefactoringAsync`.

Chapter 3

7. Add the following helper to compute *out* parameters from a parameter list:

   ```
   private static IEnumerable<ParameterSyntax>
   GetOutParameters(MethodDeclarationSyntax methodDecl)
     => methodDecl.ParameterList.Parameters.Where(parameter =>
   parameter.Modifiers.Any(m => m.Kind() ==
   SyntaxKind.OutKeyword));
   ```

8. Remove the existing method `ReverseTypeNameAsync` and replace it with `UseValueTupleAsync` and a couple of helper methods, `GenerateTupleType` and `GenerateTupleExpression`, from code at `CodeRefactoring/CodeRefactoring/CodeRefactoringProvider.cs/` Methods named `GenerateTupleType` and `GenerateTupleExpression`. Additionally, also add a new using statement at the top of the file: `using Microsoft.CodeAnalysis.Formatting;`

9. Set `CodeRefactoring.Vsix` as the Startup project and click on *F5* to build the refactoring and start debugging a new instance of Visual Studio with the refactoring enabled.

10. In the new Visual Studio instance, create a new C# class library project, say `ClassLibrary` and add the following two methods to `Class1`:

    ```
    private int MethodReturningTwoValues(out int x)
    {
     x = 0;
     return 0;
    }

    private int MethodReturningThreeValues(out int x, int y, out int z)
    {
     x = 0;
     z = 1;
     return y;
    }
    ```

11. Right-click on the **project node** | **Manage Nuget Packages** and add NuGet package reference to System.ValueTuple.
12. Put the caret on MethodReturningTwoValues and hit *Ctrl* + dot and verify that we are offered a refactoring to **Use ValueTuple return type**:

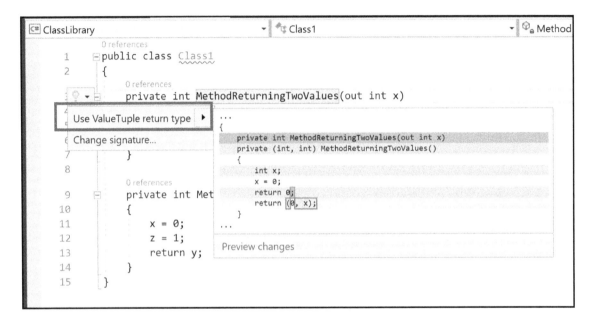

13. Apply the refactoring and verify that the method signature changes to return value tuple.
14. Similarly, put the caret on `MethodReturningThreeValues` and hit *Ctrl* + dot and verify we are offered a refactoring to **Use ValueTuple return type**:

```
public class Class1
{
    private (int, int) MethodReturningTwoValues()
    {
        int x;
        x = 0;
        return (0, x);
    }

    private int MethodReturningThreeValues(out int x, int y, out int z)
```

Use ValueTuple return type ▶
Change signature...

```
private int MethodReturningThreeValues(out int x, int y, out int z)
private (int, int, int) MethodReturningThreeValues(int y)
{
    int x;
    int z;
    x = 0;
    z = 1;
    return y;
    return (y, x, z);
}
```

Preview changes

How it works...

Code refactoring providers are VS IDE extensions that can register code actions for refactoring code to a recommended pattern without introducing any functional changes. The primary API on `CodeRefactoringProvider` is:

- `ComputeRefactoringsAsync` method (abstract): This is a method to register code actions for refactorings. This method is invoked by the code refactoring engine whenever it needs to compute the refactorings to offer on the current source line in the VS IDE. This method takes a `CodeRefactoringContext` argument, which contains the current span and document. `CodeRefactoringProvider` can map the span to syntax node in the document and analyze it to register one more code actions in the context. **CodeAction** contains the following primary members:
    - `Title` property: String that shows up with the light bulb when the code refactoring is offered.
    - `Callback` method: Delegate to be called back when the user applies a registered code action. This method returns the changed document or solution and the code refactoring engine applies the changes to the workspace.

Let's expand on the implementation details of `ComputeRefactoringsAsync` and its helpers.

The first part of `ComputeRefactoringsAsync` computes syntax node for the current span:

```
public sealed override async Task
ComputeRefactoringsAsync(CodeRefactoringContext context)
{
 var root = await
context.Document.GetSyntaxRootAsync(context.CancellationToken).ConfigureAwait(false);

 // Find the node at the selection.
 var node = root.FindNode(context.Span);
```

The next part of the method implements certain defensive checks to bail out early without registering any code action:

```
 // Only offer a refactoring if the selected node is a method declaration
 node with non-void return type and at least one 'out' var.
 var methodDecl = node as MethodDeclarationSyntax;
 if (methodDecl == null ||
  methodDecl.ReturnType.Kind() == SyntaxKind.VoidKeyword ||
```

```
    !GetOutParameters(methodDecl).Any())
{
    return;
}

// Check if the compilation references System.ValueTuple
var hasValueTuple = false;
if (context.Document.Project.SupportsCompilation)
{
    var compilation = await
context.Document.Project.GetCompilationAsync(context.CancellationToken).Con
figureAwait(false);
    var systemValueTuple =
compilation?.GetTypeByMetadataName(@"System.ValueTuple");
    if (systemValueTuple != null &&
systemValueTuple.ContainingAssembly.Name.Equals(@"System.ValueTuple"))
    {
        hasValueTuple = true;
    }
}
```

We first check if we are currently operating on a `MethodDeclarationSyntax` node with non-void return type and at least one out parameter. We also bail out if the analyzed compilation doesn't define a type named `System.ValueTuple` in `System.ValueTuple` assembly reference.

Finally, the method registers a code action with the title to display in the light bulb and a callback, `UseValueTupleAsync`, to compute the refactoring:

```
if (hasValueTuple)
{
    // Create a code action to transform the method signature to use tuples.
    var action = CodeAction.Create("Use ValueTuple return type", c =>
    UseValueTupleAsync(context.Document, methodDecl, c));

    // Register this code action.
    context.RegisterRefactoring(action);
}
```

`UseValueTupleAsync` uses the C# `SyntaxFactory` helper utility to edit the signature and body of the method declaration from the original syntax root, and returns the new document created with the new syntax root.

The first part of the method computes the new parameter list for refactored code. We remove all the *out* parameters from the parameter list and change the return type to be a tuple type. For example, for a method returning type T, and having parameters, A a, out B b, out C c, we return a `TupleTypeSyntax` (T, B, C) and change the method parameter list to contain just *A a*:

```
// Compute the new parameter list with all the out parameters removed.
var outParameters = GetOutParameters(methodDecl);
var newParameters = methodDecl.ParameterList.Parameters.Where(p =>
!outParameters.Contains(p));
var newParameterList = methodDecl.ParameterList.Update(
  methodDecl.ParameterList.OpenParenToken,
  new SeparatedSyntaxList<ParameterSyntax>().AddRange(newParameters),
  methodDecl.ParameterList.CloseParenToken);
methodDecl = methodDecl.WithParameterList(newParameterList);

// Compute the new return type: Tuple type with the original return type as first element and
// types for all original out parameters as subsequent elements.1
var newReturnType = GenerateTupleType(methodDecl.ReturnType,
outParameters);
methodDecl = methodDecl.WithReturnType(newReturnType);
```

The next part of the method adds local declaration statements at the top of the method body block for each *out* parameter in the original parameter list. For the preceding example, we will add local declaration statements `B b;` and `C c;`:

```
// Add local declaration statements as the start of the method body to
declare locals for original out parameters.
var newStatements = new List<StatementSyntax>(outParameters.Count());
foreach (var outParam in outParameters)
{
  var variableDeclarator =
SyntaxFactory.VariableDeclarator(outParam.Identifier);
  var variableDeclarationSyntax =
SyntaxFactory.VariableDeclaration(outParam.Type,
SyntaxFactory.SingletonSeparatedList(variableDeclarator));
  var localDeclarationStatement =
SyntaxFactory.LocalDeclarationStatement(variableDeclarationSyntax);
  newStatements.Add(localDeclarationStatement);
}

var statements = methodDecl.Body.Statements;
var newBody =
methodDecl.Body.WithStatements(methodDecl.Body.Statements.InsertRange(0,
newStatements));
methodDecl = methodDecl.WithBody(newBody);
```

Then, we gather all the `ReturnStatementSyntax` nodes in the original method implementation and replace their expression with a tuple expression created by concatenating the original return expression with the identifier names of the newly declared locals. For our example, this will replace statements of the form `return x;` with `return (x, b, c);`:

```
// Replace all return statement expressions with tuple expressions:
original return expression
// as the first argument and identifier name for original out parameters
as subsequent arguments.
 var returnStatements =
methodDecl.Body.DescendantNodes().OfType<ReturnStatementSyntax>();
 var replacementNodeMap = new Dictionary<ReturnStatementSyntax,
ReturnStatementSyntax>(returnStatements.Count());
 foreach (var returnStatement in returnStatements)
 {
  var tupleExpression = GenerateTupleExpression(returnStatement.Expression,
outParameters);
  var newReturnStatement = SyntaxFactory.ReturnStatement(tupleExpression);
  replacementNodeMap.Add(returnStatement, newReturnStatement);
 }

 methodDecl = methodDecl.ReplaceNodes(returnStatements,
computeReplacementNode: (o, n) => replacementNodeMap[o]);
```

Finally, we apply the formatter annotation on the method `decl` to ensure that formatting is done by the formatter engine. We then replace the updated `methodDecl` node in the original root and return the updated document:

```
// Add formatter annotation to format the edited method declaration and
body.
 methodDecl = methodDecl.WithAdditionalAnnotations(Formatter.Annotation);

// Return new document with replaced method declaration.
 var newRoot = root.ReplaceNode(originalMethodDecl, methodDecl);
 return document.WithSyntaxRoot(newRoot);
}
```

There's more…

Our current implementation of the refactoring is incomplete -- we change the method signature to return tuple types, but do not update the call sites to consume them. For example, the highlighted callsite here will be broken by our refactoring:

```
private void M()
{
 int x;
 int y = MethodReturningTwoValues(out x);
}

private int MethodReturningTwoValues(out int x)
{
 x = 0;
 return 0;
}
```

We leave it as an exercise for the reader to enhance this refactoring to use the `FindReferences` API (http://source.roslyn.io/#q=FindReferencesSearchEngine.FindReferencesAsyn) to find callsites of the method and edit the code to fix the callsite. For the preceding example, we need to replace the `MethodReturningTwoValues` invocation with the highlighted code.

```
private void M()
{
 int x;
 (int, int) t1 = MethodReturningTwoValues();
 x = t1.Item2;
 int y = t1.Item1;
}
```

Creating a CompletionProvider to provide additional intellisense items while editing code.

`CompletionProviders` are IDE extensions that provide completion items in the intellisense list when user is editing code in the Visual Studio IDE:

Chapter 3

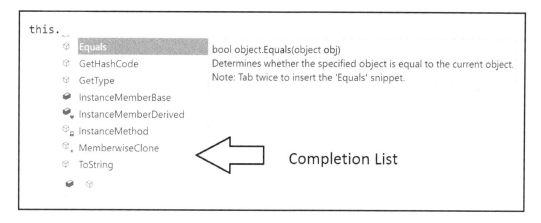

The preceding screenshot shows a completion list with all the accessible instance members from the current type and base types, and is generally shown when the user types `this.` inside executable code. Users can hit a commit character, such as *Enter* key, to invoke auto-complete with the chosen member.

In this section, we will write a `CompletionProvider` to provide the same *accessible members* completion items, but without requiring the user to have typed a `this` before a `.` character (yay! from all the lazy folks like me). Additionally, when invoked within a static method, the completion provider will provide only *static* accessible members in the completion list.

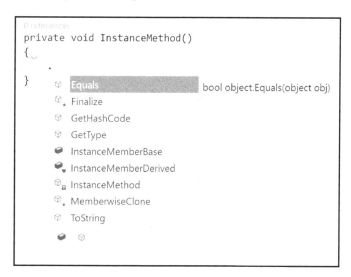

[117]

Getting ready

You will need to have Visual Studio 2017 installed on your machine to execute the recipes in this chapter. You can install a free community version of Visual Studio 2017 from `https://www.visualstudio.com/thank-you-downloading-visual-studio/?sku=Community&rel=15`.

How to do it...

1. Open Visual Studio, click on **File** | **New Project** | **Visual C#** | **Class library**, ensure the .NET framework combo box is set to *v4.6.2*, and create a project named `CompletionProvider`.
2. In solution explorer, right-click on the project node and execute the `Manage NuGet Packages` command to bring up the **NuGet Package Manager**. Add NuGet package references to `Microsoft.CodeAnalysis` and `Microsoft.CodeAnalysis.Features`, both version *2.0.0*.
3. Rename the source file `Class1.cs` to `CustomCompletionProvider.cs` and add source code for `CustomCompletionProvider` from the code sample at `CompletionProvider/CompletionProvider/CustomCompletionProvider.cs/Type` named `CustomCompletionProvider`.
4. Add a C# VSIX project named `CompletionProvider.Vsix` to the solution.
5. Replace the content of `source.extension.vsixmanifest` in the VSIX project with the following:

```xml
<?xml version="1.0" encoding="utf-8"?>
<PackageManifest Version="2.0.0"
xmlns="http://schemas.microsoft.com/developer/vsx-schema/2011"
xmlns:d="http://schemas.microsoft.com/developer/vsx-schema-design/2011">
 <Metadata>
 <Identity Id="CompletionProvider.Vsix.ccf1c2f5-d03f-42a2-a1b9-c05d10efda2c" Version="1.0" Language="en-US" Publisher="Packt publishing" />
 <DisplayName>CompletionProvider.Vsix</DisplayName>
 <Description>Roslyn completion provider.</Description>
 </Metadata>
 <Installation>
 <InstallationTarget Id="Microsoft.VisualStudio.Pro" Version="[15.0]" />
 </Installation>
 <Dependencies>
```

```xml
<Dependency Id="Microsoft.Framework.NDP"
DisplayName="Microsoft .NET Framework" d:Source="Manual"
Version="[4.5,)" />
</Dependencies>
<Assets>
<Asset Type="Microsoft.VisualStudio.MefComponent"
d:Source="Project" d:ProjectName="CompletionProvider"
Path="|CompletionProvider|"/>
</Assets>
<Prerequisites>
<Prerequisite Id="Microsoft.VisualStudio.Component.CoreEditor"
Version="[15.0,16.0)" DisplayName="Visual Studio core editor"
/>
<Prerequisite
Id="Microsoft.VisualStudio.Component.Roslyn.LanguageServices"
Version="[15.0,16.0)" DisplayName="Roslyn Language Services" />
</Prerequisites>
</PackageManifest>
```

6. Add a project-to-project reference from `CompletionProvider.Vsix` to `CompletionProvider`.
7. Set `CompletionProvider.Vsix` as the start-up project and click on *F5* to build the completion provider and start debugging a new instance of Visual Studio with the provider enabled.
8. In the new Visual Studio instance, create a new C# class library project, say `ClassLibrary` and add the following code to the source file:

```
public class Base
{
 protected static int StaticMemberBase;
 public int InstanceMemberBase;
}

public class Derived : Base
{
 private static int staticMemberDerived;
 internal int InstanceMemberDerived;

 private void InstanceMethod()
 {
  .
 }

 private static void StaticMethod()
 {
  .
```

Writing IDE Code Fixes, Refactorings, and Intellisense Completion Providers

```
    }
}
```

9. Put the caret after the `.` in `InstanceMethod` and hit *Ctrl + SpaceBar* to bring up our custom completion list. Verify all the instance members of type `Derived`, and accessible instance members of base type `Base` and `System.Object` are shown in the completion list.
10. Select a member, say `InstanceMemberDerived`, and hit the *Enter* key and verify that the `.` is replaced with `this.InstanceMemberDerived`.
11. Put the caret after the `.` in `StaticMethod` and hit *Ctrl + Spacebar* to bring up the completion list. Verify all the static members of type *Derived* and accessible static members of base type `Base` and `System.Object` are shown in the completion list.
12. Select a member, say `StaticMemberBase`, and hit the *Enter* key, and verify that the `.` is replaced with `Base.StaticMemberBase`.

How it works...

Completion providers are VS IDE extensions that can register completion items to be shown in the Visual Studio IDE when the user is editing source code. The primary APIs on `CompletionProvider` are:

- `ShouldTriggerCompletion` method (virtual): This is the method to decide if completion should be invoked for the given editing context. This method takes the following arguments: `SourceText` of the document being edited, `caretPosition` at which completion was invoked, `CompletionTrigger` (which contains the trigger kind - insertion, deletion, and so on, and the trigger character), and `OptionSet` for completion.

- `ProvideCompletionsAsync` method (abstract): This is the method to register completion items. This method is invoked by the completion engine whenever it needs to compute the completions to offer on the current completion trigger in the VS IDE. This method takes a `CompletionContext` argument, which contains the current caret position, document, completion trigger and options. `CompletionContext` exposes methods to add one or more completion items. `CompletionItem` contains the following primary components: `DisplayText` to be shown in the completion list, optional `FilterText` and `SortText` to modify the default filtering and sorting, respectively, the text `Span` of the syntax element is associated with the completion, a dictionary of `<string, string>` `Properties`, an array of `Tags`, and set of `CompletionRules` for how the completion items are handled.
- `GetDescriptionAsync` method (virtual): This method gets the description to show in the quick info for each completion item.
- `GetChangeAsync` method (virtual): This method gets the `CompletionChange` to be applied when the user commits a specific completion item. `CompletionChange` contains the set of one or more text changes to apply to the document and new caret position after committing the completion item.

Let's expand on the implementation details of each of the preceding overrides in our `CustomCompletionProvider`.

Our implementation of `ShouldTriggerCompletion` first checks whether completion is invoked for the insertion trigger:

```
public override bool ShouldTriggerCompletion(SourceText text, int caretPosition, CompletionTrigger trigger, OptionSet options)
{
 switch (trigger.Kind)
 {
  case CompletionTriggerKind.Insertion:
    return ShouldTriggerCompletion(text, caretPosition);

  default:
    return false;
 }
}
```

Writing IDE Code Fixes, Refactorings, and Intellisense Completion Providers

The helper method `ShouldTriggerCompletion` checks if the current character is . and the previous character is either a whitespace, tab, or new line character. If so, we return true; otherwise we return false.

```
private static bool ShouldTriggerCompletion(SourceText text, int position)
{
 // Provide completion if user typed "." after a whitespace/tab/newline char.
 var insertedCharacterPosition = position - 1;
 if (insertedCharacterPosition <= 0)
 {
  return false;
 }

 var ch = text[insertedCharacterPosition];
 var previousCh = text[insertedCharacterPosition - 1];
 return ch == '.' &&
   (char.IsWhiteSpace(previousCh) || previousCh == 't' || previousCh == 'r' || previousCh == 'n');
}
```

`ProvideCompletionsAsync` implementation checks up front if we should register any completion items, and bails out if we are not in the supported completion context. We also bail out if we are not editing inside a method body.

```
public async override Task ProvideCompletionsAsync(CompletionContext context)
{
 var model = await context.Document.GetSemanticModelAsync(context.CancellationToken).ConfigureAwait(false);
 var text = await model.SyntaxTree.GetTextAsync(context.CancellationToken).ConfigureAwait(false);
 if (!ShouldTriggerCompletion(text, context.Position))
 {
  return;
 }

 // Only provide completion in method body.
 var enclosingMethod = model.GetEnclosingSymbol(context.Position, context.CancellationToken) as IMethodSymbol;
 if (enclosingMethod == null)
 {
  return;
 }
```

We then compute all the accessible members in the current context using the helper methods `GetAccessibleMembersInThisAndBaseTypes` and `GetBaseTypesAndThis`:

```
private static ImmutableArray<ISymbol>
GetAccessibleMembersInThisAndBaseTypes(ITypeSymbol containingType, bool
isStatic, int position, SemanticModel model)
{
 var types = GetBaseTypesAndThis(containingType);
 return types.SelectMany(x => x.GetMembers().Where(m => m.IsStatic ==
isStatic && model.IsAccessible(position, m)))
  .ToImmutableArray();
}

private static IEnumerable<ITypeSymbol> GetBaseTypesAndThis(ITypeSymbol
type)
{
 var current = type;
 while (current != null)
 {
  yield return current;
  current = current.BaseType;
 }
}
```

We then iterate through all the members to suggest, ignoring constructors, and create and register a completion item for each member:

```
var membersToSuggest = GetAccessibleMembersInThisAndBaseTypes(
 enclosingMethod.ContainingType,
 isStatic: enclosingMethod.IsStatic,
 position: context.Position - 1,
 model: model);

// Add completion for each member.
foreach (var member in membersToSuggest)
{
 // Ignore constructors
 if ((member as IMethodSymbol)?.MethodKind == MethodKind.Constructor)
 {
  continue;
 }

 // Add receiver and description properties.
 var receiver = enclosingMethod.IsStatic ?
member.ContainingType.ToDisplayString(SymbolDisplayFormat.MinimallyQualifie
dFormat) : "this";
 var description = member.ToMinimalDisplayString(model, context.Position -
1);
```

Writing IDE Code Fixes, Refactorings, and Intellisense Completion Providers

```
    var properties = ImmutableDictionary<string, string>.Empty
     .Add(Receiver, receiver)
     .Add(Description, description);

    // Compute completion tags to display.
    var tags = GetCompletionTags(member).ToImmutableArray();

    // Add completion item.
    var item = CompletionItem.Create(member.Name, properties: properties,
    tags: tags);
     context.AddItem(item);
    }
```

We use the member's `Name` property as the `DisplayText` value for the completion item.

We compute a couple of strings, namely, `Receiver` and `Description`, and store them as string properties on the completion item. These properties are used in `GetChangeAsync` and `GetDescriptionAsync` method overrides, respectively. `Receiver` is essentially the string to add to the left of the . character when user commits a completion item: `this` for instance members, and containing type's `name` for static members. `Description` is the text to show in the quick info for each completion item. We use the symbol's minimal display string as the description, but this can be enhanced to show colored tokens and use content from the XML documentation comments on the symbol.

We also compute and attach a set of string `Tags` to the completion items. These tags determine the glyphs to show for the completion items. Examples are symbol glyph: field, method, property, and so on, and accessibility glyph: private, protected, internal, public, and so on.

`GetDescriptionAsync` override directly uses the Description property stored on the completion item to compute the `CompletionDescription`:

```
    public override Task<CompletionDescription> GetDescriptionAsync(Document
    document, CompletionItem item, CancellationToken cancellationToken)
    {
     return
    Task.FromResult(CompletionDescription.FromText(item.Properties[Description]
    ));
    }
```

`GetChangeAsync` override uses the computed *Receiver* property and the item's `DisplayText` to form the `newText` `"{receiver}.{item.DisplayText}"` to be used in the text change when the user commits the completion item. The `TextSpan` of the text change uses `item.Span.Start - 1` as the start value and `1` as the length to account for the existing . character to be removed:

```
public override Task<CompletionChange> GetChangeAsync(Document document,
CompletionItem item, char? commitKey, CancellationToken cancellationToken)
{
  // Get new text replacement and span.
  var receiver = item.Properties[Receiver];
  var newText = $"{receiver}.{item.DisplayText}";
  var newSpan = new TextSpan(item.Span.Start - 1, 1);

  // Return the completion change with the new text change.
  var textChange = new TextChange(newSpan, newText);
  return Task.FromResult(CompletionChange.Create(textChange));
}
```

Writing unit tests for a CodeFixProvider

In this section, we will show you how to write and execute unit tests for a `CodeFixProvider`.

Getting ready

You will need to have created and opened an analyzer + code fixer project, say `CSharpAnalyzers` in Visual Studio 2017. Refer to the recipe, *Creating, debugging, and executing an analyzer project in Visual Studio*, in `Chapter 1`, *Writing Diagnostic Analyzers* for guidance.

Note that the template unit test project contains unit tests for both the `DiagnosticAnalyzer` and `CodeFixProvider`. This chapter deals with `CodeFixProvider` testing only. Refer to the recipe, *Writing unit tests for an analyzer project* in `Chapter 1`, *Writing Diagnostic Analyzers* for diagnostic analyzer unit tests.

How to do it…

1. Open `UnitTests.cs` in the `CSharpAnalyzers.Test` project in the solution explorer to view the default unit tests created for the default symbol analyzer and code fix provider in the project (Type names should not contain lower case letters):

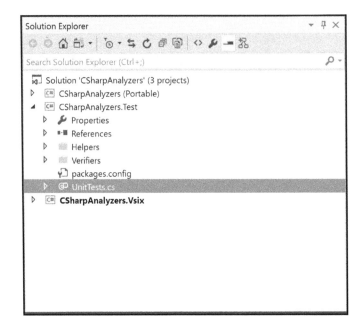

2. Click on **Test | Windows | Test Window** to open the **Test Explorer** window to view the unit tests in the project. The default project has two unit tests:
    - `TestMethod1`: This tests the scenario where analyzer diagnostic does not fire on the test code.
    - `TestMethod2`: This tests the scenario where analyzer diagnostic does fire on the test code and the code fix provider fixes the diagnostic.

   Delete `TestMethod1` as we only care about `CodeFixProvider` tests.

Chapter 3

3. Run the unit tests for the project by right-clicking on **Not Run tests** node in the **Test Explorer** and execute `Run selected tests` context menu command and verify that the `TestMethod2` passes:

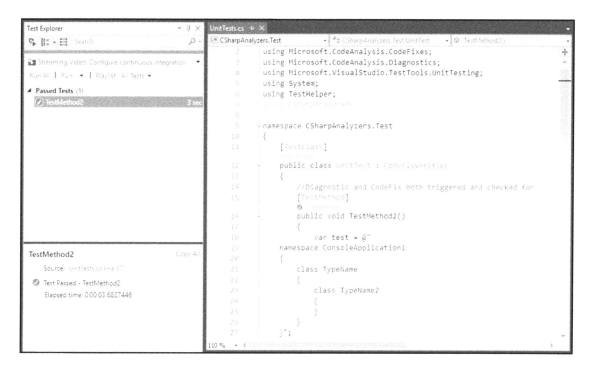

4. Edit the test source to remove all the usings and add a new nested type `TypeName2` inside `TypeName` in both the test string and `fixTest` string:

```
public void TestMethod2()
{
 var test = @"
  namespace ConsoleApplication1
  {
   class TypeName
   {
    class TypeName2
    {
    }
   }
  }";

 ...
```

[127]

Writing IDE Code Fixes, Refactorings, and Intellisense Completion Providers

```
            var fixtest = @"
             namespace ConsoleApplication1
             {
              class TYPENAME
              {
               class TypeName2
               {
               }
              }
             }";
```

5. Edit `TestMethod1` to fix the expected line number of the original expected diagnostic add a new excepted diagnostic for the new test code:
6. Right-click on `TestMethod2` in the editor and execute **Run tests** context menu command, and verify the test now fails with the diagnostic mismatch assert - expected 1, actual 2.

```
            var expected = new[] {
             new DiagnosticResult {
              Id = "CSharpAnalyzers",
              Message = String.Format("Type name '{0}' contains lowercase
            letters", "TypeName"),
              Severity = DiagnosticSeverity.Warning,
              Locations =
                new[] { new DiagnosticResultLocation("Test0.cs", 4, 15) }
             },
             new DiagnosticResult {
              Id = "CSharpAnalyzers",
              Message = String.Format("Type name '{0}' contains lowercase
            letters", "TypeName2"),
              Severity = DiagnosticSeverity.Warning,
              Locations =
                new[] { new DiagnosticResultLocation("Test0.cs", 6, 19) }
             }
            };
```

7. Fix the expected `fixTest` code to contain TYPENAME2 and verify that the test passes now.

8. Run the unit test again and note that the test still fails, but now it fails due to a difference in the fixed test code - `fixTest` has class `TypeName2` with lowercase letters, but the actual test code has `TYPENAME2`.

How it works...

An analyzer + code fix unit test project allows us to write unit tests for the execution of our analyzer/code fix provider on different code samples. Each unit test is marked with a `TestMethod` attribute and defines sample test code, expected diagnostics reported by the analyzer on that code (if any), expected fixed test code after executing the code fix provider on the sample test code, and invocation of test helper methods, here `VerifyCSharpFix`, to verify code fix.

To understand the basics of unit tests and the test framework for our unit test framework, refer to the *How it works... section* of the recipe, *Writing unit tests for an analyzer project* in `Chapter 1`, *Writing Diagnostic Analyzers* for diagnostic analyzer unit tests.

In this section, we will give a brief explanation of the abstract type that our unit test container derives from: `CodeFixVerifier`. This type contains the `VerifyCSharpFix` and `VerifyBasicFix` helper methods for running C# and VB `CodeFixProvider` unit tests, respectively. These methods call into a common helper method `VerifyFix`, which works as follows:

1. This method takes the original and expected sample test code as inputs - the original code on which to apply the code fixes, and the expected code after the code fixes have been applied.
2. It also takes the language name, analyzer, and code fix provider, along with the index of the code action to apply, in case the fixer registers multiple code actions.
3. It runs the analyzer on the original test code to get the analyzer diagnostics. It also computes the compiler diagnostics on the test code.
4. It uses the first analyzer diagnostic to create a `CodeFixContext` and invokes the code fix provider's `RegisterCodeFixesAsync` method with this context.
5. Then, it applies the registered code action at the given code fix index to compute the new document.
6. It re-executes the analyzer on the new document to get new analyzer diagnostics.
7. Until there is at least one new analyzer diagnostic, it repeats the steps 4-6 to apply the code fix on the new document.
8. Finally, it verifies the contents of the new document against the expected fixed code.

4
Improving Code Maintenance of C# Code Base

In this chapter, we will cover the following recipes:

- Configuring C# code style rules built into Visual Studio 2017
- Using the `.editorconfig` file for the configuration of code style rules
- Using the public API analyzer for API surface maintenance
- Using third-party StyleCop analyzers for code style rules

Introduction

In the current era of open source projects with numerous diverse contributors from different organizations and different parts of the world, one of the primary requirements of maintaining any repo is enforcing code style guidelines across the code base. Historically, this has been done through exhaustive documentation and code reviews to catch any violations of these coding guidelines. However, this approach has its flaws and requires a lot of man hours on maintaining the documentation and performing exhaustive code reviews.

With the automated code style and naming rules that are built into Visual Studio 2017, users can customize and configure the enforcement levels for individual rules and prompt visual indicators for violations, such as suggestions or squiggles in the editor and diagnostics in the error list, with appropriate severity (error/warning/informational message). Additionally, the rules come with a code fix that can automatically fix one or more instances of the violations across the document, project, or solution. With the new EditorConfig support in Visual Studio 2017, these rule configurations can be enforced and customized at each folder level via an `.editorconfig` file. Additionally, the `.editorconfig` files can be checked into the repo alongside the sources so that the rules are enforced for every user that contributes to the repo.

EditorConfig (http://editorconfig.org/) is an open source file format that helps developers configure and enforce formatting and code style conventions to achieve consistent, more readable codebases. EditorConfig files are easily checked into source control and are applied at repository and project levels. EditorConfig conventions override their equivalents in your personal settings, such that the conventions of the codebase take precedence over the individual developer.

In this chapter, we will introduce you to these code style rules, show you how to configure them in the Visual Studio 2017 IDE, and save these settings into an EditorConfig file. Additionally, we will introduce you to a very popular third-party Roslyn analyzer, the PublicAPI analyzer, that allows tracking the public API surface of .NET assemblies through additional non-source text files checked into the repo, and provides diagnostics and code fixes when there is a breaking API change or a new addition to the public API that is not documented in the public API files. We will also walk you through configuring StyleCop analyzers for a .NET project, a popular third-party code style analyzer, and an alternative to the built-in Visual Studio code style rules for enforcing code style.

Configuring C# code style rules built into Visual Studio 2017

In this section, we will walk you through the important categories of code style rules built into Visual Studio 2017, and also show you how to configure them in Visual Studio.

Getting ready

You will need to have Visual Studio 2017 installed on your machine to execute the recipes in this chapter. You can install a free community version of Visual Studio 2017 from `https://www.visualstudio.com/thank-you-downloading-visual-studio/?sku=Community&rel=15`.

How to do it...

1. Start Visual Studio, navigate to **File | New | Project...**, create a new C# class library project, and replace the code in `Class1.cs` with code from the code sample at `ClassLibrary/Class1.cs`.
2. Click on **Tools | Options** to bring up the tools options dialog and navigate to the C# code style options (**Text Editor | C# | Code Style | General**):

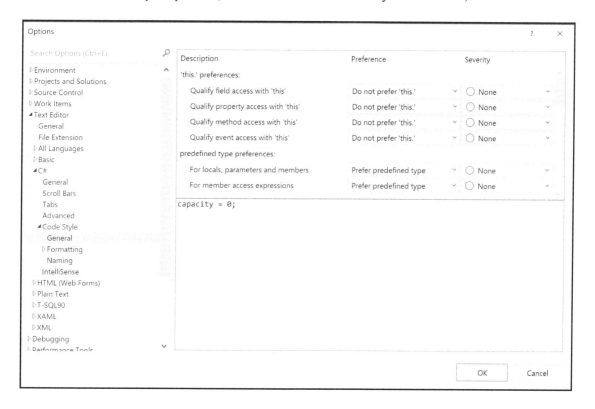

3. Change the **Severity** of **'this.' preferences** to **Suggestion**, **predefined type preferences** to **Warning**, and **'var' preferences** to **Error**. Change the **Preference** of **'var' preferences** from **Prefer explicit type** to **Prefer 'var'**:

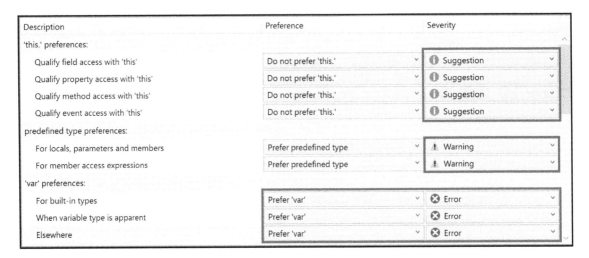

4. Change the **Severity** of **Code block preferences** to **Warning** and change the **Preference For methods** to **Prefer expression body**:

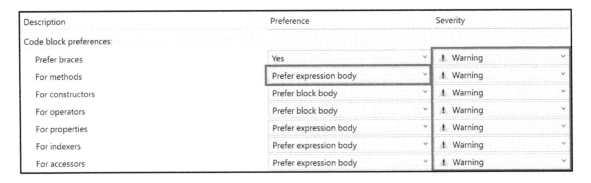

5. Ensure that all the remaining code style rules (**Expression preferences**, **Variable preferences** and '**null**' **checking**) have the severity **Suggestion**.
6. Verify the following code style diagnostics in the error list:

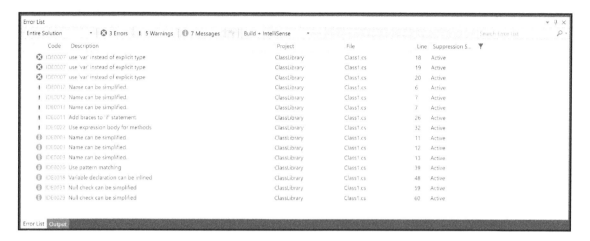

7. Double-click on the first **IDE0007** error and verify that a light bulb is offered for a code fix to **use 'var' instead of explicit type**. Verify that hitting the *Enter* key fixes the code and the diagnostic is removed from the error list. Repeat the exercise for the remaining **IDE0007** diagnostics:

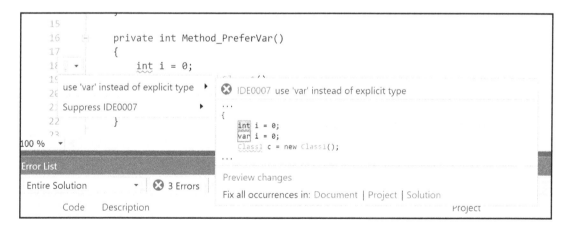

8. Now, double-click on the first **IDE0012** warning and verify that a light bulb is offered to **Simplify name 'System.Int32'**. This time, click on the **Fix all occurrences in Document** hyperlink and verify a preview changes dialog comes up that fixes all instances of *IDE0012* in the document with a single batch fix:

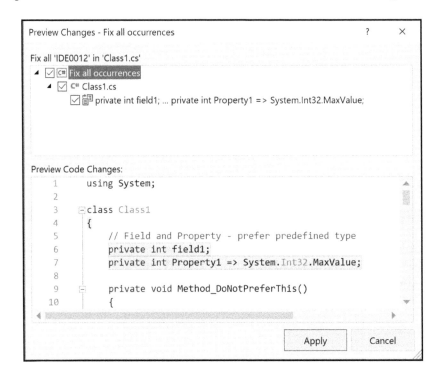

9. Apply code fixes for each of the remaining diagnostics in the error list and verify that the code is now completely clean:

```
using System;

class Class1
{
  // Field and Property - prefer predefined type
  private int field1;
  private int Property1 => int.MaxValue;

  private void Method_DoNotPreferThis()
  {
    Console.WriteLine(field1);
    Console.WriteLine(Property1);
    Method_PreferExpressionBody();
  }
```

```csharp
    private int Method_PreferVar()
    {
      var i = 0;
      var c = new Class1();
      var c2 = Method_PreferExpressionBody();
      return i;
    }

    private void Method_PreferBraces(bool flag)
    {
      if (flag)
      {
        Console.WriteLine(flag);
      }
    }

    private Class1 Method_PreferExpressionBody() =>
Method_PreferPatternMatching(null);

    private Class1 Method_PreferPatternMatching(object o)
    {
      if (o is Class1 c)
      {
        return c;
      }

      return new Class1();
    }

    private int Method_PreferInlineVariableDeclaration(string s)
    {
      if (int.TryParse(s, out var i))
      {
        return i;
      }

      return -1;
    }

    private void Method_NullCheckingPreferences(object o)
    {
      var str = o?.ToString();
      var o3 = o ?? new object();
    }
}
```

10. Add the following new method to Class1 and verify that **IDE0007** (**use 'var' instead of explicit type**) is raised for the code style violation in the newly added code:

```
private void Method_New_ViolateVarPreference()
{
    Class1 c = new Class1();
}
```

How it works...

Code style rules are built into Visual Studio 2017 and are classified into the following broad categories:

- 'this.' preferences
- predefined type preferences
- 'var' preferences
- Code block preferences
- Expression preferences
- Variable preferences
- 'null' checking

Each category has a set of one or more rules, each with two fields:

- **Preference**: A string identifying the preference for the rule. Normally, it has two possible values, one indicating that the rule should be preferred, and the other indicating the rule should not be preferred. For example, for a **'this.' preference** rule, the possible values are:
    - **Do not prefer 'this.'**: This enforces that code with the 'this.' prefix to member accesses is flagged.
    - **Prefer 'this.'**: This ensures that code without 'this.' prefix to member accesses is flagged.
- **Severity**: An enum identifying the severity of the rule. It has the following possible values and visual effects:
    - **Error**: Violations of the rule produce error diagnostics in the error list and red squiggles in the code editor.
    - **Warning**: Violations of the rule produce warning diagnostics in the error list and green squiggles in the code editor.

- **Suggestion**: Violations of the rule produce informational message diagnostics in the error list and gray dots under the first couple of characters of violating syntax in the code editor.
- **None**: Rule is not enforced in the editor and there are no diagnostics in the error list or visual indicators in the editor.

Users can configure the preference and severity of each rule as per their requirements using the **Tools** | **Options** dialog. Closing and re-opening the source documents causes the configuration changes to take effect and the violations are reported in the error list and visual indicators (squiggles/dots) appear in the code editor. Each rule comes with a code fix and FixAll support to fix one or more instances of the violation across the document, project, or solution.

Diagnostics reported for the built-in code style rules are only produced during live code editing in Visual Studio 2017 - they do not break the build and are not produced during the command-line builds. This behavior may or may not change in future versions of Visual Studio.

There is more...

Code style rule preferences are saved with user profile settings and persisted across Visual Studio sessions on the machine for the same Visual Studio install. This means that any project opened in Visual Studio will have the same code style enforcement. However, the same sources opened on a different Visual Studio installation or a different machine with a different user profile will not have the same code style enforcement. To enable same code style enforcement for a repo across all users, users need to persist the code style settings into an `.editorconfig` file and check it into the repo along with the sources. Refer to, *Using .editorconfig file for per-folder configuration for code style rules*, recipe in this chapter for further details.

Consider exploring the **Naming** rules in the **Tools** | **Options...** dialog under **Text Editor** | **C#** | **Code Style** | **Naming**. These rules allow users to enforce guidelines on how each different symbol kind should be named. For example, interface names should start with capital letter "I", type name should be Pascal cased, and so on.

Using the .editorconfig file for configuration of code style rules

In this section, we will show you how to configure the code style rules built into Visual Studio 2017 using the EditorConfig file, and how to override these settings at different folder levels. These EditorConfig files can be checked into the repo along with source files and this ensures the code style settings are persisted and enforced for all repo contributors.

Getting ready

You will need to have Visual Studio 2017 installed on your machine to execute the recipes in this chapter. You can install a free community version of Visual Studio 2017 from `https://www.visualstudio.com/thank-you-downloading-visual-studio/?sku=Community&rel=15`.

Install the `EditorConfig Language Service` VSIX from the Visual Studio extension gallery at `http://vsixgallery.com/extension/1209461d-57f8-46a4-814a-dbe5fecef941/` to get intellisense and autocompletion for `.editorconfig` files in Visual Studio.

How to do it…

1. Start Visual Studio, click on **File | New | Project…**, create a new C# class library project, and replace the code in `Class1.cs` with code from the code sample at `ClassLibrary/Class1.cs`.
2. Add a new text file named `.editorconfig` to the project with the following contents:

```
# top-most EditorConfig file
root = true

# rules for all .cs files.
[*.cs]

# 'this.' preferences
dotnet_style_qualification_for_field = false:suggestion
dotnet_style_qualification_for_property = false:suggestion
dotnet_style_qualification_for_method = false:suggestion
dotnet_style_qualification_for_event = false:suggestion
```

```
# predefined type preferences
dotnet_style_predefined_type_for_locals_parameters_members =
true:warning
dotnet_style_predefined_type_for_member_access = true:warning

# 'var' preferences
csharp_style_var_for_built_in_types = true:error
csharp_style_var_when_type_is_apparent = true:error
csharp_style_var_elsewhere = true:error

# code block preferences
csharp_new_line_before_open_brace = all
csharp_style_expression_bodied_methods = true:warning
csharp_style_expression_bodied_constructors = false:warning
csharp_style_expression_bodied_operators = false:warning
csharp_style_expression_bodied_properties = true:warning
csharp_style_expression_bodied_indexers = true:warning
csharp_style_expression_bodied_accessors = true:warning

# expression preferences
dotnet_style_object_initializer = true:suggestion
dotnet_style_collection_initializer = true:suggestion
csharp_style_pattern_matching_over_is_with_cast_check =
true:suggestion
csharp_style_pattern_matching_over_as_with_null_check =
true:suggestion
dotnet_style_explicit_tuple_names = true:suggestion

# variable preferences
csharp_style_inlined_variable_declaration = true:suggestion

# 'null' checking
csharp_style_throw_expression = true:suggestion
csharp_style_conditional_delegate_call = true:suggestion
dotnet_style_coalesce_expression = true:suggestion
dotnet_style_null_propagation = true:suggestion
```

3. Verify the following code style diagnostics in the error list:

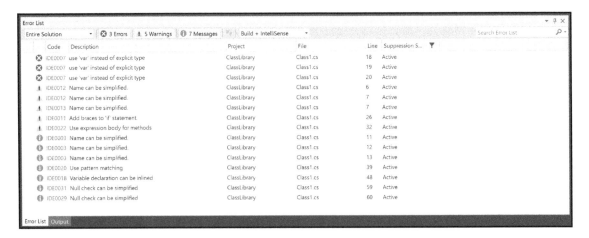

4. Double-click on the first **IDE0007** error and verify that a light bulb is offered for a code fix to **use 'var' instead of explicit type**. Verify that hitting the *Enter* key fixes the code and the diagnostic is removed from the error list. Repeat the exercise for the remaining **IDE0007** diagnostics.

5. Then, double-click on the first **IDE0012** warning and verify that a light bulb is offered to **Simplify name 'System.Int32'**. This time, click on the **Fix all occurrences in Document** hyperlink and verify that a preview changes dialog comes up, which fixes all instances of **IDE0012** in the document with a single batch fix.

6. Apply code fixes for each of the remaining diagnostics in the error list and verify the code is now completely clean:

```
using System;

class Class1
{
 // Field and Property - prefer predefined type
 private int field1;
 private int Property1 => int.MaxValue;

 private void Method_DoNotPreferThis()
 {
  Console.WriteLine(field1);
  Console.WriteLine(Property1);
  Method_PreferExpressionBody();
 }
```

```csharp
private int Method_PreferVar()
{
 var i = 0;
 var c = new Class1();
 var c2 = Method_PreferExpressionBody();
 return i;
}

private void Method_PreferBraces(bool flag)
{
 if (flag)
 {
  Console.WriteLine(flag);
 }
}

private Class1 Method_PreferExpressionBody() =>
Method_PreferPatternMatching(null);

private Class1 Method_PreferPatternMatching(object o)
{
 if (o is Class1 c)
 {
  return c;
 }

 return new Class1();
}

private int Method_PreferInlineVariableDeclaration(string s)
{
 if (int.TryParse(s, out var i))
 {
  return i;
 }

 return -1;
}

private void Method_NullCheckingPreferences(object o)
{
 var str = o?.ToString();
 var o3 = o ?? new object();
}
}
```

7. Add a new folder, say `NewFolder`, to the root of the project and add a new class, say `Class2.cs`, to the folder with the following method and verify **IDE0007** (**use 'var' instead of explicit type**) is raised for the code style violation in the newly added code.

```
private void Method_New_ViolateVarPreference()
{
 Class1 c = new Class1();
}
```

8. Add a new text file named `.editorconfig` to `NewFolder` with the following contents:

```
# rules for all .cs files in this folder.
[*.cs]

# override 'var' preferences
csharp_style_var_for_built_in_types = false:error
csharp_style_var_when_type_is_apparent = false:error
csharp_style_var_elsewhere = false:error
```

9. Close and reopen `Class2.cs` and verify the **IDE0007** is no longer reported.

How it works...

Refer to the *How it works...*, section in the recipe, *Configuring C# code style rules built into Visual Studio 2017*, in this chapter to understand the different built-in code style rules in Visual Studio 2017, the **Preference** and **Severity** settings associated with these rules and how they map to the editor config entries. For example, consider the following entry:

```
dotnet_style_qualification_for_field = false:suggestion
```

`dotnet_style_qualification_for_field` is the rule name, with the preference `false` and severity `suggestion`. These rules and their settings are enforced at each folder level, with the EditorConfig file at any folder level overriding the settings from the EditorConfig files in the ancestor directories, until the root file path is reached or an EditorConfig file with `root=true` is found. We recommend you refer to the following articles to get a detailed understanding of EditorConfig and related support in Visual Studio 2017:

- Editorconfig file format: http://EditorConfig.org/
- Editorconfig support for .NET code style in VS2017: https://blogs.msdn.microsoft.com/dotnet/2016/12/15/code-style-configuration-in-the-vs2017-rc-update/

- Editorconfig reference for .NET code style in VS2017: `https://docs.microsoft.com/en-us/visualstudio/ide/EditorConfig-code-style-settings-reference`

Using the public API analyzer for API surface maintenance

The `DeclarePublicAPIAnalyzer` analyzer is a popular third-party analyzer developed at the (`https://github.com/dotnet/roslyn-analyzers`) repo and published as a NuGet package at `https://www.nuget.org/packages/Roslyn.Diagnostics.Analyzers`. This analyzer helps track the public surface area of a project with additional readable and reviewable text files that live along with the project sources and provide API documentation as a source. For example, consider the following source file with public and non-public symbols:

```
public class Class1
{
  public int Field1;

  public object Property1 => null;

  public void Method1() { }

  public void Method1(int x) { }

  private void Method2() { }
}
```

The additional API surface text file for this type will look as follows:

```
Class1
Class1.Class1() -> void
Class1.Field1 -> int
Class1.Method1() -> void
Class1.Method1(int x) -> void
Class1.Property1.get -> object
```

There is an entry for every public symbol: type *Class1*, its constructor and it's members *Field1*, *Method1* overloads, and the *Property1* getter. Entries contain the entire symbol signature, including the return type and parameters.

With this NuGet package, users can track the shipped and unshipped public API surface at any point of time, get live and build breaking diagnostics when the public API surface is changed, and apply code fixes to update these additional files to match the local API changes. This enables richer and more focused API reviews when the actual code changes are large and spread across the code base, but the API changes can be reviewed by just looking at core signature changes in a single file.

DeclarePublicAPIAnalyzer was written primarily for tracking the public API surface of the Roslyn source base at `https://github.com/dotnet/roslyn` and is still very popular among all Roslyn contributors. The analyzer was eventually converted into a general-purpose open source analyzer that can be installed for any .NET project from `NuGet.org`.

In this section, we will show you how to install and configure the public API analyzer for a C# project, walk you through the additional text files tracking the public API surface, show you the diagnostics reported from this analyzer with API changes, and finally show you how to apply code fixes to fix one or multiple instances of these diagnostics to update the API surface text files.

Getting ready

You will need to have Visual Studio 2017 installed on your machine to execute the recipes in this chapter. You can install a free community version of Visual Studio 2017 from `https://www.visualstudio.com/thank-you-downloading-visual-studio/?sku=Community&rel=15`.

How to do it…

1. Start Visual Studio, click on **File** | **New** | **Project…**, create a new C# class library project, and replace the code in `Class1.cs` with code from the code sample at `ClassLibrary/Class1.cs` (also mentioned in the *Introduction* section of this recipe).
2. Install the `Roslyn.Diagnostics.Analyzers` NuGet package Version *1.2.0-beta2*. For guidance on how to search for and install the analyzer NuGet package in a project, refer to the recipe *Searching and installing analyzers through the NuGet package manager,* in `Chapter 2`, *Consuming Diagnostic Analyzers in .NET Projects*.

3. Escalate the severity of *RS0016* and *RS0017* from **Warning** to **Error**. For guidance on analyzer severity configuration, refer to the recipe, *Viewing and configuring analyzers in solution explorer in Visual Studio* in `Chapter 2`, *Consuming Diagnostic Analyzers in .NET Projects*.
4. Add two new text files named `PublicAPI.Shipped.txt` and `PublicAPI.Unshipped.txt` to the project.
5. Select both text files in the solution explorer, change their build action from **Content** to **AdditionalFiles** using the **Properties** window, and save the project:

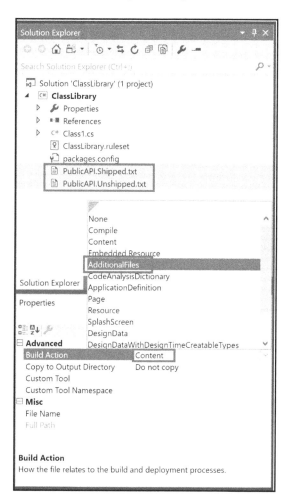

Improving Code Maintenance of C# Code Base

6. Verify squiggles in the editor and six *RS0016* errors (the '*x*' is not part of the declared API) in the error list, one for each public symbol:

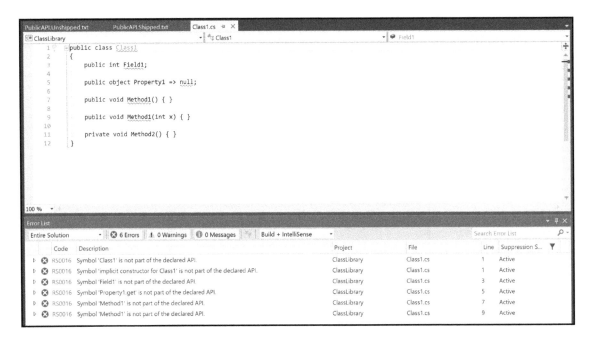

7. Move the caret to the field symbol `Field1` and hit *Ctrl* + dot(.) to get the code fix to automatically fix the diagnostic and add the symbol to the unshipped public API text file:

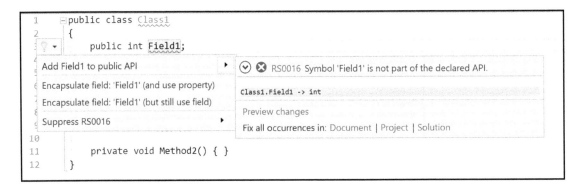

8. Apply the code fix by hitting the *Enter* key and verify the entry `Class1.Field1 -> int` is added to `PublicAPI.Unshipped.txt` and the diagnostic and squiggle for `Field1` no longer exist.

[148]

9. Move the caret to the type declaration for *Class1* and again hit *Ctrl* + dot to get the code fix, but this time apply a FixAll code fix to batch fix all RS0016 instances in the entire document and add all public symbols to the unshipped public API text file. For guidance on applying FixAll code fixes, refer to the recipe, *Applying batch code fixes (FixAll) across different scopes: document, project and solution,* in Chapter 3, *Writing IDE Code Fixes, Refactorings and Intellisense Completion Providers.*
10. Cut the entire contents of `PublicAPI.Unshipped.txt` and paste it into `PublicAPI.Shipped.txt`.
11. In `Class1.cs`, attempt to introduce a breaking API change by renaming the shipped public symbol `Field1` to `Field2`.
12. Verify *RS0016* is immediately reported for `Field2` and a code fix is offered to add a public API entry for `Field2`. Apply the code fix to add `Field2` to the public API surface and fix the diagnostic.
13. Build the project and verify that the project fails to build with the following *RS0017* diagnostic in the output window for the breaking change:
    `ClassLibraryPublicAPI.Shipped.txt(3,1,3,21): error RS0017: Symbol 'Class1.Field1 -> int' is part of the declared API, but is either not public or could not be found.`
14. Undo the changes in steps 11 and 12.
15. Change `Method2` to be a public method, verify *RS0016* is reported for it, and use the code fix to add it's API entry to `PublicAPI.Unshipped.txt`.
16. Now, rename the `unshipped` public symbol from `c` to `Method3`. Verify that *RS0016* is reported for `Method3` and the code fix replaces the public API entry for *Method2* with the entry for `Method3`:

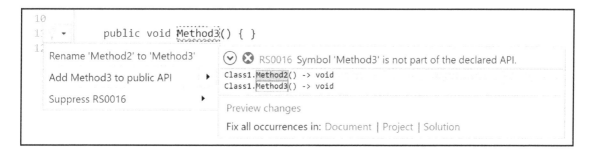

17. Apply the code fix and verify that the build succeeds and there are no diagnostics in the error list.

How it works…

`DeclarePublicAPIAnalyzer` is an additional file analyzer that works by comparing the public symbols declared in the compilation against the public API entries in the shipped and unshipped API surface text files. It uses a unique string representation for each symbol, based on its fully qualified name and signature as it's public API entry. It reports diagnostics for any missing or extra public API entries. You can find the implementation of this analyzer at https://github.com/dotnet/roslyn-analyzers/blob/master/src/Roslyn.Diagnostics.Analyzers/Core/DeclarePublicAPIAnalyzer.cs, and its corresponding code fix provided at https://github.com/dotnet/roslyn-analyzers/blob/master/src/Roslyn.Diagnostics.Analyzers/Core/DeclarePublicAPIFix.cs.

There's more…

You can read more about how to write and consume additional file analyzers, such as the DeclarePublicAPIAnalyzer, at https://github.com/dotnet/roslyn/blob/master/docs/analyzers/Using%20Additional%20Files.md.

Using third-party StyleCop analyzers for code style rules

In this section, we will introduce you to a popular third-party analyzer package for code style rules for C# projects, StyleCop analyzers. We will walk through how to install the StyleCop analyzers NuGet package, give example violations for each of the StyleCop rule categories, and show you how to configure and tune individual StyleCop rules.

Getting ready

You will need to have Visual Studio 2017 installed on your machine to execute the recipes in this chapter. You can install a free community version of Visual Studio 2017 from https://www.visualstudio.com/thank-you-downloading-visual-studio/?sku=Community&rel=15.

How to do it...

1. Start Visual Studio, navigate to **File | New | Project...**, create a new C# class library project, and replace the code in `Class1.cs` with code from the code sample at `ClassLibrary/Class1.cs`.
2. Install the `StyleCop.Analyzers` NuGet package (as of this writing, the latest prerelease version is *1.1.0-beta001*). For guidance on how to search for and install analyzer NuGet package in a project, refer to the recipe, *Searching and installing analyzers through the NuGet package manager* in `Chapter 2`, *Consuming Diagnostic Analyzers in .NET Projects*.
3. Verify the following StyleCop diagnostics show up in the error list:

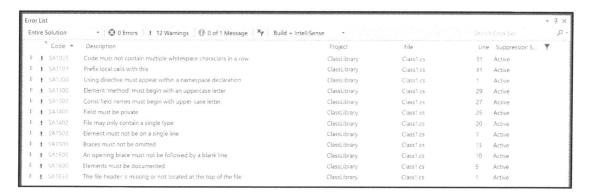

4. Build the project from the command-line or top-level Build menu in Visual Studio and verify these diagnostics are also reported from the build.

5. Double-click on the warning **SA1025 Code must not contain multiple whitespace characters in a row,** verify that the lightbulb is offered in the editor to fix the spacing violation, and applying the code fix by hitting the *Enter* key fixes it:

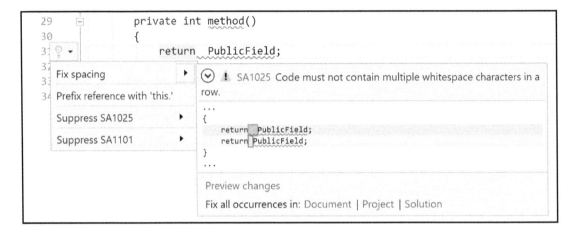

6. Then, double-click on the warning **SA1200 Using directive must appear within a namespace declaration** and verify it is reported on the using statement `using System;` due to it being outside the namespace `Namespace`.
7. Add a new file to the project named `stylecop.json`.
8. Select `stylecop.json` in the solution explorer, change its build action from **Content** to **AdditionalFiles** using the **Properties** window, and save the project:

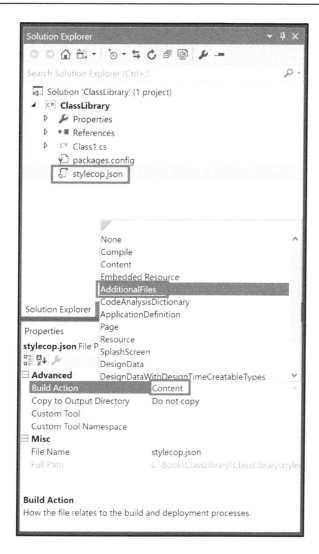

9. Add the following text to `stylecop.json` and verify that *SA1200* is no longer reported:

```
{
  "settings": {
    "orderingRules": {
      "usingDirectivesPlacement": "outsideNamespace"
    }
  }
}
```

10. Move `using System;` inside the namespace `Namespace` and verify *SA1200* (**using directive must appear outside a namespace declaration**) is now reported for the using statement being inside the namespace.

How it works...

The StypeCop analyzers contain the following categories of style rules:

- **Spacing rules (SA1000-)** (https://github.com/DotNetAnalyzers/StyleCopAnalyzers/blob/master/documentation/SpacingRules.md): Rules that enforce spacing requirements around keywords and symbols in the code
- **Readability rules (SA1100-)** (https://github.com/DotNetAnalyzers/StyleCopAnalyzers/blob/master/documentation/ReadabilityRules.md): Rules that ensure that the code is well-formatted and readable
- **Ordering rules (SA1200-)** (https://github.com/DotNetAnalyzers/StyleCopAnalyzers/blob/master/documentation/OrderingRules.md): Rules that enforce a standard ordering scheme for code contents
- **Naming rules (SA1300-)** (https://github.com/DotNetAnalyzers/StyleCopAnalyzers/blob/master/documentation/NamingRules.md): Rules that enforce naming requirements for members, types, and variables
- **Maintainability rules (SA1400-)** (https://github.com/DotNetAnalyzers/StyleCopAnalyzers/blob/master/documentation/MaintainabilityRules.md): Rules that improve code maintainability
- **Layout rules (SA1500-)** (https://github.com/DotNetAnalyzers/StyleCopAnalyzers/blob/master/documentation/LayoutRules.md): Rules that enforce code layout and line spacing
- **Documentation rules (SA1600-)** (https://github.com/DotNetAnalyzers/StyleCopAnalyzers/blob/master/documentation/DocumentationRules.md): Rules that verify the content and formatting of code documentation

The code example that we provided had the following StyleCop diagnostics by category:

- **Spacing**:
    - SA1025 (Code must not contain multiple whitespace characters in a row)
- **Readability**:
    - SA1101 (Prefix local calls with this)
- **Ordering**:
    - SA1200 (Using directive must appear within a namespace declaration)
- **Naming**:
    - SA1300 (Element "method" must begin with an uppercase letter)
    - SA1303 (Const field names must begin with uppercase letter)
- **Maintainability**:
    - SA1401 (Field must be private)
    - SA1402 (File may only contain a single type)
- **Layout**:
    - SA1502 (Element must not be on a single line)
    - SA1503 (Braces must not be omitted)
    - SA1505 (An opening brace must not be followed by a blank line)
- **Documentation**:
    - SA1600 (Elements must be documented)
    - SA1633 (The file header is missing or not located at the top of the file)

The StyleCop analyzers package also comes with code fixes for certain rules to fix the violations.

> The StyleCop analyzers can be installed either as a NuGet package (http://www.nuget.org/packages/StyleCop.Analyzers/) for specific C# projects/solutions or as a VSIX Extension enabled for all C# projects. The NuGet package enables the build-time StyleCop diagnostics and hence is the recommended way of installing the analyzers.

The code style is generally considered to be a very subjective matter, and hence it is very important that individual rules can be selectively enabled, suppressed, or configured by the end user.

- StyleCop rules can be enabled or suppressed using the code analysis ruleset files (see the recipe, *Using ruleset file and ruleset editor to configure analyzers*, in Chapter 2, *Consuming Diagnostic Analyzers in .NET Projects* for reference).
- Stylecop rules can be configured and tuned using a stylecop.json file added to the project as an additional non-source file. For example, consider the ordering rule *SA1200* (using directive must appear within a namespace declaration) at (http://www.nuget.org/packages/StyleCop.Analyzers/). By default, this rule reports violations if using directives are placed at the top of the file *outside* a namespace declaration. However, this rule can be configured to be its semantic opposite and require using directives to be outside a namespace declaration and report violations if they are *inside*, using the following stylecop.json:

```
{
  "settings": {
    "orderingRules": {
      "usingDirectivesPlacement": "outsideNamespace"
    }
  }
}
```

The StyleCop analyzers repo has thorough documentation for each category of rules, as well as individual style rules. You can find the documentation at https://github.com/DotNetAnalyzers/StyleCopAnalyzers/tree/master/documentation.

5
Catch Security Vulnerabilities and Performance Issues in C# Code

In this chapter, we will cover the following recipes:

- Identifying configuration-related security vulnerabilities in web applications
- Identifying cross-site scripting vulnerabilities in view markup files (.cshtml, .aspx files) in web applications
- Identifying insecure method calls that can lead to SQL and LDAP injection attacks
- Identifying weak password protection and management in web applications
- Identifying weak validation of data from external components to prevent attacks such as cross-site request forgery and path tampering
- Identifying performance improvements to source code using FxCop analyzers

Introduction

In this chapter, we will cover two very important and popular category of Roslyn analyzers: security and performance analyzers.

- **Security**: Given the extremely large domain of .NET applications, each of them with very domain-specific security vulnerabilities, it is critical that we have a domain-specific tools/extensions to catch these vulnerabilities. Roslyn-based security analyzers, such as **PUMA** scan analyzers, catch these vulnerabilities at compile time and report diagnostics. PUMA scan analyzer rules are classified into the following broad categories:
    - **Configuration** (`https://www.pumascan.com/rules.html#overview`): Rules to catch vulnerabilities in ASP.NET Web configuration files
    - **Cross-site Scripting** (`https://www.pumascan.com/rules.html#cross-site-scripting`): Rules to catch cross-site scripting (XSS) vulnerabilities
    - **Injection** (`https://www.pumascan.com/rules.html#injection`): Rules to catch calls to insecure method calls to external components that can cause SQL injection attacks
    - **Password Management** (`https://www.pumascan.com/rules.html#password-management`): Rules to catch vulnerabilities in password management components
    - **Validation** (`https://www.pumascan.com/rules.html#validation`): Rules to catch weak validation and authentication of external requests, which can lead to malicious attacks to other users

- **Performance**: Runtime performance is important for all applications, and there are many different aspects to it. One of the important performance criteria for .NET applications is the quality of MSIL or CIL (`https://en.wikipedia.org/wiki/Common_Intermediate_Language`) generated by the .NET compilers. The quality of MSIL is governed by both the quality of the user code and the compiler that produces MSIL. In this chapter, we will walk you through the performance rules in FxCop analyzers, which are the Microsoft code analysis rules (*CAXXXX*) written for identifying performance improvements in .NET applications to generate more efficient MSIL. These rules have been ported to the Roslyn analyzer framework and open sourced at `https://github.com/dotnet/roslyn-analyzers`.

Identifying configuration-related security vulnerabilities in web applications

ASP.NET enables you to specify configuration settings that affect all Web applications on a server, that affect only a single application, that affect individual pages, or that affect individual folders in a Web application. You can make configuration settings for features, such as compiler options, debugging, user authentication, error-message display, connection strings, and more. Configuration data is stored in XML files that are named Web.config.

You can read more details about different kind of configuration settings in the Web.config files at https://msdn.microsoft.com/en-us/library/ff400235.aspx.
In this section, we will walk you through the rules in PUMA scan analyzers to catch security vulnerabilities in web configuration in an ASP.NET Web Forms project.

Note that Roslyn analyzers are fully supported on both .NET framework projects and .NET core projects, so the PUMA scan analyzers covered here work fine on both ASP.NET and ASP.Net core web projects.

Getting ready

You will need to have Visual Studio 2017 installed on your machine to execute the recipes in this chapter. You can install a free community version of Visual Studio 2017 from https://www.visualstudio.com/thank-you-downloading-visual-studio/?sku=Community&rel=15.

How to do it...

1. Start Visual Studio and click on **File | New | Project...** and create a new **Visual C# | Web | ASP.NET Web Application** with the **Web Forms** template, say `WebApplication`:

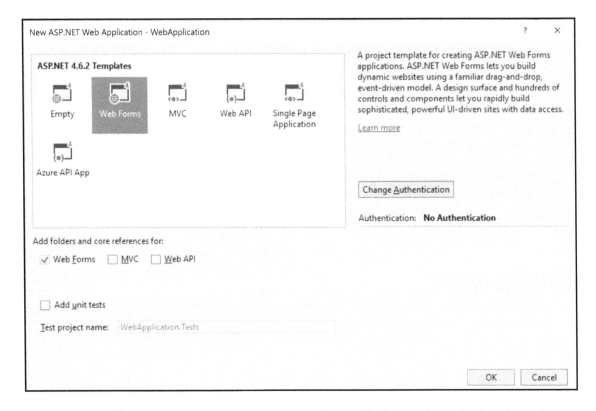

2. Install the `Puma.Security.Rules` analyzers NuGet package (at the time of writing, the latest stable version is *1.0.4*). For guidance on how to search and install analyzer NuGet package to a project, refer to the recipe, *Searching and installing analyzers through the NuGet package manager*, in `Chapter 2`, *Consuming Diagnostic Analyzers in .NET Projects*.
3. Select **Web.config** in the solution explorer and change its build action from **Content** to **AdditionalFiles** using the **Properties** window and save the project:

Chapter 5

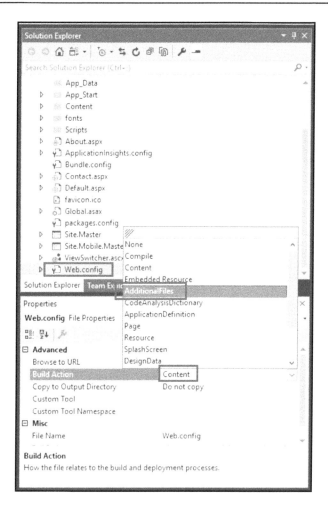

4. Open **Web.config** in the editor and replace existing system.web XML element with the following XML. You can read more about system.web XML element at https://msdn.microsoft.com/en-us/library/dayb112d(v=vs.100).aspx.

```
<system.web>
  <compilation debug="false" targetFramework="4.6.2" />
  <customErrors mode="Off" defaultRedirect="/home/error"/>
  <httpRuntime enableHeaderChecking="false"
enableVersionHeader="true" />
  <httpCookies requireSSL="false" httpOnlyCookies="false"/>
  <pages enableEventValidation="false"
enableViewStateMac="false" viewStateEncryptionMode="Never"
validateRequest="false" />
  <authentication mode="Forms">
```

[161]

Catch Security Vulnerabilities and Performance Issues in C# Code

```
          <forms loginUrl="~/Account/Login.aspx" timeout="900"
      enableCrossAppRedirects="true" protection="None" />
        </authentication>
      </system.web>
```

5. Build the project in Visual Studio or command line and verify that you get following *SECXXXX* warnings from the PUMA scan analyzer:

```
1>CSC : warning SEC0014: Insecure HTTP cookies
C:WebApplicationWeb.config(11): <httpCookies requireSSL="false"
httpOnlyCookies="false" />
1>CSC : warning SEC0015: Cookies accessible via script.
C:WebApplicationWeb.config(11): <httpCookies requireSSL="false"
httpOnlyCookies="false" />
1>CSC : warning SEC0003: Forms authentication does not set
requireSSL to true. C:WebApplicationWeb.config(14): <forms
loginUrl="~/Account/Login.aspx" timeout="900"
enableCrossAppRedirects="true" protection="None" />
1>CSC : warning SEC0004: Forms authentication does not set the
cookieless attribute to UseCookies.
C:WebApplicationWeb.config(14): <forms
loginUrl="~/Account/Login.aspx" timeout="900"
enableCrossAppRedirects="true" protection="None" />
1>CSC : warning SEC0006: Forms authentication cookie protection
attribute is not set to All. C:WebApplicationWeb.config(14):
<forms loginUrl="~/Account/Login.aspx" timeout="900"
enableCrossAppRedirects="true" protection="None" />
1>CSC : warning SEC0007: Forms authentication timeout value
exceeds the policy of 30 minutes.
C:WebApplicationWeb.config(14): <forms
loginUrl="~/Account/Login.aspx" timeout="900"
enableCrossAppRedirects="true" protection="None" />
1>CSC : warning SEC0005: Forms authentication does not set the
enableCrossAppRedirects attribute to false.
C:WebApplicationWeb.config(14): <forms
loginUrl="~/Account/Login.aspx" timeout="900"
enableCrossAppRedirects="true" protection="None" />
1>CSC : warning SEC0002: Custom errors are disabled.
C:WebApplicationWeb.config(9): <customErrors mode="Off"
defaultRedirect="/home/error" />
1>CSC : warning SEC0008: HTTP header checking is disabled.
C:WebApplicationWeb.config(10): <httpRuntime
enableHeaderChecking="false" enableVersionHeader="true" />
1>CSC : warning SEC0009: The Version HTTP response header is
enabled. C:WebApplicationWeb.config(10): <httpRuntime
enableHeaderChecking="false" enableVersionHeader="true" />
1>CSC : warning SEC0010: Event validation is disabled.
C:WebApplicationWeb.config(12): <pages
```

```
        enableEventValidation="false" enableViewStateMac="false"
        viewStateEncryptionMode="Never" validateRequest="false" />
        1>CSC : warning SEC0012: Validate request is disabled.
        C:WebApplicationWeb.config(12): <pages
        enableEventValidation="false" enableViewStateMac="false"
        viewStateEncryptionMode="Never" validateRequest="false" />
        1>CSC : warning SEC0013: Pages ViewStateEncryptionMode
        disabled. C:WebApplicationWeb.config(12): <pages
        enableEventValidation="false" enableViewStateMac="false"
        viewStateEncryptionMode="Never" validateRequest="false" />
        1>CSC : warning SEC0011: ViewStateMac is disabled.
        C:WebApplicationWeb.config(12): <pages
        enableEventValidation="false" enableViewStateMac="false"
        viewStateEncryptionMode="Never" validateRequest="false" />
```

6. Replace the `system.web` XML element in the `Web.config` file with the following contents (changes are highlighted in bold):

```
        <system.web>
          <compilation debug="false" targetFramework="4.6.2" />
          <customErrors mode="On" defaultRedirect="/home/error"/>
          <httpRuntime enableHeaderChecking="true"
        enableVersionHeader="false" />
          <httpCookies requireSSL="true" httpOnlyCookies="true"/>
          <pages enableEventValidation="true" enableViewStateMac="true"
        viewStateEncryptionMode="Always" validateRequest="true" />
          <authentication mode="Forms">
            <forms loginUrl="~/Account/Login.aspx" timeout="15"
        enableCrossAppRedirects="false" protection="All"
        requireSSL="true" cookieless="UseCookies" />
          </authentication>
        </system.web>
```

7. Build the project again and verify it compiles without any security warnings.

How it works...

PUMA scan analyzers catch security vulnerabilities in the web configuration files in C# ASP.NET web projects. In the preceding recipe, we showed you different kinds of security vulnerabilities that are caught by the PUMA scan analyzers, such as insecure forms authentication, http cookies configuration, header settings, and so on. You can read detailed description of all web configuration-related security vulnerabilities identified by the PUMA scan analyzers at `https://www.pumascan.com/rules.html#configuration`.

These security analyzers are written as additional file analyzers that analyze non-source files in the project that have been marked as `AdditionalFiles` item type. Users must mark the `web.config` file as an additional file in their project to trigger security analysis during build. You can read more about how to write and consume additional file analyzers at https://github.com/dotnet/roslyn/blob/master/docs/analyzers/Using%20Additional%20Files.md.

Identifying cross-site scripting vulnerabilities in view markup files (.cshtml, .aspx files) in web applications

Cross-site scripting (**XSS**) is a type of computer security vulnerability typically found in web applications. XSS enables attackers to inject client-side scripts into web pages viewed by other users. A cross-site scripting vulnerability may be used by attackers to bypass access controls such as the same-origin policy. Cross-site scripting carried out on websites accounted for roughly 84% of all security vulnerabilities documented by Symantec as of 2007. Their effect may range from a petty nuisance to a significant security risk, depending on the sensitivity of the data handled by the vulnerable site and the nature of any security mitigation implemented by the site's owner.

You can read more details about cross-site scripting at https://en.wikipedia.org/wiki/Cross-site_scripting.

In this section, we will walk you through the rules in PUMA scan analyzers to catch security vulnerabilities that can lead to cross-site scripting attacks in an ASP.NET web project.

Getting ready

You will need to have Visual Studio 2017 installed on your machine to execute the recipes in this chapter. You can install a free community version of Visual Studio 2017 from https://www.visualstudio.com/thank-you-downloading-visual-studio/?sku=Community&rel=15.

How to do it...

1. Start Visual Studio and click on **File** | **New** | **Project...** and create a new **Visual C#** | **Web** | **ASP.NET Web Application** with the **MVC** template, say `WebApplication`:

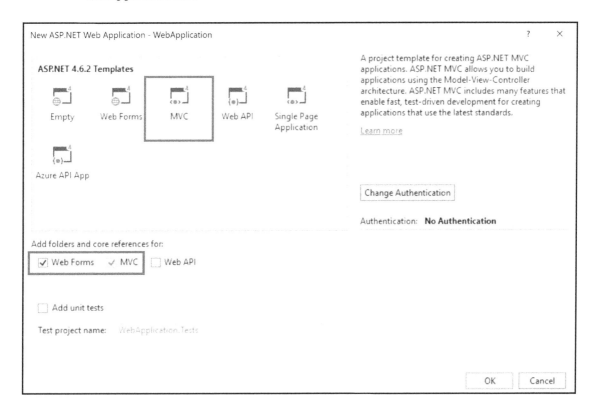

2. Install the `Puma.Security.Rules` analyzers NuGet package (at the time of writing, the latest stable version is *1.0.4*). For guidance on how to search and install analyzer NuGet package to a project, refer to the recipe *Searching and installing analyzers through the NuGet package manager* in `Chapter 2`, *Consuming Diagnostic Analyzers in .NET Projects*.

3. Open **Views | _ViewStart.cshtml** file and add the following text at the end of the file:

```
<div>
 @Html.Raw(string.Format("Welcome <span
class=\"bold\">{0}</span>!", ViewContext.ViewBag.UserName))

@{
   WriteLiteral(string.Format("Welcome <span
class=\"bold\">{0}</span>!", ViewContext.ViewBag.UserName));
 }
</div>
```

4. Select _ViewStart.cshtml in the solution explorer and change its **Build Action** from **Content** to **AdditionalFiles** using the **Properties** window below and save the project.
5. Add a new Web Form to the project, say WebForm.aspx, and the following HTML heading with a raw inline expression to the form:

```
<div>
  <h2>Welcome <%= Request["UserName"].ToString() %></h2>
</div>
```

6. Select WebForm.aspx in the solution explorer and change its **Build Action** from **Content** to **AdditionalFiles** using the **Properties** window below and save the project.
7. Build the project in Visual Studio or command line and verify you get following SECXXXX warnings from the PUMA scan analyzer:

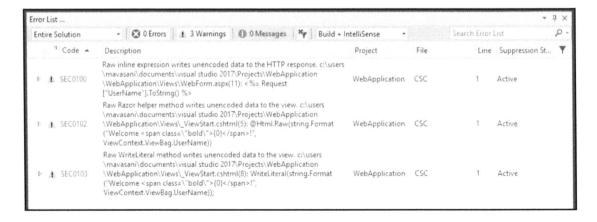

8. Replace the HTML division element added to _ViewStart.cshtml in step 3 with the following:

   ```
   <div>
    Welcome <span class=\"bold\">@ViewContext.ViewBag.UserName</span>!
   </div>
   ```

9. Replace the HTML division element added to WebForm.aspx in step 5 with the following:

   ```
   <div>
    <h2>Welcome <%: Request["UserName"].ToString() %></h2>
   </div>
   ```

10. Build the project again and verify it compiles without any security warnings.

How it works...

PUMA scan analyzers catch cross-site scripting security vulnerabilities in the view markup files (.cshtml, .aspx, .ascx) in C# ASP.NET web projects. In the preceding recipe, we showed you different kinds of security vulnerabilities that are caught by the PUMA scan analyzers, such as data from untrusted data source written to the body of an HTML document using raw inline and binding expressions, raw razor helper, and raw WriteLiteral method, and so on. It is recommended that such data is HTML encoded before being written to the browser. You can read detailed description of all cross-site scripting related security vulnerabilities identified by the PUMA scan analyzers at https://www.pumascan.com/rules.html#cross-site-scripting.

These security analyzers are written as additional file analyzers that analyze non-source files in the project that have been marked as AdditionalFiles item type. Users must mark the view markup files as additional files in their project to trigger security analysis during build. You can read more about how to write and consume additional file analyzers at https://github.com/dotnet/roslyn/blob/master/docs/analyzers/Using%20Additional%20Files.md.

Identifying insecure method calls that can lead to SQL and LDAP injection attacks

SQL injection is a code injection technique, used to attack data-driven applications, in which nefarious SQL statements are inserted into an entry field for execution (for example, to dump the database contents to the attacker). SQL injection attacks allow attackers to spoof identity, tamper with existing data, cause repudiation issues such as voiding transactions or changing balances, allow the complete disclosure of all data on the system, destroy the data or make it otherwise unavailable, and become administrators of the database server.

LDAP injection is a code injection technique used to exploit web applications, which could reveal sensitive user information or modify information represented in the **Lightweight Directory Access Protocol** (**LDAP**) data stores. LDAP injection exploits a security vulnerability in an application by manipulating input parameters passed to internal search, add, or modify functions.

You can read more details about SQL injection at (`https://en.wikipedia.org/wiki/SQL_injection`) and LDAP injection at `https://en.wikipedia.org/wiki/LDAP_injection`. In this section, we will walk you through the rules in PUMA scan analyzers to catch security vulnerabilities that can lead to SQL injection and LDAP injection attacks in data driven .NET projects.

Getting ready

You will need to have Visual Studio 2017 installed on your machine to execute the recipes in this chapter. You can install a free community version of Visual Studio 2017 from `https://www.visualstudio.com/thank-you-downloading-visual-studio/?sku=Community&rel=15`.

How to do it...

1. Start Visual Studio and click **File** | **New** | **Project...** and create a new **Visual C#** | **Class Library**, say `ClassLibrary`.
2. Install the `Puma.Security.Rules` analyzers NuGet package (at the time of writing, the latest stable version is *1.0.4*). For guidance on how to search and install analyzer NuGet package to a project, refer to the recipe, *Searching and installing analyzers through the NuGet package manager* in `Chapter 2`, *Consuming Diagnostic Analyzers in .NET Projects*.

3. Add assembly references to the following framework assemblies: *System.Data.Linq.dll* and `System.DirectoryServices.dll`.
4. Replace the default `Class1` implementation in `Class1.cs` with the following code:

```
using System.Data.Linq;
using System.Data.SqlClient;
using System.DirectoryServices;

public class Class1
{
  private void SQL_Injection(SqlConnection connection, string id)
  {
    using (DataContext context = new DataContext(connection))
    {
      context.ExecuteCommand("SELECT * FROM Items WHERE ID = " + id);
    }

    SqlCommand cmd = new SqlCommand("SELECT * FROM Items WHERE ID = " + id, connection);
    string result = cmd.ExecuteScalar().ToString();
  }

  private void LDAP_Injection(string domain, string userName)
  {
    DirectoryEntry entry = new DirectoryEntry(string.Format("LDAP://DC={0}, DC=COM/", domain));
    DirectorySearcher searcher = new DirectorySearcher(entry)
    {
      SearchScope = SearchScope.Subtree,
      Filter = string.Format("(name={0})", userName)
    };
    SearchResultCollection resultCollection = searcher.FindAll();
  }
}
```

5. Verify you get following *SECXXX* diagnostics from PUMA scan analyzers in the error list and squiggles in the editor while editing code and also when invoking an explicit build.

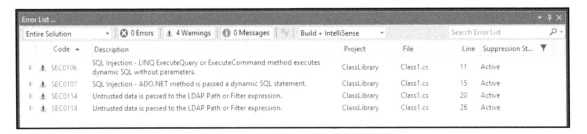

6. Fix *SEC0106* reported on `context.ExecuteCommand` in method `SQL_Injection` by passing *id* as the second argument to the invocation: `context.ExecuteCommand("SELECT * FROM Items WHERE ID = {0}", id);`

7. Fix *SEC0107* by parameterizing the query passed to *new* `SqlCommand(...)` with a *SqlParameter*:

```
SqlCommand cmd = new SqlCommand("SELECT * FROM Items WHERE ID = @id", connection);
SqlParameter parm = new SqlParameter("@id", id);
cmd.Parameters.Add(parm);
```

8. Fix *SEC0114* diagnostics by encoding the domain and `userName` arguments using the Web Protection Library (also known as AntiXSS) LDAP encoding methods.
    1. Add NuGet package reference to AntiXSS library
    2. Replace the domain argument passed to new `DirectoryEntry(...)` with `Microsoft.Security.Application.Encoder.LdapDistinguishedNameEncode(domain)`
    3. Replace the `userName` argument passed to `string.Format` invocation in the initializer for filter with `Microsoft.Security.Application.Encoder.LdapFilterEncode(userName)`

9. Verify there are no diagnostics in the error list and the project builds without any errors or warnings.

How it works...

PUMA scan analyzers catch SQL injection and LDAP injection security vulnerabilities in the source code of data-driven applications. In the preceding recipe, we showed you couple of different kinds of security vulnerabilities that are caught by these analyzers, such as concatenating untrusted data with SQL query strings, Sql command, LDAP directory entry path and filter format.

SQL injection attacks can be prevented by using parameterized queries where the untrusted data is passed as an explicit format argument.

LDAP injection attacks can be prevented by using LDAP encoding methods to encode the untrusted data. You can read detailed description of all SQL and LDAP injection security vulnerabilities identified by the PUMA scan analyzers at `https://www.pumascan.com/rules.html#injection`.

Identifying weak password protection and management in web applications

Applications responsible for password management inherit a tremendous amount of risk and responsibility. User passwords must be created with sufficient length/complexity, stored securely, and protected from brute force and cracking attempts.

In this section, we will walk you through the rules in PUMA scan analyzers to catch vulnerabilities related to weak password management vulnerabilities in ASP.NET web projects. The following password management rules are currently supported in PUMA scan analyzers:

- ASP.NET Identity Weak Password Complexity
- ASP.NET Identity Missing Password Lockout

You can read more details about these rules at `https://www.pumascan.com/rules.html#password-management`.

Getting ready

You will need to have Visual Studio 2017 installed on your machine to execute the recipes in this chapter. You can install a free community version of Visual Studio 2017 from `https://www.visualstudio.com/thank-you-downloading-visual-studio/?sku=Community&rel=15`.

How to do it...

1. Start Visual Studio and click on **File | New | Project** and create a new **Visual C# | Web | ASP.NET Web Application** with the **Web Forms** template, say `WebApplication`. Click on **Change Authentication** button and change the authentication to **Individual User Accounts**:

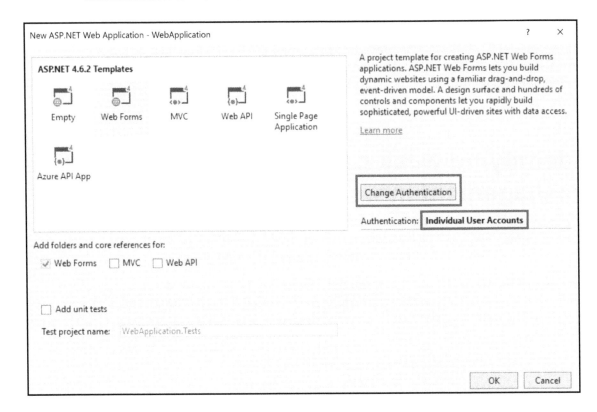

2. Install the `Puma.Security.Rules` analyzers NuGet package (at the time of writing, the latest stable version is *1.0.4*). For guidance on how to search and install analyzer NuGet package to a project, refer to the recipe, *Searching and installing analyzers through the NuGet package manager* in `Chapter 2`, *Consuming Diagnostic Analyzers in .NET Projects*.

3. Build the project and verify that you get a bunch of *SECXXXX* diagnostics from the PUMA scan analyzers, including a couple of password protection related diagnostics (*SEC0017* and *SEC0018*):

   ```
   WebApplicationApp_StartIdentityConfig.cs(50,41,57,14): warning
   SEC0017: Password validator settings do not meet the
   requirements - Minimum Length (12), Numeric Character (True),
   Lowercase Character (True), Uppercase Character (True), Special
   Character (True)
   ...
   WebApplicationAccountLogin.aspx.cs(36,121,36,126): warning
   SEC0018: Password lockout is disabled. To protect accounts from
   brute force attacks, set the shouldLockout parameter to true.
   ```

4. Open `WebApplicationApp_StartIdentityConfig.cs` and change the required minimum password length to be `12`:

   ```
   // Configure validation logic for passwords
   manager.PasswordValidator = new PasswordValidator
   {
       RequiredLength = 12,
       RequireNonLetterOrDigit = true,
       RequireDigit = true,
       RequireLowercase = true,
       RequireUppercase = true,
   };
   ```

5. Open `WebApplicationAccountLogin.aspx.cs` and change the `shouldLockout` argument to `PasswordSignIn` invocation to be true:

   ```
   var result = signinManager.PasswordSignIn(Email.Text,
   Password.Text, RememberMe.Checked, shouldLockout: true);
   ```

6. Build the project and verify there are no *SEC0017* and *SEC0018* diagnostics.

Identifying weak validation of data from external components to prevent attacks such as cross-site request forgery and path tampering

In this section, we will walk you through the rules in PUMA scan analyzers to catch security vulnerabilities that can lead to following types of security attacks due to insufficient validation of input:

- **Cross-Site request forgery** (https://en.wikipedia.org/wiki/Cross-site_request_forgery): Cross-site request forgery, also known as one-click attack or session riding and abbreviated as CSRF or XSRF, is a type of malicious exploit of a website where unauthorized commands are transmitted from a user that the web application trusts. Unlike cross-site scripting (XSS), which exploits the trust a user has for a particular site, CSRF exploits the trust that a site has in a user's browser

- **Path tampering** (https://en.wikipedia.org/wiki/Directory_traversal_attack): A directory traversal (or path traversal) consists in exploiting insufficient security validation/sanitization of user-supplied input filenames, so that characters representing traverse to parent directory are passed through to the file APIs. The goal of this attack is to use an affected application to gain unauthorized access to the filesystem

- **Unvalidated redirect** (https://www.owasp.org/index.php/Unvalidated_Redirects_and_Forwards_Cheat_Sheet): Unvalidated redirects and forwards are possible when a web application accepts untrusted input that could cause the web application to redirect the request to a URL contained within untrusted input. By modifying untrusted URL input to a malicious site, an attacker may successfully launch a phishing scam and steal user credentials

Getting ready

You will need to have Visual Studio 2017 installed on your machine to execute the recipes in this chapter. You can install a free community version of Visual Studio 2017 from https://www.visualstudio.com/thank-you-downloading-visual-studio/?sku=Community&rel=15.

How to do it...

1. Start Visual Studio and click **File** | **New** | **Project...** and create a new **Visual C#** | **Web** | **ASP.NET Web Application** with the **MVC** template, say `WebApplication`.

2. Install the `Puma.Security.Rules` analyzers NuGet package (at the time of writing, the latest stable version is *1.0.4*). For guidance on how to search and install analyzer NuGet package to a project, refer to the recipe, *Searching and installing analyzers through the NuGet package manager,* in `Chapter 2`, *Consuming Diagnostic Analyzers in .NET Projects*.

3. Add a new class `Class1` to the project and replace the file contents with the following code:

```
using System.Configuration;
using System.Net.Http;
using System.Web.Mvc;

namespace WebApplication
{
  public class Class1
  {
    [AllowHtml]
    public string AllowHtmlProperty { get; set; }

    [HttpPost]
    [ValidateInput(false)]
    public ActionResult Missing_AntiForgeryToken()
    {
      return null;
    }

    [HttpPost]
    public FileResult Path_Tampering(string fileName)
    {
      string filePath =
ConfigurationManager.AppSettings["DownloadDirectory"].ToString();
      return new FilePathResult(filePath + fileName,
"application/octet-stream");
    }

    private void Certificate_Validation_Disabled()
    {
```

```
                using (var handler = new WebRequestHandler())
                {
                    handler.ServerCertificateValidationCallback += (sender,
             cert, chain, sslPolicyErrors) => true;
                }
            }
        }
    }
```

4. Verify you get following **SECXXX** diagnostics from PUMA scan analyzers in the error list and squiggles in the editor while editing code and also when invoking an explicit build:

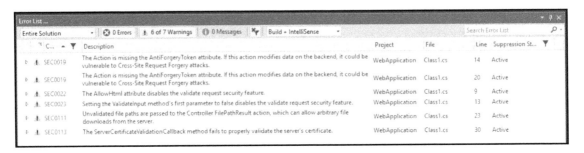

5. Fix the first two *SEC0019* diagnostics by applying the `[ValidateAntiForgeryToken]` attribute to methods `Missing_AntiForgeryToken` and `Path_Tampering`.
6. Fix *SEC0022* by deleting the `[AllowHtml]` attribute on `AllowHtmlProperty`.
7. Fix *SEC0023* by deleting the `[ValidateInput(false)]` attribute on `Missing_AntiForgeryToken`.
8. Fix *SEC01111* by adding the following `ValidatedFileResult` type and replacing `return new FilePathResult(...)` with `return new ValidatedFileResult(...)` in `Path_Tampering` method.

```
            private class ValidatedFileResult : FileResult
            {
              public ValidatedFileResult(string filePath, string fileName,
            string contentType)
                : base(contentType)
              {
                // Add validation logic.
              }

              protected override void WriteFile(HttpResponseBase response)
```

```
        {
            // Add write logic
        }
    }
```

9. Fix *SEC0113* by deleting the line `handler.ServerCertificateValidationCallback += (sender, cert, chain, sslPolicyErrors) => true;`.
10. Build the project again and verify it compiles without any security warnings.

> You can read further details about PUMA scan validation rules at `https://www.pumascan.com/rules.html#validation`.

Identifying performance improvements to source code using FxCop analyzers

In this section, we will introduce you to a popular third-party analyzer package for C# projects, FxCop analyzers.
We will walk through how to install the FxCop analyzers NuGet package and give examples violations for different performance rules and show you how to automatically fix some of these issues with the code fixes that come along with the analyzers in the NuGet package.

Getting ready

You will need to have Visual Studio 2017 installed on your machine to execute the recipes in this chapter. You can install a free community version of Visual Studio 2017 from `https://www.visualstudio.com/thank-you-downloading-visual-studio/?sku=Community&rel=15`.

How to do it...

1. Start Visual Studio and click **File | New | Project...** and create a new C# class library project and replace the code in `Class1.cs` with code from the code sample at `ClassLibrary\Class1.cs`.
2. Install the `Microsoft.CodeAnalysis.FxCopAnalyzers` NuGet package (the latest prerelease version at the time of writing is *1.2.0-beta2*). For guidance on how to search and install analyzer NuGet package to a project, refer to the recipe, *Searching and installing analyzers through the NuGet package manager*, in Chapter 2, *Consuming Diagnostic Analyzers in .NET Projects*.
3. Unload the project file by right-clicking on `ClassLibrary1` in the solution explorer and then open the project file for editing in Visual Studio by right clicking on the unloaded project in the solution explorer.
4. Add the following `PropertyGroup` to the project to enable the new Roslyn `IOperation` feature used by the FxCop analyzers:

   ```
   <PropertyGroup>
     <Features>IOperation</Features>
   </PropertyGroup>
   ```

5. Reload the project and verify the following FxCop diagnostics show up in the error list:

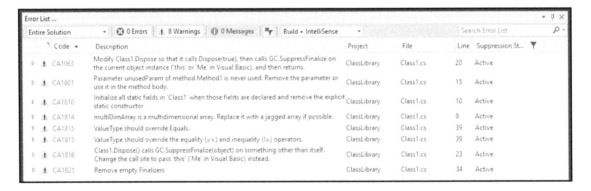

6. Build the project from the command line or top level **Build** menu in Visual Studio and verify these diagnostics are also reported from build.
7. Double click on the warning *CA1815* (**ValueType should override Equals**) and verify lightbulb is offered in the editor to implement the overrides for equals, `GetHashCode` and == and != operator methods:

Chapter 5

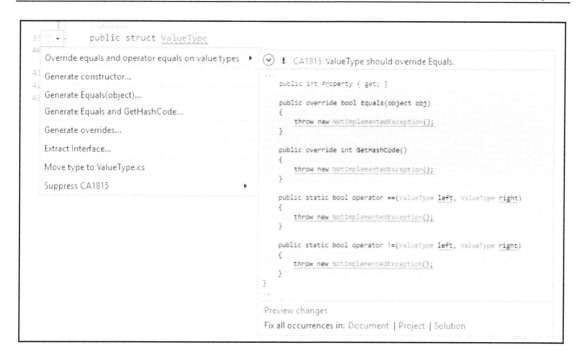

8. Verify that applying the code fix by hitting the *Enter* key fixes *CA1815* diagnostics. Note that this introduces new *CAXXXX* diagnostics due to the default implementation of the overrides.

9. Replace the content of `Class1.cs` with following code and verify all *CAXXXX* diagnostics are fixed:

```
using System;

namespace Namespace
{
  public class Class1: IDisposable
  {
    private static int staticField = 3;
    private int[][] jaggedArray;

    public void Method1(int usedParam)
    {
      Console.WriteLine(usedParam);
    }

    public void Dispose()
    {
      Dispose(true);
```

```csharp
      GC.SuppressFinalize(this);
    }

    protected virtual void Dispose(bool disposing)
    {
      if (disposing)
      {
        // Dispose resources.
      }
    }
  }

  public struct ValueType: IEquatable<ValueType>
  {
    public int Property { get; }

    public override bool Equals(object obj)
    {
      return Equals((ValueType)obj);
    }

    public bool Equals(ValueType other)
    {
      return other.Property == Property;
    }

    public override int GetHashCode()
    {
      return Property.GetHashCode();
    }

    public static bool operator ==(ValueType left, ValueType right)
    {
      return left.Property == right.Property;
    }

    public static bool operator !=(ValueType left, ValueType right)
    {
      return left.Property != right.Property;
    }
  }
}
```

How it works...

FxCop analyzers are a port of the most important Microsoft code analysis rules (CAXXXX), which were implemented as an MSIL-based binary analysis. Compared to the post-build binary analysis, the FxCop analyzers have added advantage of live analysis and diagnostics while editing code, as well as rich code fixes to fix these issues.

FxCop contains rules in various different categories such as performance, security, code style, API design, maintainability, and so on. In the example covered in this section, we focused on the following performance rules:

- *CA1801* (Review unused parameters) (https://msdn.microsoft.com/en-us/library/ms182268.aspx): A method signature includes a parameter that is not used in the method body.
- *CA1810* (Initialize reference type static fields inline) (https://msdn.microsoft.com/en-us/library/ms182275.aspx): When a type declares an explicit static constructor, the just-in-time (JIT) compiler adds a check to each static method and instance constructor of the type to make sure that the static constructor was previously called. Static constructor checks can decrease performance.
- *CA1814* (Prefer jagged arrays over multidimensional) (https://msdn.microsoft.com/en-us/library/ms182277.aspx): A jagged array is an array whose elements are arrays. The arrays that make up the elements can be of different sizes, which can result in less wasted space for some sets of data.
- *CA1815* (Override equals and operator equals on value types) (https://msdn.microsoft.com/en-us/library/ms182276.aspx): For value types, the inherited implementation of equals uses the Reflection library and compares the contents of all fields. Reflection is computationally expensive, and comparing every field for equality might be unnecessary. If you expect users to compare or sort instances, or to use instances as hash table keys, your value type should implement equals.
- *CA1816* (Call `GC.SuppressFinalize` correctly) (https://msdn.microsoft.com/en-us/library/ms182269.aspx): A method that is an implementation of `Dispose` does not call `GC.SuppressFinalize`, or a method that is not an implementation of `Dispose` calls `GC.SuppressFinalize`, or a method calls `GC.SuppressFinalize` and passes something other than this.
- *CA1821* (Remove empty finalizers) (https://msdn.microsoft.com/en-us/library/bb264476.aspx): Whenever you can, avoid finalizers because of the additional performance overhead that is involved in tracking object lifetime. An empty finalizer incurs added overhead without any benefit.

You can read detailed documentation about all the FxCop performance rules at https://msdn.microsoft.com/en-us/library/ms182260(v=vs.140).aspx.

Note that even though majority of Microsoft Code Analysis performance rules have been ported to FxCop analyzers package, not all rules are enabled by default in the NuGet package. You can view and configure the suppression state and severity of each FxCop rule by using the ruleset editor. For further guidance on using the ruleset editor, refer to recipe *Using ruleset file and ruleset editor to configure analyzers,* in Chapter 2, *Consuming Diagnostic Analyzers in .NET Projects.*

6
Live Unit Testing in Visual Studio Enterprise

In this chapter, we will cover the following recipes:

- Running **live unit tests** (**LUT**) in Visual Studio for unit test projects based on NUnit, XUnit, and MSTest frameworks
- Viewing and navigating live unit test results
- Understanding incremental live unit test execution with code changes
- Understanding start/stop/pause/continue/restart functionalities for fine grained control of LUT
- Including and excluding subsets of tests for live execution
- Configuring different options for live unit testing using the **Tools** | **Options** dialog

Introduction

This chapter enables developers to use the new Roslyn-based feature in the Visual Studio 2017 Enterprise edition that enables smart live unit test execution in the background. The following snippet and screenshot from this (`https://blogs.msdn.microsoft.com/visualstudio/2016/11/18/live-unit-testing-visual-studio-2017-rc/`) Visual Studio blog post on LUT gives a nice gist about this feature.

Live Unit Testing in Visual Studio Enterprise

Live unit testing automatically runs the impacted unit tests in the background as you edit code and visualizes the results and code coverage live, in the editor, in real time. In addition to giving feedback on the impact that your changes had on the existing tests, you also get immediate feedback on whether the new code you added is already covered by one or more existing tests. This will gently remind you to write unit tests as you are making bug fixes or adding features. You will be on your way to the promised land, where there is no test debt in your code base!

As mentioned in the post, there are three potential states for any given line:

- A line of executable code that is covered by at least one failing test is decorated with a red cross (✖)
- A line of executable code that is covered by only passing tests is decorated with a green tick (✓)
- A line of executable code that is not covered by any test is decorated it with a blue dash (−)

LUT uses the Roslyn APIs to analyze snapshots to your product and test code and determines the set of unit tests that need to be run for your projects. Additionally, it also uses the Roslyn APIs to analyze incremental updates to your code to smartly determine subset of unit tests that need to be re-run from your prior test runs. These are the same set of analysis APIs that are used by the Visual Studio IDE diagnostic engine to incrementally update the intellisense/live diagnostics in the error list and squiggles in the editor.

Once the set of unit tests to execute have been determined, it schedules them for execution in the background, and as and when the tests complete, it automatically shows their pass/fail/exclusion status with the glyphs on test methods. Users can start/stop/pause/resume live test execution at any given time. Additionally, they can exclude/include a subset of tests/files projects for LUT execution. They can also pause/restart/stop LUT anytime and configure different options for LUT, such as automatic pause on low battery, test execution timeout, and so on.

Running live unit tests in Visual Studio for unit test projects based on NUnit, XUnit, and MSTest frameworks

In this section, we will walk you through the steps to enable LUT for your unit test projects, viewing and understanding the live results from the test execution. In VS2017, live unit testing is supported for unit test projects, based on the following unit test frameworks:

- **NUnit**: Documentation at `https://www.nunit.org/`
- **XUnit**: Documentation at `https://xunit.github.io/`
- **MSTest**: Documentation at (`https://en.wikipedia.org/wiki/MSTest`) and (`https://msdn.microsoft.com/en-us/library/ms182489.aspx`)

We will cover LUT for unit test projects, based on each of the preceding test frameworks.

Getting started

You will need to have the Visual Studio 2017 Enterprise edition installed on your machine to execute this recipe. You can install a licensed enterprise edition from https://www.visualstudio.com/thank-you-downloading-visual-studio/?sku=Enterprise&rel=15.

How to do it...

1. Open Visual Studio and create a new C# class library project, say `ClassLibrary`, with the following source code:

   ```
   namespace ClassLibrary
   {
     public class Class1
     {
       public bool Method1()
       {
         return true;
       }

       public bool Method2()
       {
         return false;
       }

       public bool Method3(Class1 c)
       {
         return c.Method1();
       }

       public bool Method4(Class1 c)
       {
         return c.Method2();
       }
     }
   }
   ```

2. [NUnit] Add a C# unit test project, say `NUnitBasedTestProject`, to the solution and add a reference to `ClassLibrary` to this project.
3. Open **NuGet Package Manager** for the project and uninstall the existing NuGet package references in `MSTest.TestAdapter` and `MSTest.TestFramework`:

Chapter 6

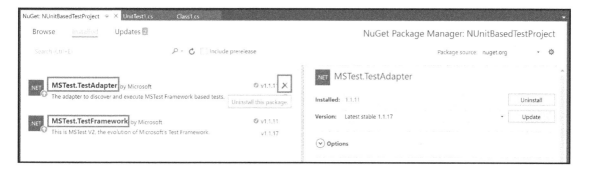

4. Add NuGet package references to the latest stable versions of NUnit and **NUnit3TestAdapter** to the project.
5. Replace the source code in file `UnitTest1.cs` with the following code:

```
using NUnit.Framework;

namespace NUnitBasedTestProject
{
  [TestFixture]
  public class UnitTest1
  {
    [Test]
    public void TestMethod1()
    {
      var c = new ClassLibrary.Class1();
      Assert.True(c.Method1());
    }

    [Test]
    public void TestMethod2()
    {
      var c = new ClassLibrary.Class1();
      Assert.True(c.Method2());
    }
  }
}
```

6. Start live unit testing for the project by executing the **Test | Live Unit Testing | Start** command.

7. Wait for a few seconds and note that the added unit tests execute in the background, and that `TestMethod1` passes and `TestMethod2` fails as expected and the corresponding green and red glyphs show up in the editor. Also, verify that the **Output** window switches to **Live Unit Testing** view and shows the test execution log with execution time stamps:

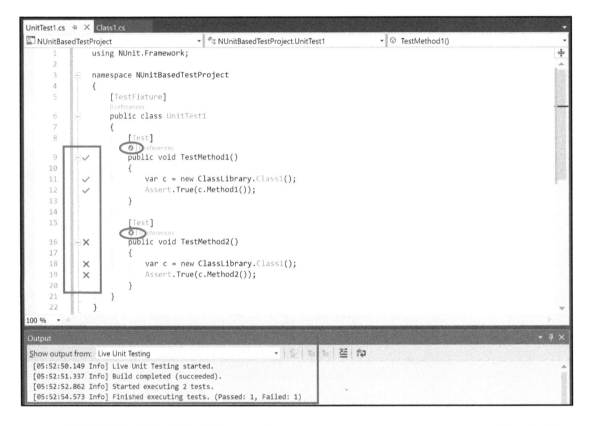

8. [XUnit] Add a C# unit test project, say `XUnitBasedTestProject`, to the solution and add a reference to `ClassLibrary` to this project.
9. Open **NuGet Package Manager** for the project and uninstall the existing NuGet package references to `MSTest.TestAdapter` and `MSTest.TestFramework`.
10. Add the NuGet package references to the latest stable versions of XUnit and `xunit.runner.visualstudio` (later than 2.2.0).

11. Replace the source code in the `UnitTest1.cs` file with the following source code:

    ```
    using Xunit;

    namespace XUnitBasedTestProject
    {
      public class UnitTest1
      {
        [Fact]
        public void TestMethod1()
        {
          var c = new ClassLibrary.Class1();
          Assert.True(c.Method1());
        }

        [Fact]
        public void TestMethod2()
        {
          var c = new ClassLibrary.Class1();
          Assert.True(c.Method2());
        }
      }
    }
    ```

12. Wait for a few seconds and note that unit tests execute in the background and `TestMethod1` passes and `TestMethod2` fails. Verify that the green and red glyphs shows up in the editor for these tests, respectively.
13. [MSTest] Add a C# unit test project, say `MSTestBasedTestProject`, to the solution and add a reference to `ClassLibrary` to this project.
14. Open the **NuGet Package Manager** for the project and update the existing NuGet package references for `MSTest.TestAdapter` and `MSTest.TestFramework` to latest stable version (later than *1.1.17*)
15. Replace the source code in file `UnitTest1.cs` with the following source code:

    ```
    using Microsoft.VisualStudio.TestTools.UnitTesting;

    namespace MSTestBasedTestProject
    {
      [TestClass]
      public class UnitTest1
      {
        [TestMethod]
        public void TestMethod1()
        {
    ```

```
        var c = new ClassLibrary.Class1();
        Assert.IsTrue(c.Method1());
    }

    [TestMethod]
    public void TestMethod2()
    {
        var c = new ClassLibrary.Class1();
        Assert.IsTrue(c.Method2());
    }
  }
}
```

16. Wait for a few seconds and note that unit tests execute in the background and `TestMethod1` passes and `TestMethod2` fails. Verify that the green and red glyphs shows up in the editor for these tests, respectively.
17. Open `Class1.cs` in the project `ClassLibrary` and verify that the test coverage and pass/fail details are shown for each method in the editor:

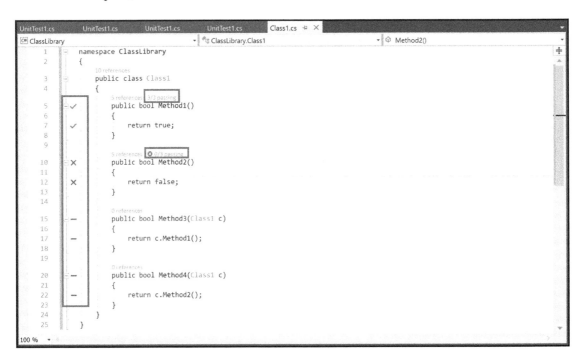

Chapter 6

Viewing and navigating live unit test results

In this section, we will show you how to view and navigate the results from live test execution using the **Test Explorer** and the tool tip in the Visual Studio editor.

Getting started

You will need to have the Visual Studio 2017 Enterprise edition installed on your machine to execute this recipe. You can install a licensed enterprise edition from https://www.visualstudio.com/thank-you-downloading-visual-studio/?sku=Enterprise&rel=15.

How to do it...

1. Open Visual Studio and create a new C# class library project, say `ClassLibrary`.
2. Replace the existing code in the source file `Class1.cs` with the code in attached sample `ClassLibrary\Class1.cs`.
3. Add a C# unit test project, say `UnitTestProject`, to the solution and add a reference to `ClassLibrary` to this project.
4. Open the **NuGet Package Manager** for the project and update the existing NuGet package references for `MSTest.TestAdapter` and `MSTest.TestFramework` to latest stable version (later than *1.1.17*)
5. Replace the source code in the `UnitTest1.cs` file with the code in the attached sample `UnitTestProject\UnitTest1.cs`.
6. Open the **Test Explorer** window by clicking on **Test | Window | Test Explorer**.
7. Start live unit testing for the project by executing **Test | Live Unit Testing | Start** command.
8. Wait for a few seconds and note that the added unit tests execute on the background and `TestMethod1` passes and `TestMethod2` fails as expected.

Live Unit Testing in Visual Studio Enterprise

9. Verify that the results are shown in the **Test Explorer** and there are corresponding green and red glyphs in the editor:

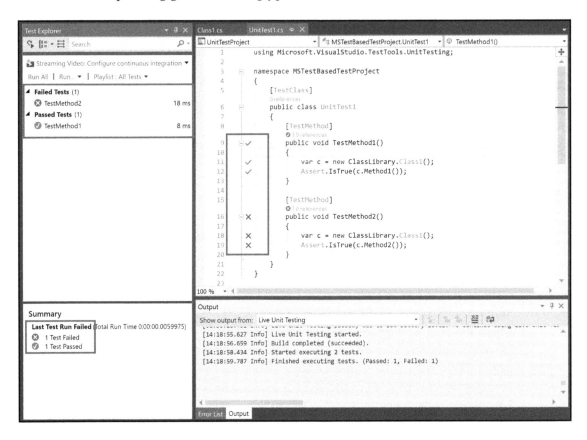

10. Open source file `Class1.cs` in `ClassLibrary` and click on the test indicator on top of `Method1`, which reads `1/1 passing`. Verify that a tool bar pops up with the name and status of the test, `TestMethod1`.

Chapter 6

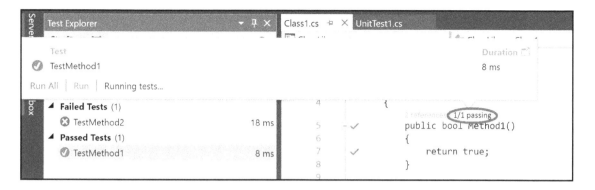

11. Double-click on the method name `TestMethod1` in the tool bar and make sure to navigate to the definition of this method in `UnitTest1.cs`.
12. Switch back to `Class1.cs` and hover near the green tick (✓) near `Method1` to view that the method is **Covered by 1 test.**:

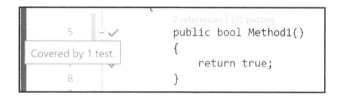

13. Click on the tick (✓) to bring up another toolbar with the method name and verify that double-clicking on it takes you to the test method definition.

Understanding incremental live unit test execution with code changes

In this section, we will show you how live unit tests run incrementally on making changes to test and product code on a solution configured to run live unit tests.

Getting started

You will need to have the Visual Studio 2017 Enterprise edition installed on your machine to execute this recipe. You can install a licensed enterprise edition from `https://www.visualstudio.com/thank-you-downloading-visual-studio/?sku=Enterprise&rel=15`.

Additionally, clone the solution `ClassLibrary.sln` attached from the previous recipe in this chapter, *Viewing and navigating live unit test results*. Alternatively, you can manually execute the steps in that recipe before executing this recipe.

How to do it...

1. Open the `ClassLibrary.sln` solution with two projects: `ClassLibrary` and `UnitTestProject` and start live unit testing by navigating to **Test | Live Unit Testing | Start**.
2. Add a new source file `Class2.cs` with the following code to the `ClassLibrary` project:

   ```
   namespace ClassLibrary
   {
     public class Class2
     {
       public bool Method5()
       {
         return false;
       }

       public bool Method6()
       {
         return true;
       }
     }
   }
   ```

3. Open the **Output** window, switch the **Show output from:** combo box to **Live Unit Testing**, and clear all the contents in the window by pressing the highlighted button:

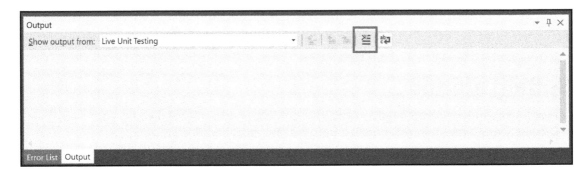

4. Add a new source file `UnitTest2.cs` with the following code to the `UnitTestProject` project:

```
using Microsoft.VisualStudio.TestTools.UnitTesting;

namespace MSTestBasedTestProject
{
  [TestClass]
  public class UnitTest2
  {
    [TestMethod]
    public void TestMethod5()
    {
      var c = new ClassLibrary.Class2();
      Assert.IsTrue(c.Method5());
    }

    [TestMethod]
    public void TestMethod6()
    {
      var c = new ClassLibrary.Class2();
      Assert.IsTrue(c.Method6());
    }
  }
}
```

5. Wait for a few seconds and note that the added unit tests execute on the background and `TestMethod5` passes and `TestMethod6` fails as expected.

Live Unit Testing in Visual Studio Enterprise

6. Also, note that the text in the **Output** window states that only two unit tests were executed (newly added ones `TestMethod5` and `TestMethod6`). Additionally, the **Test Explorer** shows the old tests `TestMethod1` and `TestMethod2` as grayed out, because these tests did not execute when we added new test code:

7. Switch back to the `Class1.cs` file in `ClassLibrary` project and edit `Method1` to return `true`.
8. Wait a few seconds for the tests to execute in the background and see that `TestMethod1` now shows as passed.
9. Note that `TestMethod5` and `TestMxethod6` are now grayed out in the **Test Explorer**, indicating that they did not execute with the last code change:

How it works...

In this recipe, we showed you how the live unit test execution is designed to analyze incremental product and test changes and execute only the subset of tests in the unit test projects, which could be semantically affected by those changes. As mentioned in the introduction section of this chapter, LUT uses the Roslyn APIs to analyze these incremental code updates from your prior test runs. These are the same set of analysis APIs that are used by the Visual Studio IDE diagnostic engine to incrementally update the intellisense/live diagnostics in the error list and squiggles in the editor.

In this recipe, we started with a single class, `Class1`, in the `ClassLibrary` project and a single unit test class, `UnitTest1`, in `UnitTestProject`. `UnitTest1` contains two methods `TestMethod1` and `TestMethod2`, that tested methods `Method1` and `Method2` in `Class1`, respectively. We added a new class, `Class2`, in `ClassLibrary` project with methods `Method5` and `Method6`. Then, we added a new unit test class, `UnitTest2` containing methods `TestMethod5` and `TestMethod6`, that test methods `Method5` and `Method6`, respectively. On adding these methods, LUT determined that the existing tests in type `UnitTest1` are unaffected by newly added `Class2` and `UnitTest2` and hence did not re-execute them. Subsequently, when we edited `Class1.Method1`, LUT only re-executed `UnitTest1.TestMethod1` and `UnitTest1.TestMethod2` but not the test methods in `UnitTest2`.

Understanding Start/Stop/Pause/Continue/Restart functionality for fine grain control of LUT

In this section, we will show you how to control the live unit test execution in Visual Studio using the start, stop, pause, continue, and restart commands.

Getting started

You will need to have Visual Studio 2017 Enterprise edition installed on your machine to execute this recipe. You can install a licensed enterprise edition from https://www.visualstudio.com/thank-you-downloading-visual-studio/?sku=Enterprise&rel=15.

Additionally, clone the solution `ClassLibrary.sln` attached from the recipe, *Viewing and navigating live unit test results*, in this chapter. Alternatively, you can manually execute the steps in that recipe before executing this recipe.

How to do it...

1. Open the solution `ClassLibrary.sln`, with two projects: `ClassLibrary` and `UnitTestProject` and start live unit testing by clicking on **Test | Live Unit Testing | Start**. Also, bring up the **Test Explorer** window by clicking on **Test | Windows | Test Explorer**.
2. Change `Class1.Method1` to return true instead of false.

3. Wait for a few seconds and note that the unit tests execute on the background, and `TestMethod1` and `TestMethod2` are both passed:

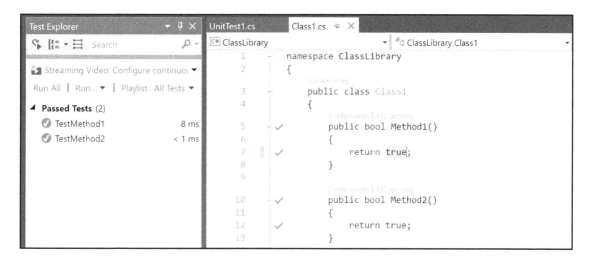

4. Click on **Test** | **Live Unit Testing** | **Pause** to temporarily pause LUT execution. Note that green tick (✓) marks in the editor disappear as soon as LUT is paused:

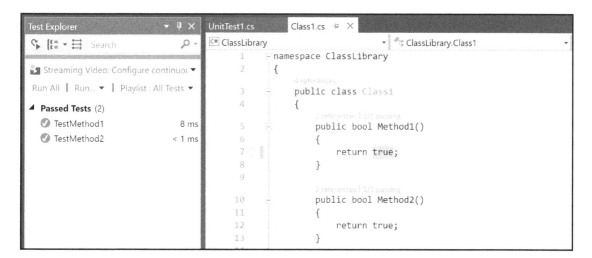

Live Unit Testing in Visual Studio Enterprise

5. Change `Class1.Method1` to again return false. This should cause `TestMethod1` to fail when re-executed, but note that the test still shows as passing in **Test Explorer** window because tests are not running live:

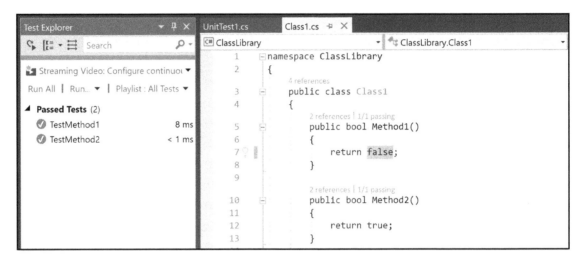

6. Navigate to **Test | Live Unit Testing | Continue** to resume LUT and note that `TestMethod1` immediately executes and is now shown as failing in the **Test Explorer** and gylph in the editor:

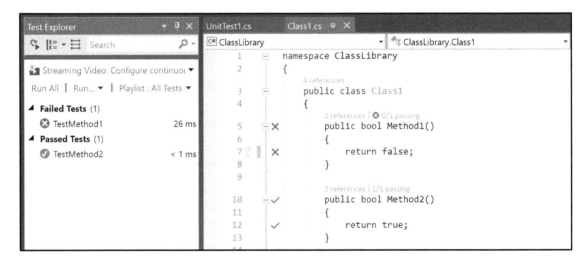

7. Click on **Test | Live Unit Testing | Restart** and note that all the test results are wiped out momentarily in the editor and **Test Explorer** window.

[200]

8. Note that **Output** window's **Live Unit Testing** pane shows the message: **Build completed (succeeded)**, indicating the projects were built again and all tests re-executed.
9. Navigate to **Test | Live Unit Testing | Stop** and note that all the test results are wiped out permanently in the editor and **Test Explorer** window:

10. Note that the **Output** window's **Live Unit Testing** pane shows the message: **Live Unit Testing stopped.**, confirming that LUT execution was stopped.

Including and excluding subset of tests for live execution

In this section, we will show you how to selectively include and/or exclude subset of tests from live unit test execution. This features is extremely helpful in improving responsiveness for very large solutions where building the entire solution and then executing all the unit tests could be time consuming and resource intensive.

Getting started

You will need to have the Visual Studio 2017 Enterprise edition installed on your machine to execute this recipe. You can install a licensed enterprise edition from `https://www.visualstudio.com/thank-you-downloading-visual-studio/?sku=Enterprise&rel=15`.

How to do it...

1. Open Visual Studio 2017 and create a C# solution with 10 `ClassLibrary` projects, say `ClassLibrary, ClassLibrary1, ..., ClassLibrary9` and one unit test project `UnitTestProject`:

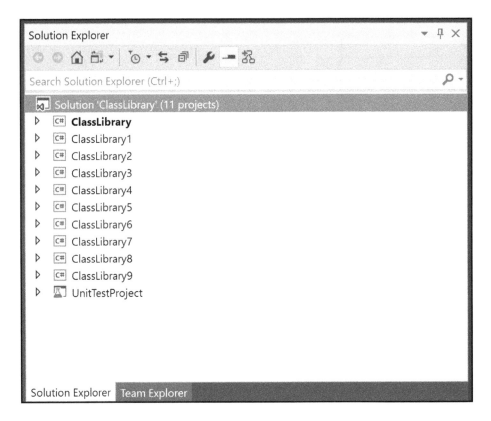

2. Add a project reference to all the class library projects in `UnitTestProject`.
3. Add a new test class `UnitTest2` in `UnitTestProject` and rename the test method to `TestMethod2`.

4. Navigate to **Test | Live Unit Testing | Start** and notice the following dialog prompting that the solution is large and responsiveness will improve if subset of the tests are included:

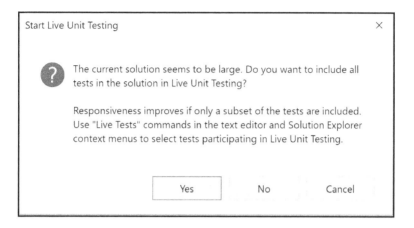

5. Click on **No** so that none of the tests are included for live execution.
6. Verify the blue dash (−) in front of the test methods in `UnitTestProject`, confirming the exclusion of unit tests from live execution:

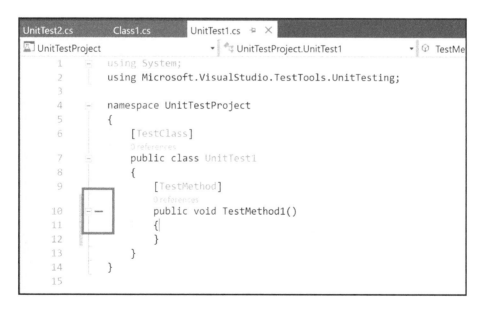

Live Unit Testing in Visual Studio Enterprise

7. Right-click on class `UnitTest1` in the editor and execute **Live Tests | Include** to include unit tests in this class for LUT.

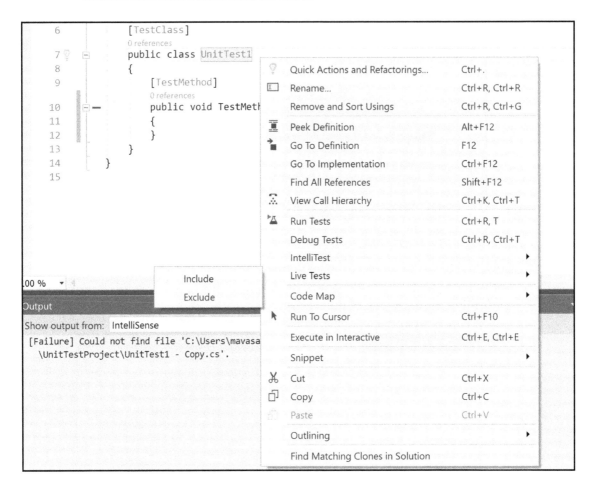

8. Verify that `UnitTest1.TestMethod1` executes immediately with LUT and is shown as passed, but `UnitTest2.TestMethod2` is not executed.
9. Right-click on class `UnitTest1` in the editor again and execute **Live Tests | Exclude** to exclude unit tests in this class for LUT.
10. Edit the method `UnitTest1.TestMethod1` by hitting the *Enter* key and verify the test is now excluded from LUT and test result is also cleared from the editor and **Test Explorer** window:

[Screenshot of Visual Studio Test Explorer and UnitTest1.cs code editor]

 You can include/exclude all tests from a unit test project for LUT by right-clicking on the project node in the solution explorer and clicking on **Live Tests | Include/Exclude**.

Configuring different options for live unit testing using the Tools Options dialog

In this section, we will show you how to configure LUT execution options, such as starting LUT on solution load, configuring the minimum battery percentage required to keep LUT enabled in order to save battery power, and so on. This enables users to control when to automatically start/pause LUT and to control the level of logging to meet their requirements.

Getting started

You will need to have the Visual Studio 2017 Enterprise edition installed on your machine to execute this recipe. You can install a licensed enterprise edition from https://www.visualstudio.com/thank-you-downloading-visual-studio/?sku=Enterprise&rel=15.

Additionally, clone the `ClassLibrary.sln` solution attached from the recipe, *Viewing and navigating live unit test results*, in this chapter. Alternatively, you can manually execute the steps in that recipe before proceeding with this recipe.

How to do it...

1. Open the solution `ClassLibrary.sln` with two projects, `ClassLibrary` and `UnitTestProject`, and start live unit testing by navigating to **Test** | **Live Unit Testing** | **Start**. Also, bring up the **Test Explorer** window by clicking on **Test** | **Windows** | **Test Explorer**.
2. Click on **Tools** | **Options**, and search `Live Unit Testing` in the search bar, and click on the **General** tab to view the LUT configuration options:

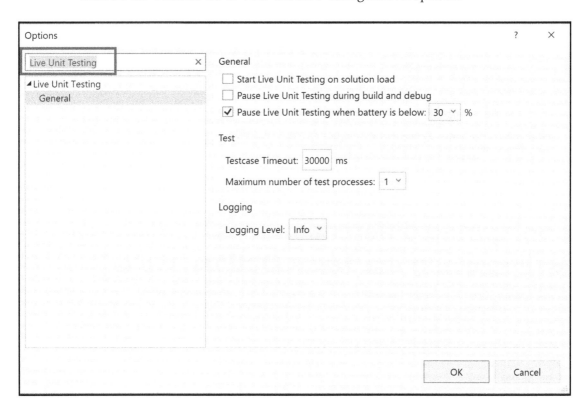

3. Check **Start Live Unit Testing on solution load** and click on **OK** on the dialog.
4. Stop live unit testing for the solution by navigating to **Test | Live Unit Testing | Stop**.
5. Close and re-open the solution and verify that all unit tests are automatically executed with LUT on completion of the solution load.
6. Open the LUT configuration options using **Tools | Options** again and change the minimum battery percentage to pause LUT from 30% to 100%
7. Disconnect the power cord from your laptop and verify the LUT is immediately paused, and that editing any test method doesn't cause tests to be re-executed with LUT.
8. Connect the laptop power cord and verify the unit tests again; start executing in the background with LUT.

C# Interactive and Scripting

In this chapter, we will cover the following recipes:

- Writing a simple C# script and evaluating it within the Visual Studio interactive window
- Using script directives and REPL commands in the C# interactive window
- Using keyboard shortcuts for evaluating and navigating through script sessions in the C# interactive window
- Initializing a C# interactive session from an existing C# project
- Executing a C# script on a Visual Studio developer command prompt using `csi.exe`
- Using the Roslyn scripting API to execute C# code snippets

Introduction

This chapter gives a basic introduction to one of the most powerful features/tools based on the Roslyn compiler API: **C# interactive and scripting.** You can read an overview about C# scripting at `https://msdn.microsoft.com/en-us/magazine/mt614271.aspx`. Here is a small gist of this feature from the preceding article:

C# scripting is a tool for testing out your C# and .NET snippets without the effort of creating multiple unit testing or console projects. It provides an easy means to explore and understand an API without the overhead of a yet another `CSPROJ` file in your `%TEMP%` directory. The C# read-evaluate-print-loop (REPL) is available as an interactive window within Visual Studio 2015 and after and as a new command-line interface (CLI) called CSI.

C# Interactive and Scripting

Here is a screenshot of the C# interactive window in Visual Studio:

The following is a screenshot of the C# interactive command-line interface (`csi.exe`) executed from a Visual Studio 2017 developer command prompt:

Writing a simple C# script and evaluating it within the Visual Studio interactive window

In this section, we will walk you through the basics of C# scripting and show you how to use the Visual Studio interactive window to evaluate a C# script.

Getting started

You will need to have Visual Studio 2017 Community edition installed on your machine to execute this recipe. You can install a free community edition from `https://www.visualstudio.com/thank-you-downloading-visual-studio/?sku=Community&rel=15`

How to do it…

1. Open Visual Studio and start the **C# Interactive** window by clicking on **View | Other Windows | C# Interactive**:

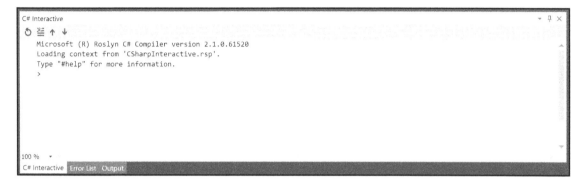

2. Type `Console.WriteLine("Hello, World!")` in the interactive window and hit the *Enter* key to evaluate the C# expression.
3. Verify that `Hello, World!` is output as a result in the interactive window:

4. Now, type a variable declaration statement of type `List<int>` with a collection initializer: `var myList = new List<int> { 3, 2, 7, 4, 9, 0 };` and press the *Enter* key.
5. Next, type an expression statement that accesses the `myList` variable declared in the previous statement and filter the list to all the even numbers in the list using a linq expression: `myList.Where(x => x % 2 == 0)`.
6. Press the *Enter* key to evaluate the expression and verify that a nicely formatted enumerable list is output as the result of the evaluation: `Enumerable.WhereListIterator<int> { 2, 4, 0 }`.
7. Type the command `$"The current directory is { Environment.CurrentDirectory }."`. This accesses the current directory environment variable and verifies your current directory output.

8. Now, type the following commands into the interactive window and verify that pressing the *Enter* key leads to a 10-second UI delay as per the entered `await` expression:

```
> using System.Threading.Tasks;
> await Task.Delay(10000)
>
```

9. Type the following class declaration in the interactive window and press the *Enter* key:

```
class C
{
  public void M()
  {
    Console.WriteLine("C.M invoked");
  }
}
```

10. Instantiate type `C` declared earlier and invoke method `M` on the instance by evaluating the following statement: `new C().M();`.
11. Verify that the output in the interactive window is: `C.M invoked`.

You can view the entire contents of the interactive window for this recipe in the attached text file `InteractiveWindowOutput.txt`.

How it works...

In this recipe, we wrote a simple set of C# interactive script commands to perform a bunch of operations that are common in regular C# code, but without having to declare a stub type/main method or having to create a source file/project. The operations performed during the interactive session were:

1. Evaluating an expression that outputs a string to the console (`Console.WriteLine(...)`).
2. Declaring a local variable for the lifetime of the interactive session and initialize it with a collection `initializer` (`myList`).
3. Accessing the preceding declared variable in a subsequent linq statement and evaluating the resultant value (`myList.Where(...)`).

4. Accessing environment variables in C# expression evaluations (`Environment.CurrentDirectory`).
5. Importing namespace in the session through a using declaration (`using System.Threading.Tasks;`).
6. Awaiting an async expression (`await Task.Delay(10000)`).
7. Declaring a C# class with a method (`class C` and `method M`) for the lifetime of the interactive session.
8. Instantiating the preceding declared class and invoking the method in a subsequent statement (`new C().M()`).

Let's briefly walk through the implementation of the C# interactive compiler that enables all the preceding regular C# operations in the interactive mode.

`Csi.main` (http://source.roslyn.io/#csi/Csi.cs,14) is the primary entry point into the C# interactive compiler. After initialization of the compiler, the control eventually reaches `CommandLineRunner.RunInteractiveLoop` (http://source.roslyn.io/#Microsoft.CodeAnalysis.Scripting/Hosting/CommandLine/CommandLineRunner.cs,7c8c5cedadd34d79), which is, the REPL, or read-evaluate-print-loop, that reads interactive commands and evaluates them in a loop until the user exits by pressing *Ctrl + C*.

For each entered line, the REPL loop executes `ScriptCompiler.ParseSubmission` (http://source.roslyn.io/#Microsoft.CodeAnalysis.Scripting/ScriptCompiler.cs,54b12302e519f660) to parse the given source text into a syntax tree. If the submission is incomplete (for example, if the first line of a class declaration has been entered), then it outputs . and continues waiting for more text for the submission. Otherwise, it creates a script using the current submission text chained to the end of the prior submissions and runs the new submission by invoking into the core C# compiler APIs. The result of the submission is output to the interactive window.

Further details on how the submission chains to the prior submissions and executes within the interactive compiler are out of the scope of this chapter. You may navigate the script compiler's code base at (http://source.roslyn.io/#q=RunSubmissionsAsync) to understand the internal workings.

Using script directives and REPL commands in the C# interactive window

In this section, we will walk you through the common directives and REPL commands available in C# interactive scripting and show you how to use them in the Visual Studio interactive window.

Getting started

You will need to have the Visual Studio 2017 Community edition installed on your machine to execute this recipe. You can install a free community edition from https://www.visualstudio.com/thank-you-downloading-visual-studio/?sku=Community&rel=15.

How to do it...

1. Open Visual Studio and start the **C# Interactive** window by clicking on **View** | **Other Windows** | **C# Interactive**.
2. Copy `Newtonsoft.Json.dll` from the attached sample for the recipe into your temp directory `%TEMP%`.
3. Execute the following `#r` directive to load this assembly into the interactive session:

   ```
   #r "<%YOUR_TEMP_DIRECTORY%>\Newtonsoft.Json.dll"
   ```

4. Verify that you can now reference types from this assembly as well as create objects and invoke methods. For example, type the following code snippet into the interactive window:

   ```
   using Newtonsoft.Json.Linq;
   JArray array = new JArray();
   array.Add("Manual text");
   array.Add(new DateTime(2000, 5, 23));

   JObject o = new JObject();
   o["MyArray"] = array;

   o.ToString()
   ```

5. Verify the string representation of the array that is the output to the interactive window:

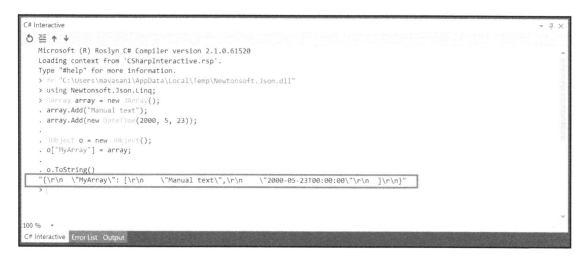

6. Execute the REPL command `#clear` (or `#cls`) and verify this clears all the text from the interactive window.
7. Copy `MyScript.csx` from the attached sample for the recipe into your temp directory `%TEMP%`.
8. Execute the following `#load` directive to load and execute this script in the interactive session:

   ```
   #load "<%YOUR_TEMP_DIRECTORY%>\MyScript.csx"
   ```

9. Verify that the script executes, and you get the following output from the execution:

10. Execute the `#reset` REPL command to reset the interactive session.

C# Interactive and Scripting

11. Now, attempt to refer to the Newtonsoft.Json namespace in the interactive session, which was added prior to the reset, and verify that you get an error, as the assembly is no longer loaded in the session:

12. Finally, execute the #help REPL command to print the help text for available keyboard shortcuts, directives, and REPL commands in the interactive window:

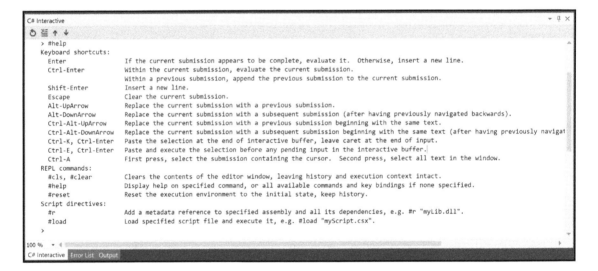

You can view the entire contents of the interactive window for this recipe in the attached text file InteractiveWindowOutput.txt.

[216]

Using keyboard shortcuts for evaluating and navigating through script sessions in the C# interactive window

In this section, we will walk you through the common keyboard shortcuts available in C# interactive scripting and show you how to use them in the Visual Studio interactive window.

As demonstrated in the last step of the previous recipe, you can use the *#help* REPL command in the interactive window to see the entire list of keyboard shortcuts available in the C# interactive window.

Getting started

You will need to have the Visual Studio 2017 Community edition installed on your machine to execute this recipe. You can install a free community edition from https://www.visualstudio.com/thank-you-downloading-visual-studio/?sku=Community&rel=15.

How to do it...

1. Open Visual Studio and open the **C# Interactive** window by clicking on **View | Other Windows | C# Interactive**.
2. Type the string constant `"World!"` and hit the *Enter* key to evaluate and output the string.
3. Type `"Hello, "` + and move the cursor to the previous submission from the step 2, and hit the *Ctrl + Enter* keys to append the text from the previous submission to the current submission. The current submission text should change to `"Hello, "` + `"World!"`, and pressing the *Enter* key should output the text `"Hello, World!"`.

4. Type @"Hello, World and press the *Shift* + *Enter* keys to add a new line within the current submission. Typing with a new line!" on the next line and hitting the *Enter* key should output the text "Hello, World\r\nwith a new line!", as shown here:

```
C# Interactive
Microsoft (R) Roslyn C# Compiler version 2.1.0.61520
Loading context from 'CSharpInteractive.rsp'.
Type "#help" for more information.
> "World!"
"World!"
> "Hello, " + "World!"
"Hello, World!"
> @"Hello, World
. with a new line!"
"Hello, World\r\nwith a new line!"
>
```

5. Type Hello and press the *Esc* key; this should clear the text on the current line.
6. Press the *Alt* + *Up* arrow keys together; this should change the current submission text to be the same as the previous submission, in our case, @"Hello, World
   . with a new line!".
7. Press the *Enter* key to output "Hello, World\r\nwith a new line!" again.
8. Press the quote key ". This should automatically add another quote for the string. Press the *Delete* key to remove this automatically and add the second quote.
9. Now, press the *Ctrl* + *Alt* + *Up* arrow keys together; this should change the current submission text to be the same as the last among the previous submissions that started with the same character, that is, ". In our case, this was the submission "Hello, " + "World!".
10. Press the *Enter* key to output "Hello, World!".
11. Now, place the cursor on our very first submission in the session, that is, the submission at step 2.
12. Press the *Ctrl* + *A* keys together to select the entire text in the first submission, that is, "World!". Then, press the *Ctrl* + *Enter* keys together to copy this text into the current submission.
13. Press the *Enter* key to output "World!".
14. Place the cursor back on the previous submission and press the *Ctrl* + *A* keys twice to select the entire contents of the interactive window.

You can view the entire contents of the interactive window for this recipe in the attached text file `InteractiveWindowOutput.txt`.

Initializing the C# interactive session from the existing C# project

In this section, we will walk you through the steps to initialize a C# interactive scripting session from an existing C# project and then use the types from the project in the Visual Studio interactive window.

Getting started

You will need to have Visual Studio 2017 Community edition installed on your machine to execute this recipe. You can install a free community edition from `https://www.visualstudio.com/thank-you-downloading-visual-studio/?sku=Community&rel=15`.

How to do it...

1. Open Visual Studio and start the **C# Interactive** window by clicking on **View | Other Windows | C# Interactive**.
2. Declare a local variable `int x = 0;` in the interactive window and press the *Enter* key.
3. Execute `Console.WriteLine(x)` and verify the output `0` to confirm that the variable `x` is declared in the current session.
4. Create a new C# class library project, say `ClassLibrary`.
5. Add the following method `M` to type `Class1` in the created project:

    ```
    public void M()
    {
      Console.WriteLine("Executing ClassLibrary.Class1.M()");
    }
    ```

C# Interactive and Scripting

6. Right-click on the project in the solution explorer and click on **Initialize Interactive with Project**:

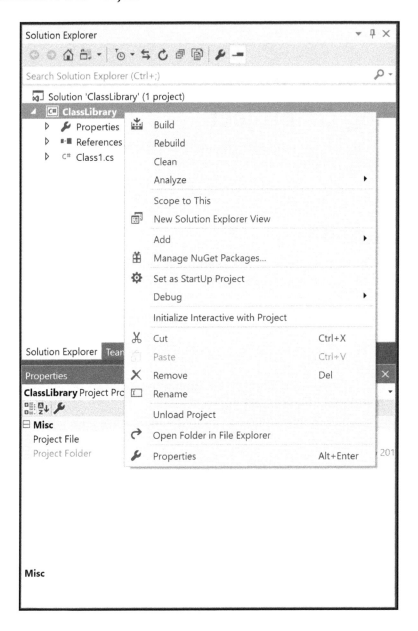

7. Verify that the project build has started, and that the C# interactive session has been reset with the project references and output assembly (`ClassLibrary.dll`):

```
C# Interactive
Microsoft (R) Roslyn C# Compiler version 2.1.0.61520
Loading context from 'CSharpInteractive.rsp'.
Type "#help" for more information.
> int x = 0;
> Console.WriteLine(x);
0
> #reset
Resetting execution engine.
Loading context from 'CSharpInteractive.rsp'.
> #r "C:\Program Files (x86)\Reference Assemblies\Microsoft\Framework\.NETFramework\v4.6\System.dll"
> #r "C:\Program Files (x86)\Reference Assemblies\Microsoft\Framework\.NETFramework\v4.6\System.Core.dll"
> #r "C:\Program Files (x86)\Reference Assemblies\Microsoft\Framework\.NETFramework\v4.6\System.Xml.Linq.dll"
> #r "C:\Program Files (x86)\Reference Assemblies\Microsoft\Framework\.NETFramework\v4.6\System.Data.DataSetExtens
> #r "C:\Program Files (x86)\Reference Assemblies\Microsoft\Framework\.NETFramework\v4.6\Microsoft.CSharp.dll"
> #r "C:\Program Files (x86)\Reference Assemblies\Microsoft\Framework\.NETFramework\v4.6\System.Data.dll"
> #r "C:\Program Files (x86)\Reference Assemblies\Microsoft\Framework\.NETFramework\v4.6\System.Net.Http.dll"
> #r "C:\Program Files (x86)\Reference Assemblies\Microsoft\Framework\.NETFramework\v4.6\System.Xml.dll"
> #r "ClassLibrary.dll"
> using ClassLibrary;
>
```

8. Type the following text `new Class1().M();` in the interactive window and press the *Enter* key to execute the submission.
9. Verify that `Executing ClassLibrary.Class1.M()` is output as a result, confirming that the interactive session was initialized with the `ClassLibrary` project.
10. Attempt to reference the variable *x* that was defined in step2, that is, prior to initializing the interactive session with the project by executing `Console.WriteLine(x);`.
11. Verify that this leads to the following compile time error, confirming that the session state was completely reset when we initialized it from the project:

> `> Console.WriteLine(x);`
> `(1,19): error CS0103: The name 'x' does not exist in the current context`

You can view the entire contents of the interactive window for this recipe in the attached text file `InteractiveWindowOutput.txt`.

Executing the C# script on a Visual Studio developer command prompt using csi.exe

In this section, we will show you how to use the command-line interface for executing C# scripts and their interactive mode. `csi.exe` (CSharp Interactive) is the CLI executable for C# interactive that ships with the C# compiler toolset, along with Visual Studio.

Getting started

You will need to have the Visual Studio 2017 Community edition installed on your machine to execute this recipe. You can install a free community edition from `https://www.visualstudio.com/thank-you-downloading-visual-studio/?sku=Community&rel=15`.

How to do it…

1. Start the Visual Studio 2017 develop command prompt and execute the command `csi.exe` to start the C# interactive session.
2. Type `Console.WriteLine("Hello, World!")` on the console and click on the *Enter* key to execute the command in interactive mode:

3. Press *Ctrl + C* to exit the interactive mode.
4. Create a script file `MyScript.csx` with the following code to output the arguments to the script:

   ```
   var t = System.Environment.GetCommandLineArgs();

   foreach (var i in t)
   {
      System.Console.WriteLine(i);
   }
   ```

5. Execute the script with arguments 1 2 3 and verify the following output. Also, note that after executing the script, we return back to the command prompt, not the interactive session:

   ```
   c:\>csi MyScript.csx 1 2 3
   csi
   MyScript.csx
   1
   2
   3
   ```

6. Now, execute the same script with an additional `-i` argument prepended and verify the same output as earlier, this time however, we return to an interactive prompt:

   ```
   c:\>csi -i MyScript.csx 1 2 3
   csi
   -i
   MyScript.csx
   1
   2
   3
   >
   ```

7. Execute `Console.WriteLine(t.Length)` and verify that the output is 6, confirming that the variable *t* declared in the script and initialized with the command-line arguments is still alive in the current interactive session.
8. Press *Ctrl + C* to exit the interactive mode.

C# Interactive and Scripting

9. Execute `csi -i` to start `csi.exe` in interactive mode and execute the *#help* command to get the list of available keyboard shortcuts, REPL commands, and script directives:

```
c:\>csi -i
Microsoft (R) Visual C# Interactive Compiler version 2.1.0.61520
Copyright (C) Microsoft Corporation. All rights reserved.

Type "#help" for more information.
> #help
Keyboard shortcuts:
  Enter      If the current submission appears to be complete, evaluate it.  Otherwise, insert a new line.
  Escape     Clear the current submission.
  UpArrow    Replace the current submission with a previous submission.
  DownArrow  Replace the current submission with a subsequent submission (after having previously navigated backwards).
  Ctrl-C     Exit the REPL.
REPL commands:
  #help      Display help on available commands and key bindings.
Script directives:
  #r         Add a metadata reference to specified assembly and all its dependencies, e.g. #r "myLib.dll".
  #load      Load specified script file and execute it, e.g. #load "myScript.csx".
>
```

10. Note that the set of available keyboard shortcuts, REPL commands, and script directives in `csi.exe` is a subset of the corresponding sets in the Visual Studio interactive window. Refer to the earlier recipes *Using script directives and REPL commands in the C# interactive window* and *Using keyboard shortcuts for evaluating and navigating through script sessions in the C# interactive window*, in this chapter for available shortcuts, commands, and directives in the Visual Studio interactive window.

11. Press *Ctrl* + *C* to exit the interactive mode.

12. Attempt to execute `csi.exe` with arguments, but no script name, and verify error *CS2001* about missing source file:

```
c:\>csi.exe 1
error CS2001: Source file 'c:\1' could not be found.
```

You can read more about the command-line REPL and the arguments to `csi.exe` at https://github.com/dotnet/roslyn/wiki/Interactive-Window#repl.

Using the Roslyn scripting API to execute C# code snippets

In this section, we will show you how to to write a C# console application that uses Roslyn scripting APIs to execute C# code snippets and consume their output. The scripting APIs enable .NET applications to instantiate a C# engine and execute code snippets against host-supplied objects. The scripting APIs can also be used directly in an interactive session.

Getting started

You will need to have the Visual Studio 2017 Community edition installed on your machine to execute this recipe. You can install a free community edition from https://www.visualstudio.com/thank-you-downloading-visual-studio/?sku=Community&rel=15.

How to do it...

1. Open Visual Studio and create a new C# console application targeting .NET Framework 4.6 or higher, say `ConsoleApp`.
2. Install the `Microsoft.CodeAnalysis.CSharp.Scripting` NuGet package (at the time of writing, the latest stable version is *2.1.0*). For guidance on how to search for and install the NuGet package to a project, refer to the recipe, *Searching and installing analyzers through the NuGet package manager* in `Chapter 2`, *Consuming Diagnostic Analyzers in .NET Projects*.
3. Replace the source code in `Program.cs` with the source code from the attached code sample `\ConsoleApp\Program.cs`.
4. Press *Ctrl* + *F5* to build and start the project `.exe` without debugging.
5. Verify the first output from the evaluation of `EvaluateSimpleAsync`:

    ```
    Executing EvaluateSimpleAsync...
    3
    ```

6. Press any key to continue the execution.
7. Verify the second output from the evaluation of `EvaluateWithReferencesAsync`:

   ```
   Executing EvaluateWithReferencesAsync...
   <%your_machine_name%>
   ```

8. Press any key to continue the execution.
9. Verify the third output from the evaluation of `EvaluateWithImportsAsync`:

   ```
   Executing EvaluateWithImportsAsync...
   1.4142135623731
   ```

10. Press any key to continue the execution.
11. Verify last output from the evaluation of `EvaluateParameterizedScriptInLoopAsync`:

    ```
    Executing EvaluateParameterizedScriptInLoopAsync...
    0
    1
    4
    9
    16
    25
    36
    49
    64
    81
    Press any key to continue . . .
    ```

12. Press any key to exit the console.

Refer to the article (`https://github.com/dotnet/roslyn/wiki/Scripting-API-Samples`) for more examples of the scripting API.

How it works...

In this recipe, we wrote a C# console application based on Roslyn scripting APIs to perform various common scripting operations. The rich scripting APIs provides a powerful object model for the evaluation, creation, and execution of scripts with configuration options.

Let us walk through the code in this recipe and understand how we implemented some of these operations:

```
public static void Main(string[] args)
{
    EvaluateSimpleAsync().Wait();

    Console.ReadKey();
    EvaluateWithReferencesAsync().Wait();

    Console.ReadKey();
    EvaluateWithImportsAsync().Wait();

    Console.ReadKey();
    EvaluateParameterizedScriptInLoopAsync().Wait();
}
```

The `Main` method invokes individual methods to perform following operations:

- `EvaluateSimpleAsync`: A simple evaluation of a binary add expression
- `EvaluateWithReferencesAsync`: An evaluation involving a reference assembly passed down to the script options
- `EvaluateWithImportsAsync`: An evaluation involving the importing of a system namespace and invoking an API from the namespace
- `EvaluateParameterizedScriptInLoopAsync`: A creation and evaluation of a script parameterized by parameters and invoked over a loop of values.

`EvaluateSimpleAsync` invokes the most common scripting API, `CSharpScript.EvaluateAsync` (http://source.roslyn.io/#q=CSharpScript.EvaluateAsync), with an expression as the argument to evaluate that expression. In our case, we pass in `1 + 2` as the argument to `EvaluateAsync`, which outputs the result 3:

```
private static async Task EvaluateSimpleAsync()
{
    Console.WriteLine("Executing EvaluateSimpleAsync...");
    object result = await CSharpScript.EvaluateAsync("1 + 2");
    Console.WriteLine(result);
}
```

`EvaluateWithReferencesAsync` invokes the same `CSharpScript.EvaluateAsync` API (http://source.roslyn.io/#q=CSharpScript.EvaluateAsync), but using an additional reference assembly passed down through the script options with the `ScriptOptions.WithReferences` API (http://source.roslyn.io/#q=ScriptOptions.WithReferences).

In our case, we pass in `typeof(System.Net.Dns).Assembly` as an additional reference for the evaluation of `System.Net.Dns.GetHostName()`, which outputs the machine name:

```
private static async Task EvaluateWithReferencesAsync()
{
   Console.WriteLine("Executing EvaluateWithReferencesAsync...");
   var result = await
CSharpScript.EvaluateAsync("System.Net.Dns.GetHostName()",
   ScriptOptions.Default.WithReferences(typeof(System.Net.Dns).Assembly));
   Console.WriteLine(result);
}
```

`EvaluateWithImportsAsync` invokes the `CSharpScript.EvaluateAsync` API (http://source.roslyn.io/#q=CSharpScript.EvaluateAsync) with a namespace import passed down through the script options with the `ScriptOptions.WithImports` API (http://source.roslyn.io/#q=ScriptOptions.WithImports). In our case, we pass in `System.Math` as an additional namespace import for the evaluation of `Sqrt(2)`, which outputs the result `1.4142135623731`:

```
private static async Task EvaluateWithReferencesAsync()
{
   Console.WriteLine("Executing EvaluateWithReferencesAsync...");
   var result = await
CSharpScript.EvaluateAsync("System.Net.Dns.GetHostName()",
   ScriptOptions.Default.WithReferences(typeof(System.Net.Dns).Assembly));
   Console.WriteLine(result);
}
```

`EvaluateParameterizedScriptInLoopAsync` creates a parameterized C# script using the `CSharpScript.Create` API (http://source.roslyn.io/#Microsoft.CodeAnalysis.CSharp.Scripting/CSharpScript.cs,3beb8afb18b9c076), which takes the script code to execute and a global type as arguments:

```
private static async Task EvaluateParameterizedScriptInLoopAsync()
{
   Console.WriteLine("Executing EvaluateParameterizedScriptInLoopAsync...");
   var script = CSharpScript.Create<int>("X*Y", globalsType:
typeof(Globals));
   script.Compile();
   for (int i = 0; i < 10; i++)
   {
      Console.WriteLine((await script.RunAsync(new Globals { X = i, Y = i
})).ReturnValue);
   }
}
```

It then invokes the `Script.Compile` API (http://source.roslyn.io/#q=Script.Compile) to compile the script. The compiled script is then executed in a loop using the `Script.RunAsync` API (http://source.roslyn.io/#q=Script.RunAsync) with different instances of global type Globals, with incremented values of fields X and Y. Each iteration computes the result of the expression `X * Y`, which in our case is just square of all the numbers in the loop from zero to nine.

8
Contribute Simple Functionality to Roslyn C# Compiler Open Source Code

In this chapter, we will cover the following recipes:

- Setting up Roslyn enlistment
- Implementing a new syntax error in the C# compiler code base
- Implementing a new semantic error in the C# compiler code base
- Writing unit tests for a new error in C# compiler code base
- Using Roslyn Syntax Visualizer to view Roslyn syntax tokens and nodes for a source file
- Sending a Roslyn Pull request to contribute to next version of C# compiler and VS IDE

Contribute Simple Functionality to Roslyn C# Compiler Open Source Code

Introduction

This chapter enables developers to add new functionality to the Roslyn C# compiler. Let's briefly walk through the different parts of the Roslyn source tree. You can take a quick look at the topmost source folder of the Roslyn repo in the VS2017 branch:
https://github.com/dotnet/roslyn/tree/Visual-Studio-2017/src

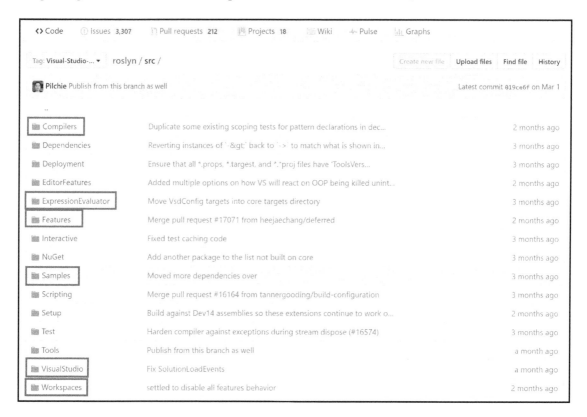

The most important source folders and corresponding components are:

- Compilers: This implements the Roslyn C# and VB compilers and the core Microsoft Code Analysis layer, which exposes the rich-language agnostic API to perform syntactic and semantic analysis of source code. Core concepts of this layer are SyntaxTree (source file), SemanticModel (semantics of a source file), Symbol (declaration in source), and Compilation (collection of source files and options).

- `Workspaces`: This implements the Workspaces layer and the corresponding APIs to do workspace-level code analysis and refactoring of projects and solutions. This layer is completely agnostic to the host operating on the workspace, such as Visual Studio or command-line tools. Core concepts of this layer are Document (syntax tree with an associated semantic model), Project (collection of documents and assembly references comprising a compilation and properties for configuring a compilation), Solution (collection of projects), and Workspace-level Options.
- `Features`: Extensible IDE features built on top of the Workspaces layer, such as Code fixes, refactorings, intellisense, completion, find references, navigate to definition, edit and continue (EnC), diagnostics, and so on, lie in this layer. This layer is not coupled to Visual Studio and can be hosted within different hosts or command-line tools.
- `VisualStudio`: Visual Studio-specific components built on top of the Features and Workspaces layers provide an end-to-end C# and VB IDE experience. Core concepts of this layer are the *Visual Studio Workspace*, Project system (component that bridges the gap between static program representation to a live IDE representation by populating the workspace and lighting up the above noted IDE features), and Language services (core language semantic services exposed to the project system).
- `ExpressionEvaluator`: C# and VB expression evaluators to parse and evaluate simple expressions and compute the runtime results.
- `Samples`: Samples and walkthroughs to demonstrate Roslyn API usage. You can read more details at `https://github.com/dotnet/roslyn/wiki/Samples-and-Walkthroughs`.

> You can read a more detailed Roslyn overview at `https://github.com/dotnet/roslyn/wiki/Roslyn%20Overview`.

Setting up Roslyn enlistment

In this section, we will walk you through the steps to install the required tools, enlist in Roslyn, build the Roslyn compiler sources and deploy, debug, and run tests for the locally-built compiler toolset.

Getting Started

You will need to have Visual Studio 2017 installed on your machine to execute the recipes in this chapter. You can install a free community version of Visual Studio 2017 from `https://www.visualstudio.com/thank-you-downloading-visual-studio/?sku=Community&rel=15`. Ensure that C#, VB, MSBuild, and Visual Studio Extensibility are included in the selected workloads. More specifically, add the .NET desktop development workload and Visual Studio Extensibility tools workloads to your VS install.

How to do it...

1. Install GitHub for desktop by following the steps at `https://desktop.github.com/` and sign in to GitHub using your GitHub profile. If you do not have a profile, you can create one at `https://github.com/join`.
2. Execute the following commands from the *Git Shell* to enlist and restore Roslyn compiler sources with VS2017 tag:
    - git clone https://github.com/dotnet/roslyn c:\Roslyn
    - cd c:\Roslyn
    - git checkout tags/Visual-Studio-2017
    - Restore.cmd
3. Build the Roslyn compiler subtree from a VS2017 admin developer command prompt: `msbuild /m /v:m Compilers.sln`. You can also build the entire Roslyn source tree using either `Build.cmd` or `msbuild /m /v:m Roslyn.sln`. This step builds the sources and deploys the locally-built compiler toolset (or entire Roslyn IDE + compiler toolset) into the **RoslynDev** hive.

NOTE: If you get build errors due to strong name signing failures, execute the following command from an admin developer command prompt to disable strong name verification: `sn -Vr *`, and then execute the build.

4. Open `Roslyn.sln` in VS2017 and set `Compilers\CompilerExtension.csproj` as the startup project.
5. Click on *Ctrl + F5* to deploy the locally built compiler toolset into a separate Visual Studio hive and start a new Visual Studio instance from this hive (RoslynDev).
6. In the new instance of Visual Studio, create a new C# class library project.

Chapter 8

7. Change the **msbuild** output verbosity from *Minimal* to *Normal* by opening **Tools | Options | Projects and Solutions | Build and Run | MSBuild project build output verbosity**.
8. Build the C# class library project and open the Output Window to confirm that locally built *csc.exe* was used to build the library and it was executed from the Visual Studio RoslynDev hive:
   `C:\USERS\<%USER_NAME%>\APPDATA\LOCAL\MICROSOFT\VISUALSTUDIO\15.0_XXXXXXXXROSLYNDEV\EXTENSIONS\MICROSOFT\ROSLYN COMPILERS\42.42.42.42424\csc.exe`
9. Right-click on `Compilers\CSharpCompilerSemanticTest.csproj` and open project **Properties | Debug** page. Execute the C# compiler semantic unit tests by executing the xunit console exe specified in the **Start external program** textbox with arguments from the **Command line arguments** textbox:
   `C:\Users\<%USER_NAME%>\.nuget\packages\xunit.runner.console\<%VERSION%>\tools\xunit.console.x86.exe`
   `"<%REPO_ROOT%>\Binaries\Debug\UnitTests\CSharpCompilerSemanticTest\\Roslyn.Compilers.CSharp.Semantic.UnitTests.dll" -html "<%REPO_ROOT%>\Binaries\Debug\UnitTests\CSharpCompilerSemanticTest\\xUnitResults\Roslyn.Compilers.CSharp.Semantic.UnitTests.html" -noshadow`

You can get more detailed instructions on enlisting, building, and testing Roslyn sources at `https://github.com/dotnet/roslyn/blob/dev16/docs/contributing/Building,%20Debugging,%20and%20Testing%20on%20Windows.md`.

Implementing a new syntax error in the C# compiler code base

This section will enable Roslyn contributors to make changes to the C# parser to add a new syntax error. The C# parser reports a diagnostic *CS0106* (*the modifier 'modifier' is not valid for this* item) (`https://msdn.microsoft.com/en-us/library/3dd3ha66.aspx`) when an incorrect modifier is used in symbol declarations such as fields, methods, locals, and so on. For example, the following erroneous code generates three *CS0106* instances:

```
class Class
{
  // Error CS0106: The modifier 'async' is not valid for this item
  async int field;
  // Error CS0106: The modifier 'readonly' is not valid for this item
```

```
    readonly static void M()
    {
        // Error CS0106: The modifier 'readonly' is not valid for this item
        readonly int local = 0;
        System.Console.WriteLine(local);
    }
}
```

However, if you declare a parameter with an incorrect modifier, say `readonly int param`, it doesn't generate *CS0106*, instead it generates a large number of unhelpful syntax errors and squiggles related to missing tokens, invalid identifiers, and so on. Consider the following example:

```
class Class
{
    static void M(readonly int param)
    {
    }
}
```

This generates the following set of errors and squiggles:

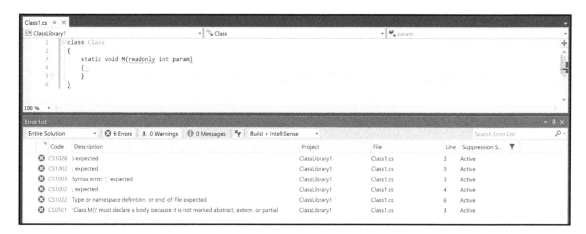

In this section, we will modify the C# parser to implement a better error recovery mechanism for such invalid parameter modifiers and report a single *CS0106* syntax error, which is more helpful to the end user.

Getting Started

You need to ensure that you have installed *Git* tools, VS2017, with .NET development and VS Extensiblity workloads and have enlisted and built Roslyn sources with the VS2017 tag. For reference, see the recipe *Setting up Roslyn enlistment*, at the start of this chapter.

How to do it...

1. Open `Roslyn.sln` at the root of the Roslyn repo in VS2017.
2. Open source file `<%ROOT%>\src\Compilers\CSharp\Portable\Parser\LanguageParser.cs`.
3. Navigate to private method `IsPossibleParameter` (line 4060) and add the highlighted || clause to the default case return statement:

   ```
   default:
       return IsPredefinedType(this.CurrentToken.Kind) ||
   GetModifier(this.CurrentToken) != SyntaxModifier.None;
   ```

4. Navigate to private method `ParseParameterModifiers` (line 4234), and replace the existing `while (IsParameterModifier(this.CurrentToken.Kind, allowThisKeyword))` with a `while (true)` loop, add the following if statement at the start of the while loop:

   ```
   while (true)
   {
     if (!IsParameterModifier(this.CurrentToken.Kind,
   allowThisKeyword))
     {
       if (GetModifier(this.CurrentToken) != SyntaxModifier.None)
       {
         // Misplaced modifier
         var misplacedModifier = this.EatToken();
         misplacedModifier = this.AddError(misplacedModifier,
   ErrorCode.ERR_BadMemberFlag, misplacedModifier.Text);
         modifiers.Add(misplacedModifier);
         continue;
       }

       break;
     }
     ...
   ```

5. Build the solution.
6. Set `VisualStudio\VisualStudioSetup.Next.csproj` as the startup project and click on *Ctrl + F5* to start a new VS instance with the locally built compiler and IDE toolset.
7. Create a new C# class library project, say `ClassLibrary`, and add the following code:

    ```
    class Class
    {
        static void M(readonly int param)
        {
        }
    }
    ```

8. Verify that there is a single *CS0106* diagnostic in the error list for the invalid `readonly` modifier and also that the editor has a single squiggle.

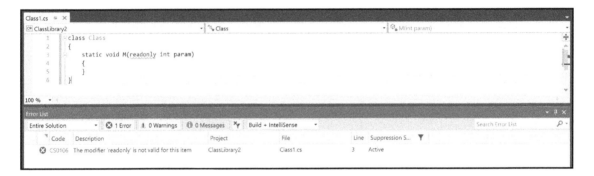

9. Build the project and verify that the build output has a single *CS0106* diagnostic.

You can view all the parser changes made in this recipe at https://github.com/mavasani/roslyn/commit/02b7be551b46fa9a8e054c3317bc2ae7957b563c.

How it works...

Parsing, syntax analysis, or syntactic analysis is the process of analyzing a string of symbols, either in natural language or in computer languages, conforming to the rules of a formal grammar.

The C# language parser is the first phase of the compiler tool chain that parses the source files according to the C# language specification to produce syntax trees. The primary entry point for parsing each source file is `SyntaxFactory.ParseCompilationUnit` (http://source.roslyn.io/#q=SyntaxFactory.ParseCompilationUnit), which transforms the given source text into a `CompilationUnitSyntax` with syntax nodes, tokens, and trivia.

Use http://source.roslyn.io/ for a rich semantic search and navigation of Roslyn source code. Note that the version of source code indexed at this website corresponds to the latest sources in the *master* branch of the Roslyn repo and may differ from the sources for the *Visual-Studio-2017* tag.

`LanguageParser.ParseCompilationUnitCore` (http://source.roslyn.io/#q=LanguageParser.ParseCompilationUnitCore) is the core method of the LanguageParser that parses the outermost namespace declaration, if any, and then parses type and member declarations within the namespace body. It uses the **Lexer** (http://source.roslyn.io/#q=Lexer.cs) to read the next token and uses a very sophisticated error recovery mechanism to provide meaningful syntax errors for erroneous code with misplaced or invalid tokens. In this recipe, we identified a case of invalid modifiers on parameters, where the C# compiler doesn't perform optimal error recovery and changed the parser code to look for invalid modifiers on parameters and parse them with the *CS0601* diagnostic.

The following highlighted change in step 3 to the default case return statement in `IsPossibleParameter` ensures that we don't completely skip over the parameter list when we encounter a member-level modifier such as readonly, public, private, and so on, in the modifier list of a parameter declaration. Instead, we associate the modifier with the parameter.

```
default:
    return IsPredefinedType(this.CurrentToken.Kind) ||
    GetModifier(this.CurrentToken) != SyntaxModifier.None;
```

The `If` statement added in the while loop of the `ParseParameterModifiers` method in step 4 ensures that we parse both valid and invalid modifiers into the parameter modifier list (as opposed to just the valid modifiers in the original code) and generate appropriate *CS0106* syntax errors on the invalid modifiers.

Implementing a new semantic error in the C# compiler code base

This section will enable the Roslyn contributor to make changes to the C# binder/semantic analysis phase to add a new semantic diagnostic. Additionally, we will also show how to extend an existing semantic diagnostic reported during the local rewriting (lowering) phase to cover more cases.

Usage of implicitly typed declarations with the `var` keyword is a very subjective matter. The C# compiler only reports non-subjective semantic errors on implicitly typed declarations where the type cannot be inferred or is invalid. However, there are certain cases where the type of the initializer is valid and can be inferred, but not at all apparent due to conversions in the initializer expression. For example, consider the expressions `var x = 1 + 1.0, var y = "string" + 1`. The initializers for *x* and *y* contain implicit conversions on the left/right sides of the binary expression, which may also involve user defined implicit operator conversions, hence, the inferred type of the variables is not apparent. We will extend the C# binder to report a new warning **CS0823** for such cases:
`Warning CS0823: Use an explicit type for declaration as the initializer type '{0}' is not apparent due to conversions.`

Additionally, in this recipe we will extend *CS1717* (Assignment made to same variable; did you mean to assign something else?) (`https://docs.microsoft.com/en-us/dotnet/csharp/misc/cs1717`) to be reported on self-assigning property access. Currently, it only covers self-assigning field, local, parameter, and event access.

With both the preceding changes, we will see the following new warnings for the code here:

```
class Class
{
  int X { get; set; }

  void M(int x)
  {
    // Warning CS1717 Assignment made to same variable; did you mean to
    //assign something else?
    X = X;
    // Warning CS0823 Use an explicit type for declaration as the
    //initializer type 'string' is not apparent due to conversions
    var y = x + "" ;
  }
}
```

Getting Started

You need to ensure that you have installed *Git* tools, VS2017 with .NET development, and VS Extensiblity workloads, and have enlisted and built Roslyn sources with the VS2017 tag. For reference, see the recipe *Setting up Roslyn enlistment* at the start of this chapter.

How to do it…

1. Open `Roslyn.sln` at the root of the Roslyn repo in VS2017.
2. Open source file `<%ROOT%>\src\Compilers\CSharp\Portable\Errors\ErrorCode.cs` and add the following new Warning ID at line 566:
   `WRN_ImplicitlyTypedVariableNotRecommended = 823,`
3. Open the resx file `<%ROOT%>\src\Compilers\CSharp\Portable\CSharpResources.resx` and add the following new resource strings for warning messages:

   ```
   <data name="WRN_ImplicitlyTypedVariableNotRecommended"
   xml:space="preserve">
     <value>
        Use an explicit type for declaration as the initializer
   type '{0}' is not apparent due to conversions
     </value>
   </data>

   <data name="WRN_ImplicitlyTypedVariableNotRecommended_Title"
   xml:space="preserve">
     <value>
        Use an explicit type for declaration as the initializer
   type is not apparent due to conversions
     </value>
   </data>
   ```

4. Open source file `<%ROOT%>\src\Compilers\CSharp\Portable\Errors\ErrorFacts.cs` and add a new switch case in the method `GetWarningLevel` at line 320: `ErrorCode.WRN_ImplicitlyTypedVariableNotRecommended`:

5. Open source file `<%ROOT%>\src\Compilers\CSharp\Portable\Binder\Binder_Statements.cs` and add the following if statement in method `BindInferredVariableInitializer` at line 702:

```
if (expression.Kind == BoundKind.BinaryOperator)
{
  var binaryOperation = (BoundBinaryOperator)expression;
  if (!binaryOperation.Left.GetConversion().IsIdentity ||
!binaryOperation.Right.GetConversion().IsIdentity)
  {
    // Use an explicit type for declaration as the initializer type '{0}' is
    //not apparent due to conversions.
    Error(diagnostics,
ErrorCode.WRN_ImplicitlyTypedVariableNotRecommended,
errorSyntax, expression.Display);
  }
}
```

6. Open source file `<%ROOT%>\src\Compilers\CSharp\Portable\Lowering\DiagnosticsPass_Warnings.cs` and add the following switch section in method `IsSameLocalOrField` at line 204:

```
case BoundKind.PropertyAccess:
  var prop1 = expr1 as BoundPropertyAccess;
  var prop2 = expr2 as BoundPropertyAccess;
  return prop1.PropertySymbol == prop2.PropertySymbol &&
    (prop1.PropertySymbol.IsStatic ||
IsSameLocalOrField(prop1.ReceiverOpt, prop2.ReceiverOpt));
```

7. Build the solution.
8. Set `VisualStudio\VisualStudioSetup.Next.csproj` as the startup project and click on *Ctrl + F5* to start a new VS instance with the locally built compiler and IDE toolset.
9. Create a new C# class library project, say `ClassLibrary`, and add the following code:

```
class Class
{
  int X { get; set; }

  void M(int x)
  {
```

Chapter 8

```
            X = X;
            var y = x + "" ;
        }
    }
```

10. Verify the new warnings *CS0823* and *CS1717* show up in the error list and squiggles appear in the editor:

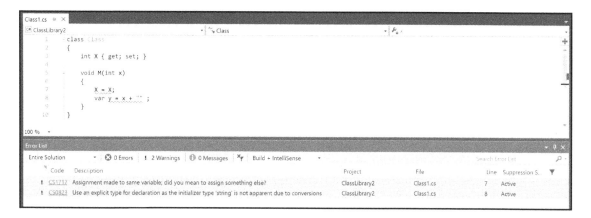

11. Build the project and verify that the build output also has the new diagnostics.

You can view all the source changes made in this recipe for *CS0823* at `https://github.com/mavasani/roslyn/commit/a155824a41150414966c6f03493b0bb05a45a59e` and for *CS1717* at `https://github.com/mavasani/roslyn/commit/9f33d6809202d9b2b7ef5e0fa79df0b56ea46110`

How it works...

Semantic analysis, also context sensitive analysis, is a process in compiler construction, usually after parsing, to gather necessary semantic information from the source code.

C# binder is the second phase of the compiler tool chain that operates on syntax trees, nodes, tokens, and trivia that comes out from the parser and analyzes the semantics of the code according to the C# language specification. This phase produces **BoundTrees** and reports semantic diagnostics. A bound tree is essentially an abstract syntax tree with rich semantic information associated with each node in the tree. All the semantic information provided by the **SemanticModel** APIs at the CodeAnalysis layer is from the bound nodes associated with the syntax. The primary entry points for binding statements and expressions are `Binder.BindStatement` and `Binder.BindExpression`, respectively.

Use http://source.roslyn.io/ for rich semantic search and navigation of Roslyn source code. Note that the version of source code indexed at this website corresponds to the latest sources in the *master* branch of the Roslyn repo, and may differ from the sources for the *Visual-Studio-2017* tag.

In this recipe, we showed you how to make the following changes in the binder to add a new diagnostic *CS0823*:

1. Add a new error code to the `ErrorCode` enum.
2. Add new resource strings for the compiler diagnostic message.
3. Add a new semantic diagnostic to the method to bind the implicit variable initializer when the initializer is a binary expression involving non-apparent implicit conversions.

C# local rewriter or lowering is the third phase of the compiler tool chain that simplifies the bound trees into very simple bound nodes. Additionally, it also performs flow analysis and reports flow analysis diagnostics (such as unreachable code). Then output of the local rewriter is fed to the code generator that generates MSIL for the simplified bound tree. In this recipe, we extended the existing local rewriting diagnostic pass to report *CS1717* for self-assigning property access expressions.

Writing unit tests for a new error in the C# compiler code base

This section will enable you to add unit tests to the C# compiler. This has the following set of unit test projects in Roslyn.sln:

- `CSharpCompilerSyntaxTest`: Unit tests for parsing and syntax errors
- `CSharpCompilerSemanticTest`: Unit tests for semantic errors and semantic model APIs
- `CSharpCompilerSymbolTest`: Unit tests for symbols defined in the compiler layer
- `CSharpCommandLineTest`: Unit tests for the compiler's command-line options
- `CSharpCompilerEmitTest`: Unit tests for the code generation phase that verify the generated MSIL

In this section, we will add unit tests to `CSharpCompilerSemanticTest` for a newly added semantic error.

Getting Started

You need to ensure that you have executed the previous recipe in this chapter, *Implementing a new semantic error in the C# compiler code base*, to add a new semantic diagnostic to the C# compiler: `Warning CS0823: Use an explicit type for declaration as the initializer type '{0}' is not apparent due to conversions.`

How to do it...

1. Open `Roslyn.sln` at the root of the Roslyn repo in VS2017.
2. Open source file `<%ROOT%>\src\Compilers\CSharp\Test\Semantic\Semantics\ImplicitlyTypedLocalsTests.cs`.
3. Add the following new unit test to the source file:

   ```
   [Fact]
   public void VarInferredTypeNotApparent()
   {
     var source = @"
     class Class
     {
       void M(int x, string y)
       {
         var z = x + y;
       }
     }";

     CreateCompilationWithMscorlib(source).VerifyDiagnostics();
   }
   ```

4. Build the test project and execute the unit test on a command-line console using the command line copied from the project's `Debug` property page, appending -method switch for the newly added unit test:

   ```
   <%USERS_FOLDER%>\.nuget\packages\xunit.runner.console\2.2.0-beta4-build3444\tools\xunit.console.x86.exe
   "<%ROOT%>\Binaries\Debug\UnitTests\CSharpCompilerSemanticTest\Roslyn.Compilers.CSharp.Semantic.UnitTests.dll" -html
   "C:\roslyn\Binaries\Debug\UnitTests\CSharpCompilerSemanticTest\xUnitResults\Roslyn.Compilers.CSharp.Semantic.UnitTests.html" -noshadow -method
   Microsoft.CodeAnalysis.CSharp.UnitTests.ImplicitlyTypedLocalTests.VarInferredTypeNotApparent
   ```

Contribute Simple Functionality to Roslyn C# Compiler Open Source Code

5. Verify the unit test fails with the missing *CS0823* diagnostic:

   ```
   Expected:
   Actual:
       // (6,7): warning CS0823: Use an explicit type for
   declaration as the initializer type 'string' is not apparent
   due to conversions
       // var z = x + y;
   Diagnostic(ErrorCode.WRN_ImplicitlyTypedVariableNotRecommended,
   "z = x + y").WithArguments("string").WithLocation(6, 7)

   Diff:
   ++>
   Diagnostic(ErrorCode.WRN_ImplicitlyTypedVariableNotRecommended,
   "z = x + y").WithArguments("string").WithLocation(6, 7)
   ```

6. Add the missing diagnostic as an argument to the `VerifyDiagnostics` invocation in our unit test:

![Screenshot of ImplicitlyTypedLocalsTests.cs in Visual Studio showing the VarInferredTypeNotApparent() test method with the added Diagnostic argument in the VerifyDiagnostics call.]

7. Re-execute the unit test by repeating step 4 and verify that the test passes now.

> If you get a `DirectoryNotFoundException`, ensure that the test results directory exists on the machine:
> `<%ROOT%>\Binaries\Debug\UnitTests\CSharpCompilerSemanticTest\xUnitResults`.

8. Add another unit test to verify that the diagnostic does not fire for a case where the initializer binary expression has no implicit conversions:

   ```
   [Fact]
   public void VarInferredTypeApparent_NoDiagnostic()
   ```

[246]

```
    {
      var source = @"
      class Class
      {
        void M(int x, string y)
        {
          var z = (string)(x + y);
        }
      }";

      CreateCompilationWithMscorlib(source).VerifyDiagnostics();
    }
```

9. Execute the new unit test and verify that it passes.

 You can also execute the unit tests inside Visual Studio using the **Test Explorer** window, but the test discovery for `Roslyn.sln` is quite slow due to thousands of unit tests across the solution. Hence, you might have to wait for a few minutes before you can execute the first unit test.

Using Roslyn Syntax Visualizer to view Roslyn syntax tokens and nodes for a source file

The **Syntax Visualizer** is a Visual Studio extension that facilitates the inspection and exploration of Roslyn syntax trees and can be used as a debugging aid when you develop your own applications atop the .NET Compiler Platform (Roslyn) APIs.

In this section, we will show you how to install and use the Roslyn **Syntax Visualizer** to view the syntax tree, nodes, and properties of C# and Visual Basic source code in Visual Studio. You can also view the semantics associated with the syntax nodes, such as symbol information, type information, and compile time constant value of expressions.

Getting Started

You need to install the `.NET Compiler Platform SDK` to install the Roslyn **Syntax Visualizer**. For guidance on installing the SDK, refer to the recipe, *Creating, debugging, and executing an analyzer project in Visual Studio*, in `Chapter 1`, *Writing Diagnostic Analyzers*.

How to do it…

1. Open Visual Studio and start the Roslyn **Syntax Visualizer** with the command **View** | **Other Windows** | **Syntax Visualizer** and dock it to the left side of the Visual Studio window.
2. Create a new C# class library project, say `ClassLibrary`, and add the following method to `Class1.cs`:

   ```
   public void Method()
   {
       Console.WriteLine("Hello world!");
   }
   ```

3. Select the code for the invocation `Console.WriteLine("Hello world!")` and view the **Syntax Visualizer** hierarchical tree view: `CompilationUnit` containing a `NamespaceDeclaration`, which contains a `ClassDeclaration`, which contains a `MethodDeclaration` with a `Block` whose first statement is an `ExpressionStatement` with an `InvocationExpression`:

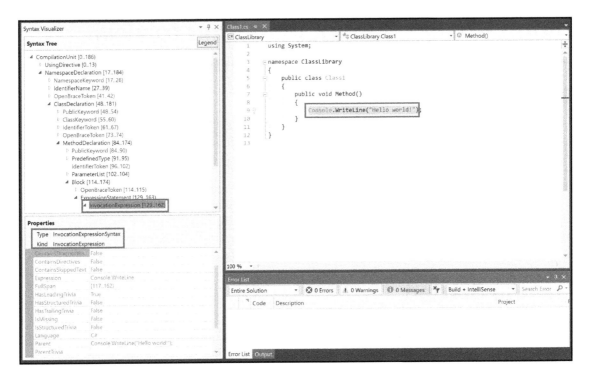

4. Right-click on the **InvocationExpression** node in **SyntaxTree** pane of the **Syntax Visualizer** and click on **View Symbol (if any)** command.

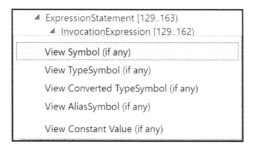

5. You can view the `Properties` of the PE metadata symbol `System.Console.WriteLine` that is bound to the invocation.

6. Add a new VB class library project to the solution, say `ClassLibrary1`, and add the following method to the existing class:

   ```
   Public Sub Method()
      Console.Write("Hello World!")
   End Sub
   ```

7. Select the invocation expression `Console.Write("Hello World!")` in the editor and you can view the Syntax tree, nodes, and properties of the VB code in the **Syntax Visualizer**:

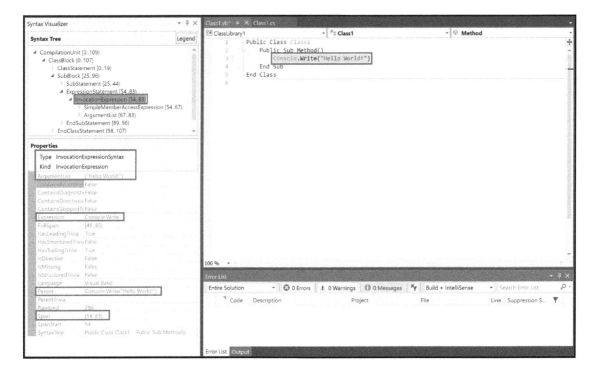

You can read a more detailed overview of the **Syntax Visualizer** tool at `https://github.com/dotnet/roslyn/wiki/Syntax%20Visualizer`.

Sending a Roslyn pull request to contribute to next version of C# compiler and VS IDE

In this section, we will walk you through the steps to follow to send a pull request to contribute to the next version of the Roslyn compilers and Visual Studio IDE.

Getting Started

You need to ensure that you have installed Git tools, VS2017 with .NET development and VS Extensiblity workloads and have enlisted and built Roslyn sources. For reference, see the recipe, *Setting up Roslyn enlistment*, at the start of this chapter.

How to do it...

1. It is recommended that you create a Roslyn issue at `https://github.com/dotnet/roslyn/issues` for your planned work and also discuss it with Roslyn team members prior to coding to avoid any unnecessary or redundant work.
2. Make the source changes that you would like to contribute to the Roslyn code base in your local enlistment. For example, execute the recipe, *Implementing a new semantic error in the C# compiler code base,* covered earlier in this chapter.
3. Add sufficient unit tests for your code changes. For example, execute the recipe, *Writing unit tests for a new error in C# compiler code base,* covered earlier in this chapter.
4. Execute `Test.cmd` at the root of the repo to build and run all the tests to confirm that there are no regressions with your changes. For reference, see the recipe, *Setting up Roslyn enlistment* at the start of this chapter.
5. Create a new git branch, add and commit your changes, and push them to the origin. For git help, search at `https://help.github.com/`.
6. Sign the .NET **Contributor License Agreement** (**CLA**) at `http://cla2.dotnetfoundation.org/` before sending the pull request.
7. Follow the steps at `https://help.github.com/articles/creating-a-pull-request/` to start a new pull request with your branch.

8. Fill out the pull request template in the description tab of the pull request. You can edit this information even after creating a pull request.
9. After creating a pull request, add a new comment tagging the compiler and/or the IDE team to review the changes:
    - Compiler team: `@dotnet/roslyn-compiler`
    - IDE team: `@dotnet/roslyn-ide`
10. Make the requested code changes from the reviewers and ensure there are no merge conflicts in your branch.
11. After you get at least two approvals and all the tests pass on the pull request, you can request your changes to be merged in by the team members.

You can read the **Contributing Code** guidelines for the Roslyn repo at `https://github.com/dotnet/roslyn/wiki/Contributing-Code` for further details.

9
Design and Implement a New C# Language Feature

In this chapter, we will cover the following recipes:

- Designing syntax and grammar for a new C# language feature
- Implementing parser support for a new C# language feature
- Implementing binding/semantic analysis support for a new C# language feature
- Implementing lowering/code generation support for a new C# language feature
- Writing unit tests for C# parsing, binding, and codegen phases

Introduction

This chapter enables developers to design a new C# language feature and implement various compiler phases for this language feature. On a high level, the C# compiler has following important phases:

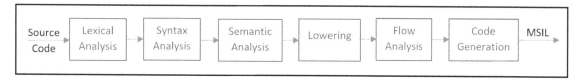

- **Lexical Analysis** (https://en.wikipedia.org/wiki/Lexical_analysis): This transforms the sequence of characters in a source file to into tokens such as keywords, identifiers, operators, and so on. `Lexer.Lex` (http://source.roslyn.io/#Microsoft.CodeAnalysis.CSharp/Parser/Lexer.cs, 5ad0cc36317d33e7) is the primary entry point into the C# lexer that fetches the next token and increments the current position within the source text. For example, consider the following source code:

    ```
    class C
    {
     void Method(int x)
     {
       x = x + 1;
     }
    }
    ```

This gets transformed into the following sequence of tokens during lexical analysis (white space and newline trivia excluded for brevity):

```
class (Keyword) C (IdToken)
{ (OpenBraceToken)
 void (Keyword) Method (IdToken) ( (OpenParenToken) int (Keyword) x
(IdToken) ) (CloseParenToken)
 { (OpenBraceToken)
   x (IdToken) = (EqualsToken) x (IdToken) + (PlusToken) 1
(NumericalLiteralToken) ; (SemiColonToken)
 } (CloseBraceToken)
} (CloseBraceToken)
```

- **Syntax Analysis** (https://en.wikipedia.org/wiki/Parsing): This transforms the sequence of tokens generated from the lexical analysis phase into a syntax tree with nodes, tokens, and trivia. It also verifies that the syntax conforms to the C# language specification and generates syntax diagnostics. `SyntaxFactory.ParseCompilationUnit` (http://source.roslyn.io/#q=SyntaxFactory.ParseCompilationUnit) is the primary entry point into the C# language parser that generates a `CompilationUnitSyntax` node, which is then used to create a `SyntaxTree` rooted at this node (see `CSharpSyntaxTree.Create` (http://source.roslyn.io/#Microsoft.CodeAnalysis.CSharp/Syntax/CSharpSyntaxTree.cs, d40da3b7b4e39486)). For the preceding example source code and lexical tokens, we get the following syntax tree:

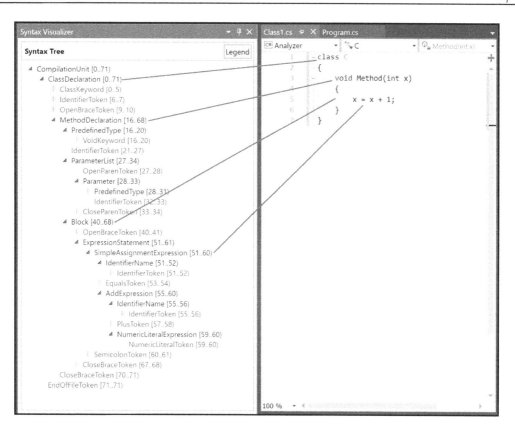

- **Semantic Analysis or Binding** (https://en.wikipedia.org/wiki/Semantic_analysis_(compilers)): Transforms the syntax tree generated from the parsing phase into a bound tree with `BoundNodes`. A bound tree is essentially an abstract syntax tree with rich semantic information associated with each node in the tree. All the semantic information provided by the `SemanticModel` APIs at the CodeAnalysis layer is from the bound nodes associated with the syntax. This phase analyzes the semantics of source code, such as type checking, method overload resolution, conversions, and so on, and generates semantic diagnostics. The primary entry points for binding statements and expressions are `Binder.BindStatement` (http://source.roslyn.io/#q=Binder.BindStatement) and `Binder.BindExpression` (http://source.roslyn.io/#q=Binder.BindExpression), respectively. For the preceding example, the following bound tree is generated for the method body for `Method`:

```
BoundBlockStatement (1 statements) (Syntax: '{ ... }')
    BoundExpressionStatement (Syntax: 'x = x + 1;')
        BoundSimpleAssignmentExpression (Type: System.Int32)
```

```
            (Syntax: 'x = x + 1')
                Left: BoundParameterReferenceExpression (Type:
            System.Int32) (Syntax: 'x')
                Right: BoundBinaryOperatorExpression (IntegerAdd) (Type:
            System.Int32) (Syntax: 'x + 1')
                    Left: BoundParameterReferenceExpression (Type:
            System.Int32) (Syntax: 'x')
                    Right: BoundLiteralExpression (Type: System.Int32,
            Constant: 1) (Syntax: '1')
```

- **Lowering**: This transforms the bound tree generated from the binding phase into a simplified bound tree. For example, a bound *for* loop node gets rewritten into a bound block with labels and conditional jumps (see `LocalRewriter.RewriteForStatement` (http://source.roslyn.io/#q=RewriteForStatement)). `LocalRewriter.Rewrite` (http://source.roslyn.io/#Microsoft.CodeAnalysis.CSharp/Lowering/LocalRewriter/LocalRewriter.cs,c30511823bc3c19f) is the primary entry point to lower each method block in the compilation.
- **Flow analysis** (https://en.wikipedia.org/wiki/Data-flow_analysis): This phase performs basic data flow and control flow analysis of the lowered bound tree to generate unreachable code and uninitialized variable diagnostics. `FlowAnalysisPass.Rewrite` (http://source.roslyn.io/#q=FlowAnalysisPass.Rewrite) is the primary entry point into the flow analysis phase.
- **Code generation** (https://en.wikipedia.org/wiki/Code_generation_(compiler)): This transforms lowered bound tree into MSIL represented with a sequence of bytes that gets emitted into a .NET assembly. `CodeGenerator.Generate` (http://source.roslyn.io/#Microsoft.CodeAnalysis.CSharp/CodeGen/CodeGenerator.cs,c28190700f8e314c) is the primary entry point into the code generator. For the preceding code example, the C# compiler generates the following MSIL for `Method`:

```
            .method private hidebysig instance void Method(int32 x) cil
            managed
            {
              // Code size 7 (0x7)
              .maxstack 8
              IL_0000: nop
              IL_0001: ldarg.1
              IL_0002: ldc.i4.1
              IL_0003: add
              IL_0004: starg.s x
              IL_0006: ret
            } // end of method C::Method
```

You can read a more detailed overview of Roslyn at `https://github.com/dotnet/roslyn/wiki/Roslyn%20Overview`.

New language feature: Switch Operator (?::)

In this chapter, we will design a new C# langauge feature that we call *Switch operator (?::)*. This feature is derived from two existing C# language constructs: switch statement (`https://docs.microsoft.com/en-us/dotnet/csharp/language-reference/keywords/switch`) and conditional operator (`?:`) (`https://docs.microsoft.com/en-us/cpp/cpp/conditional-operator-q`). It allows writing conditional expressions that can switch on multiple values of the expression and return a corresponding value or a default value. For example, consider the following switch statement that computes a string representation for an integral expression:

```
public string GetString(int expression)
{
 string expressionStr;
 switch (expression)
 {
  case 1:
   expressionStr = "One";
   break;

  case 2:
   expressionStr = "Two";
   break;

  case 3:
   expressionStr = "Three";
   break;

  default:
   expressionStr = "More than three";
   break;
 }

 return expressionStr;
}
```

This code basically switches on different possible values of the *expression* and returns a descriptive string for its runtime value. The underlying intent of the user is to just return a mapped expression for different possible values of *expression*, with some default value. The switch operator designed in this chapter will allow you to rewrite the preceding code using a single expression:

```
string expressionStr = expression ?: [1, 2, 3] : ["One", "Two", "Three", "More than three"];
```

Designing syntax and grammar for a new C# language feature

Syntax and **Grammar** are the core elements for implementing a new language feature. This section will enable you to define the syntax (nodes and tokens) and grammar for a new C# language feature: Switch operator (?::). For details on the intended functionality of this operator, read the section *New language feature: Switch Operator (?::)* at the start of this chapter.

Getting Started

You need to ensure that you have enlisted and built Roslyn sources with *VS2017* tag on your machine. For further guidance, refer to the recipe, *Setting up Roslyn enlistment* in Chapter 8, *Contribute Simple Functionality to Roslyn C# Compiler Open Source Code*.

> For the steps in the recipe that mention *Define ... in the C# language specification*, the reader should create a new GitHub issue on (https://github.com/dotnet/roslyn/issues/new) with labels Language-C# and Area-Language Design and get the specification reviewed by the language team. If approved, the reviewers will ensure that it gets added to the C# language specification.

How to do it...

1. Define the grammar for the new ternary operator ?:: in the C# language specification :

    ```
    switch-expression:
      null-coalescing-expression
    ```

```
null-coalescing-expression ?: bracketed-argument-list :
bracketed-argument-list

bracketed-argument-list:
[ argument-list ]
```

2. Define the compile time semantics associated with the new operator and the switch expression in C# language specification:

   A switch expression of the form `expr ?: [label1, label2, ..., labeln] : [val1, val2, ..., valn, valn+1]` has the following compile time semantics:

   - The governing type of the switch expression is established by the same set of rules as the governing type of a switch statement.
   - The first bracketed argument list `[label1, label2, ..., labeln]` must contain expressions labeli with a constant value that is implicitly convertible to the switch governing type. A compile-time error occurs if two or more `labeli` in the same switch expression specify the same constant value.
   - The second bracketed argument list `[val1, val2, ..., valn, valn+1]` controls the type of the switch expression resultant value. Applying the following checks to each pair vali and valj in the list must yield the same value for type Z; otherwise, a compile time error occurs:
       - If `vali` has type X and `valj` has type Y then:
           - If an implicit conversion exists from X to Y, but not from Y to X, then Y is the type of the expression (Z = Y).
           - If an implicit conversion exists from Y to X, but not from X to Y, then X is the type of the expression (Z = X).
           - Otherwise, no expression type can be determined, and a compile-time error occurs.
       - If only one of `vali` and `valj` has a type, and both `vali` and `valj` are implicitly convertible to a type Z, then that is the type of the expression.
       - Otherwise, no expression type can be determined, and a compile-time error occurs.

3. Define the associativity and precedence for the new operator in the C# language specification:

   The switch operator is right-associative, meaning that operations are grouped from right to left.
   The switch operator has the same precedence as other ternary operators (such as conditional operator ?:).

4. Define the runtime execution semantics of the switch expression in the C# language specification:

   A switch expression is evaluated as follows:

   - The expression expr is evaluated and converted to the governing type.
   - If one of the n constants, say `labeli`, specified in the first bracketed list in the same switch expression is equal to the value of the expression `expr`, then expression `vali` in the second bracketed list is evaluated and converted to type Z and becomes the resultant value of the expression.
   - If none of the n constants specified in the first bracketed list in the same switch expression is equal to the value of the expression `expr`, then the last expression `valn+1` in the second bracketed list is evaluated and converted to type Z and becomes the resultant value of the expression.

5. Open `Roslyn.sln` in Visual Studio 2017 and open source file `%REPO_ROOT%\src\Compilers\CSharp\Portable\Syntax\SyntaxKind.cs`. Add new `SyntaxKinds` for the `QuestionColonToken` and `SwitchExpression` at lines 77 and 334, respectively:

   ```
   QuestionColonToken = 8284,
   ...
   SwitchExpression = 8658,
   ```

6. Open source file `%REPO_ROOT%\src\Compilers\CSharp\Portable\Syntax\Syntax.xml` and add XML definition for the new syntax node `SwitchExpressionSyntax` with fields `Expression`, `QuestionColonToken`, `Labels`, `ColonToken`, and `Values` at line 686:

   ```
   <Node Name="SwitchExpressionSyntax" Base="ExpressionSyntax">
     <Kind Name="SwitchExpression"/>
     <Field Name="Expression" Type="ExpressionSyntax">
       <PropertyComment>
         <summary>ExpressionSyntax node representing the
   ```

```xml
      expression of the switch expression.</summary>
    </PropertyComment>
  </Field>
  <Field Name="QuestionColonToken" Type="SyntaxToken">
    <Kind Name="QuestionColonToken"/>
    <PropertyComment>
      <summary>SyntaxToken representing the question mark.</summary>
    </PropertyComment>
  </Field>
  <Field Name="Labels" Type="BracketedArgumentListSyntax">
    <PropertyComment>
      <summary>BracketedArgumentListSyntax node representing comma separated labels to switch on.</summary>
    </PropertyComment>
  </Field>
  <Field Name="ColonToken" Type="SyntaxToken">
    <Kind Name="ColonToken"/>
    <PropertyComment>
      <summary>SyntaxToken representing the colon.</summary>
    </PropertyComment>
  </Field>
  <Field Name="Values" Type="BracketedArgumentListSyntax">
    <PropertyComment>
      <summary>BracketedArgumentListSyntax node representing the comma separated expression results.</summary>
    </PropertyComment>
  </Field>
  <TypeComment>
    <summary>Class which represents the syntax node for switch expression.</summary>
  </TypeComment>
  <FactoryComment>
    <summary>Creates a SwitchExpressionSyntax node.</summary>
  </FactoryComment>
</Node>
```

7. Build the project `CSharpCodeAnalysis` to auto generate the source code for the new `SwitchExpressionSyntax` node added earlier. Note that the build will fail with a bunch of *RS0016* errors as we haven't added the new public types to the public API surface.

8. Switch back to source file `%REPO_ROOT%\src\Compilers\CSharp\Portable\Syntax\SyntaxKind.cs` and invoke the code fix at line 334 defining the `SwitchExpression` using *Ctrl + .* and apply **Fix all occurrences** in **Projec**t to fix all *RS0016* diagnostics:

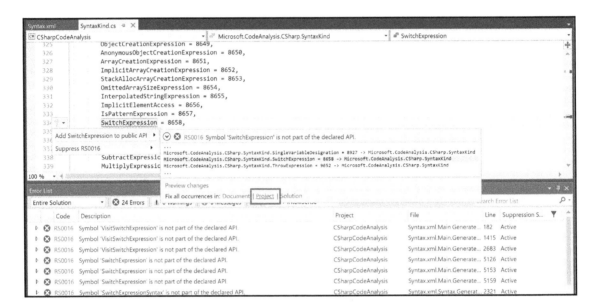

9. Build the project again and verify it succeeds this time.

You can view all the source changes made in this recipe at `https://github.com/mavasani/roslyn/commit/4b50f662c53e1b9fc83f81a819f29d11b85505d5`.

How it works...

In the first half of this recipe, we walked through the steps to define the grammar, compile time, and runtime semantics, associativity and precedence of the new switch expression/operator. In the second half, we defined the new syntax kinds and syntax node in the compiler.

The grammar, associativity, and precedence for the new switch expression is identical to the grammar for the existing conditional ternary expression.

As both the ternary operators come just after the null coalescing operator (??) in the precedence order, the grammar specifies:

```
switch-expression:
 null-coalescing-expression
 null-coalescing-expression ?: bracketed-argument-list : bracketed-
 argument-list
```

The grammar specifies the labels and the values for the switch expression to be a comma separated argument list within square brackets, for example, [arg_1, arg_2, ..., arg_n]. Some examples of expressions:

```
// Valid syntax cases
expression ?: [1, 2, 3] : ["One", "Two", "Three", "More than three"];
expression ?: [MethodCall1()] : ["One", "Two", "Three", "More than three"];
// invalid semantics

// Invalid syntax cases
expression ?: [MethodCall1(), 2] : "One"; // argument lists must be
bracketed
expression ?: [MethodCall1(), MethodCall2()]; // missing colon and argument
list
```

Compile time semantics enforce that the type of the expression being switched on has the same semantic requirements as the switch governing type for a switch statement:

The governing type of a switch statement is established by the switch expression. If the type of the switch expression is sbyte, byte, short, ushort, int, uint, long, ulong, char, string, or an enum-type, then that is the governing type of the switch statement. Otherwise, exactly one user-defined implicit conversion (Section 6.4) must exist from the type of the switch expression to one of the following possible governing types: sbyte, byte, short, ushort, int, uint, long, ulong, char, string. If no such implicit conversion exists, or if more than one such implicit conversion exists, a compile-time error occurs.

Compile time semantics also enforce that:

- The first bracketed argument list be all constant labels, such that there is an implicit conversion to the switch governing type
- The second argument list be of length one greater than the first list and all arguments be expressions, such that they are convertible to a common type Z with implicit conversions

The following are some examples of semantically valid and invalid switch expressions:

```
string expression = ...

// Valid syntax and semantics
expression ?: [1, 2, 3] : ["One", "Two", "Three", "More than three"];

// Invalid semantics, valid syntax
expression ?: [MethodCall1(), 2] : ["One", "Two", "Three"]; // non constant label
expression ?: [1.0] : ["One", "Two"]; // No implicit conversion from label to switch governing type
expression ?: [1] : ["One", 1.0]; // No implicit conversions to a common type between "One" and 1.0
```

Runtime semantics of the switch expression are identical to the switch statement. The expression on which we switch is first evaluated, and its value compared against each label in the first argument list. For a match, we evaluate the corresponding expression in the second list and convert it to type Z and that becomes the result of the expression. If there is no match, the last expression in the second argument list is evaluated and converted to type Z and becomes the default result of the expression:

```
Console.WriteLine(expression ?: [1, 2, 3] : ["One", "Two", "Three", "More than three"]);

// expression == 1, prints "One"
// expression == 2, prints "Two"
// expression == 3, prints "Three"
// otherwise, prints "More than three"
```

Implementing parser support for a new C# language feature

Lexical analysis and **Syntax analysis** (**Parsing**) are initial phases of the C# compiler that transform the input source text into a syntax tree with nodes and tokens and reports syntax diagnostics. This section will enable you to add the lexer and parser support for a new C# language feature: *Switch operator (?::)*. For details on the intended functionality of this operator, read the section *New language feature: Switch Operator (?::)* at the start of this chapter. For details on the grammar and syntax definitions for this operator, read the previous recipe.

Getting Started

You need to ensure that you have enlisted and built Roslyn sources with *VS2017* tag on your machine. For further guidance, refer to the recipe, *Setting up Roslyn, enlistment* in `Chapter 8`, *Contribute Simple Functionality to Roslyn C# Compiler Open Source Code*.

Additionally, git commit `https://github.com/mavasani/roslyn/commit/4b50f662c53e1b9fc83f81a819f29d11b85505d5` on your enlistment to get the syntax definitions and build `CSharpCodeAnalysis` project.

How to do it...

1. Open `Roslyn.sln` in Visual Studio 2017
2. Open source file `%REPO_ROOT%\src\Compilers\CSharp\Portable\Parser\Lexer.cs` and add the highlighted `else if` statement at line 565 in the method `ScanSyntaxToken`:

   ```
   case '?':
     if (TextWindow.PeekChar() == '?')
     { ...
     }
     else if (TextWindow.PeekChar() == ':')
     {
      TextWindow.AdvanceChar();
      info.Kind = SyntaxKind.QuestionColonToken;
     }
     else
     { ...
     }
   ```

3. Open source file `%REPO_ROOT%\src\Compilers\CSharp\Portable\Parser\LanguageParser.cs` and add the highlighted `else if` statement at line 9426 in the method `ParseSubExpressionCore`:

   ```
   if (tk == SyntaxKind.QuestionToken && precedence <= Precedence.Ternary)
   { ...
   }
   else if (tk == SyntaxKind.QuestionColonToken && precedence <= Precedence.Ternary)
   {
   ```

```
       var questionColonToken = this.EatToken();
       var labels = this.ParseBracketedArgumentList();
       var colon = this.EatToken(SyntaxKind.ColonToken);
       var values = this.ParseBracketedArgumentList();
       leftOperand = _syntaxFactory.SwitchExpression(leftOperand,
    questionColonToken, labels, colon, values);
    }

    return leftOperand;
```

4. Go to line 10552 in the same file (method `CanFollowCast`) add the highlighted case clause:

```
       case SyntaxKind.EndOfFileToken:
       case SyntaxKind.QuestionColonToken:
        return false;
```

5. Open source file `%REPO_ROOT%\src\Compilers\CSharp\Portable\Syntax\SyntaxKindFacts.cs` and add the highlighted case clause at line 1278 in the method `GetText`:

```
       case SyntaxKind.XmlProcessingInstructionEndToken:
        return "?>";
       case SyntaxKind.QuestionColonToken:
        return "?:";
       ...
```

6. Set `Roslyn.csproj` as the startup project.
7. Change the **solution configuration** from **Debug** to **Release** (to avoid asserts in the binder) and rebuild the solution.
8. Hit *Ctrl* + *F5* to start new instance of VS from the `RoslynDev` hive with our local changes.
9. In the new instance of VS, create a new C# class library project and add the following code, which uses the new switch operator:

```
    class Class
    {
     void M(int expr)
     {
       var exprStr = expr ?: [1, 2, 3] : ["One", "Two", "Three",
    "More than three"];
        System.Console.WriteLine(exprStr);
     }
    }
```

10. Open the Roslyn syntax visualizer from **View | Other Windows | Syntax Visualizer** and select the switch expression in the editor to view the parsed syntax nodes and tokens for the expression. For guidance on the syntax visualizer, refer to the recipe, *Using Roslyn syntax visualizer to view Roslyn syntax tokens and nodes for a source file* in `Chapter 8`, *Contribute Simple Functionality to Roslyn C# Compiler Open Source Code*.

11. Verify that there are no squiggles or intellisense errors in the error list:

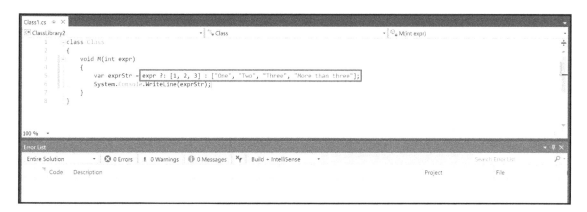

12. Remove the colon token and the second bracketed argument list, that is, `: ["One", "Two", "Three", "More than three"]`, and verify you get syntax errors for missing tokens in the switch expression:

```
Error CS1003 Syntax error, ':' expected ClassLibrary
<%PROJECT_DIR%>\ClassLibrary\Class1.cs 5
Error CS1003 Syntax error, '[' expected ClassLibrary
<%PROJECT_DIR%>\ClassLibrary\Class1.cs 5
```

```
Error CS1003 Syntax error, ']' expected ClassLibrary
<%PROJECT_DIR%>\ClassLibrary\Class1.cs 5
```

13. Revert step 11 and try to build the project and verify it fails with `CSC : error CS7038: Failed to emit module 'ClassLibrary'` as we have not implemented any binding or code generation for the new construct.

You can view all the source changes made in this recipe at https://github.com/mavasani/roslyn/commit/24144442e4faa9c54fe2a4b519455a1a45c29569.

How it works...

In this recipe, we added basic lexer and parser support for the switch operator (?:). Lexer is primarily responsible for scanning the text and generating tokens. LanguageParser is responsible for parsing the lexed tokens and generate syntax tree with nodes and tokens.

Let's walk through our code changes in this recipe. We added the following highlighted code to the lexer:

```
case '?':
  if (TextWindow.PeekChar() == '?')
  { ...
  }
  else if (TextWindow.PeekChar() == ':')
  {
    TextWindow.AdvanceChar();
    info.Kind = SyntaxKind.QuestionColonToken;
  }
  else
  { ...
  }
```

In the original code, when we were scanning the text and identify a '?' character, we peeked at the next character to identify it is another '?' character (the ?? null coalescing operator) or a whitespace (the ? token for the conditional operator). Our new code adds an additional check for whether the next character is ':' (the ?: token for the switch operator). If so, it advances the current character in the text window and sets the syntax kind for the current token to `SyntaxKind.QuestionColonToken`.

We added the following highlighted code to the parser:

```
if (tk == SyntaxKind.QuestionToken && precedence <= Precedence.Ternary)
{ ...
}
else if (tk == SyntaxKind.QuestionColonToken && precedence <=
Precedence.Ternary)
{
 var questionColonToken = this.EatToken();
 var labels = this.ParseBracketedArgumentList();
 var colon = this.EatToken(SyntaxKind.ColonToken);
 var values = this.ParseBracketedArgumentList();
 leftOperand = _syntaxFactory.SwitchExpression(leftOperand,
questionColonToken, labels, colon, values);
}
```

We extended the original code that parsed the `QuestionToken` in the parser to also check for the `QuestionColonToken` and ternary precedence. If so, we eat the next token as the `questionColonToken`. Then, we attempt to parse the `labels` as a bracketed argument list by invoking `ParseBracketedArgumentList` (this code already exists in the language parser for parsing the bracketed argument list for a dictionary initializer). This is followed by parsing the colon token by invoking `EatToken` with the expected syntax kind for the colon token. This method handles both the valid and invalid token cases:

```
protected SyntaxToken EatToken(SyntaxKind kind)
{
 Debug.Assert(SyntaxFacts.IsAnyToken(kind));

 var ct = this.CurrentToken;
 if (ct.Kind == kind)
 {
  MoveToNextToken();
  return ct;
 }

 //slow part of EatToken(SyntaxKind kind)
 return CreateMissingToken(kind, this.CurrentToken.Kind, reportError:
true);
}
```

For a valid token of the expected kind, it moves to the next token and returns the current colon token. If the next token is not of the expected kind, it generates a missing token and also reports a syntax diagnostic for the missing token:

Error CS1003 Syntax error, ':' **expected** *ClassLibrary*
<%PROJECT_DIR%>\ClassLibrary\Class1.cs 5

Finally, we parse the *values* as another bracketed argument list. We invoke the newly auto generated syntax factory helper `SwitchExpression` to generate a `SwitchExpressionSyntax` node with the parsed tokens.

Implementing binding/semantic analysis support for a new C# language feature

Semantic analysis (**Binding**) is the intermediate phase of the C# compiler that transforms syntax trees into C# bound trees and reports semantic diagnostics. This section will enable you to add the binding support for a new C# language feature: `Switch operator (?::)`. For details on the intended functionality of this operator, read the section, *New language feature: Switch Operator (?::)* at the start of this chapter. For details on the grammar and syntax definitions for this operator, read the first recipe of this chapter, *Designing syntax and grammar for a new C# language feature*.

Getting Started

You need to ensure that you have enlisted and built Roslyn sources with *VS2017* tag on your machine. For further guidance, refer to the recipe, *Setting up Roslyn enlistment* in `Chapter 8`, *Contribute Simple Functionality to Roslyn C# Compiler Open Source Code*.

Additionally, the following two git commits on your enlistment to get the syntax definitions and parser support, respectively, and build `CSharpCodeAnalysis` project:

- https://github.com/mavasani/roslyn/commit/4b50f662c53e1b9fc83f81a819f29d11b85505d5
- https://github.com/mavasani/roslyn/commit/24144442e4faa9c54fe2a4b519455a1a45c29569

How to do it...

1. Open `Roslyn.sln` in Visual Studio 2017
2. Open source file `%REPO_ROOT%\src\Compilers\CSharp\Portable\BoundTree\BoundNodes.xml` and add the following `BoundSwitchOperator` definition at line 437:

```
        <Node Name="BoundSwitchOperator" Base="BoundExpression">
        <!-- Non-null type is required for this node kind -->
        <Field Name="Type" Type="TypeSymbol" Override="true"
        Null="disallow"/>

        <Field Name="Expression" Type="BoundExpression"/>
        <Field Name="Labels"
        Type="ImmutableArray&lt;BoundExpression&gt;"/>
        <Field Name="Values"
        Type="ImmutableArray&lt;BoundExpression&gt;"/>
        </Node>
```

3. Open source file %REPO_ROOT%\src\Compilers\CSharp\Portable\Binder\Binder_Expression.cs and add the switch section at line 535 in the method BindExpressionInternal:

```
        case SyntaxKind.SwitchExpression:
          return BindSwitchOperator((SwitchExpressionSyntax)node,
        diagnostics);
```

4. Copy the method implementations for BindSwitchOperator and BindSwitchOperatorArguments from the attached code sample source file CSharpCodeAnalysis\Binder_Operators.cs and paste them into source file %REPO_ROOT%\src\Compilers\CSharp\Portable\Binder\Binder_Operators.cs at line 3521.

5. Copy the partial type definition for BoundSwitchOperator from the attached code sample source file CSharpCodeAnalysis\Expression.cs and paste it into source file %REPO_ROOT%\src\Compilers\CSharp\Portable\BoundTree\Expression.cs at line 1221.

6. Add a new source file %REPO_ROOT%\src\Compilers\CSharp\Portable\Lowering\LocalRewriter\LocalRewriter_SwitchOperator.cs to the project CSharpCodeAnalysis with a stub implementation of the lowering for the switch operator copied from CSharpCodeAnalysis\LocalRewriter_SwitchOperator.cs:

```
        public override BoundNode
        VisitSwitchOperator(BoundSwitchOperator node)
        {
         // TODO: Implement lowering for switch operator.
         return MakeLiteral(node.Syntax,
           ConstantValue.Create($"CodeGen not yet implemented for:
        '{node.Syntax.ToString()}'"),
```

```
        _compilation.GetSpecialType(SpecialType.System_String));
}
```

7. Add stub flow analysis implementation for the switch operator to `%REPO_ROOT%\src\Compilers\CSharp\Portable\FlowAnalysis\PreciseAbstractFlowPass_Switch.cs` at line 260:

    ```
    public override BoundNode
    VisitSwitchOperator(BoundSwitchOperator node)
    {
      // TODO: Implement flow analysis for switch operator.
      return null; }
    ```

8. Build project `csc.csproj` to generate `%REPO_ROOT%\Binaries\Debug\Exes\csc\csc.exe` with our local changes.

9. Create a new source file, say `test.cs`, with the following source code:

    ```
    class Class
    {
     public static void Main(string[] args)
     {
       System.Console.WriteLine(args.Length ?: [0, 1, 2] : ["Zero", "One", "Two", "More than two"]);
     }}
    ```

10. Compile this source file with locally built `csc.exe` and verify that the build succeeds.

11. Run the generated executable `test.exe` and verify it runs fine, but the output is still not the expected result due to a stub codegen implementation for the switch operator:

You can view all the source changes made in this recipe at https://github.com/mavasani/roslyn/commit/7a666595c8bf8d5e8c897540ec85ae3fa9fc5236.

How it works...

In this recipe, we added basic binding/semantic analysis support for the switch operator (?:), which enabled us to compile and execute source code with this new operator. Note that this is not a comprehensive implementation of the binding phase for this operator, and requires further work such as enhanced error reporting. See the next section, *There's more...*, in this recipe for further details.

The C# binder is responsible for semantic analysis of the syntax tree produced by the parser. It transforms the syntax tree into a bound tree with BoundNodes, which is essentially an abstract syntax tree with rich semantic information associated with each node in the tree.

We first added a new BoundNode definition for the switch operator, BoundSwitchOperator, into a template file BoundNodes.xml:

```
<Node Name="BoundSwitchOperator" Base="BoundExpression">
  <!-- Non-null type is required for this node kind -->
  <Field Name="Type" Type="TypeSymbol" Override="true" Null="disallow"/>

  <Field Name="Expression" Type="BoundExpression"/>
  <Field Name="Labels" Type="ImmutableArray&lt;BoundExpression&gt;"/>
  <Field Name="Values" Type="ImmutableArray&lt;BoundExpression&gt;"/>
</Node>
```

Note the difference between syntax nodes and bound nodes for the switch operator. We no longer store any purely syntactic information, such as the question colon token or the brackets around the argument list. The expression on which the switch operates is expected to bind to a BoundExpression, and labels and values are also expected be a list of bound expressions.

Building the project CSharpCodeAnalysis runs a generator tool over BoundNodes.xml file as a pre-build step to auto-generate BoundNodes.generated.cs file with the source definitions for the bound nodes.

Design and Implement a New C# Language Feature

BoundNodes.generated.cs is no longer automatically generated during the build of CSharpCodeAnalysis project in the latest Roslyn master branch, which was a post *VS2017* change. On the latest sources, you must explicitly run the following script to auto-generate this code: https://github.com/dotnet/roslyn/blob/master/build/scripts/generate-compiler-code.cmd.

The core binding support involved appending the switch case in BindExpressionInternal to handle the syntax node of SyntaxKind.SwitchExpression and invoke BindSwitchOperator method.

We added the new method BindSwitchOperator to the binder to handle top level binding of the SwitchExpressionSyntax node:

```
private BoundSwitchOperator BindSwitchOperator(SwitchExpressionSyntax node,
DiagnosticBag diagnostics)
{
 BoundExpression switchExpr = BindValue(node.Expression, diagnostics,
BindValueKind.RValue);
 ImmutableArray<BoundExpression> labelsExpr =
BindSwitchOperatorArguments(node.Labels, diagnostics);
 ImmutableArray<BoundExpression> valuesExpr =
BindSwitchOperatorArguments(node.Values, diagnostics);

 // TODO: Add semantic validation for arguments and diagnostics.
 TypeSymbol type = valuesExpr.Length > 1 ? valuesExpr[0].Type :
CreateErrorType();
 bool hasErrors = type.IsErrorType();

 return new BoundSwitchOperator(node, switchExpr, labelsExpr, valuesExpr,
type, hasErrors);
}
```

We bind the expression of the switch operator as a value using BindValue (http://source.roslyn.io/#Microsoft.CodeAnalysis.CSharp/Binder/Binder_Expressions.cs, 608d49de0066ede1, references) invocation. This guarantees that we have an actual expression with a value, rather than a type, as the node's expression. For example, we get the following semantic error when this is violated:

```
Administrator: Developer Command Prompt for VS 2017

c:\roslyn>type test.cs
class Class
{
    public static void Main(string[] args)
    {
        System.Console.WriteLine(Class ?: [0, 1, 2] : ["Zero", "One", "Two", "More than two"]);
    }
}
c:\roslyn>c:\roslyn\Binaries\Debug\Exes\csc\csc.exe test.cs
Microsoft (R) Visual C# Compiler version 42.42.42.42424
Copyright (C) Microsoft Corporation. All rights reserved.

test.cs(5,34): error CS0119: 'Class' is a type, which is not valid in the given context

c:\roslyn>
```

We added the new method, `BindSwitchOperatorArguments`, to bind the `Labels` and `Values` of the switch operator:

```
private ImmutableArray<BoundExpression>
BindSwitchOperatorArguments(BracketedArgumentListSyntax node, DiagnosticBag
diagnostics)
{
 AnalyzedArguments analyzedArguments = AnalyzedArguments.GetInstance();
 ImmutableArray<BoundExpression> arguments;
 try
 {
  BindArgumentsAndNames(node, diagnostics, analyzedArguments);
  arguments = BuildArgumentsForErrorRecovery(analyzedArguments);
 }
 finally
 {
  analyzedArguments.Free();
 }

 return arguments;
}
```

This method invokes the existing binder method, `BindArgumentsAndNames` (http://source.roslyn.io/#q=BindArgumentsAndNames), to bind the argument list and then build arguments for error recovery.

We also added a stub partial type implementation for `BoundSwitchOperator` for implementing `IOperation` (http://source.roslyn.io/#Microsoft.CodeAnalysis/Operations/IOperation.cs,7743f66521e66763) APIs:

```
// TODO: Implement IOperation support for switch operator.
internal partial class BoundSwitchOperator
```

```
{
  protected override OperationKind ExpressionKind => OperationKind.None;

  public override void Accept(OperationVisitor visitor)
  {
   visitor.VisitNoneOperation(this);
  }

  public override TResult Accept<TArgument,
TResult>(OperationVisitor<TArgument, TResult> visitor, TArgument argument)
  {
   return visitor.VisitNoneOperation(this, argument);
  }
}
```

IOperation is a new experimental feature that is currently being implemented in the compiler layers to expose the semantics associated with the compiler bound nodes as a publically supported API. The API is not released or publically supported as of VS2017, which may or may not change in a future release.

Additionally, we added stub implementations for flow analysis and lowering to enable us to build source code with the switch operator, though the generated MSIL or the output of the compiled executable is not the same as the expected final outcome. More specifically, the lowering implementation just replaced the entire BoundSwitchOperator node with a bound string literal stating that codegen is not yet implemented for the new switch operator:

```
return MakeLiteral(node.Syntax,
  ConstantValue.Create($"CodeGen not yet implemented for:
'{node.Syntax.ToString()}'"),
  _compilation.GetSpecialType(SpecialType.System_String));
```

Refer to the next recipe in this chapter for implementing lowering support for the operator.

There's more...

The current binder implementation of the switch operator has a bunch of pending work items, primarily related to more comprehensive semantic validation and error generation. The validation items to be implemented are:

1. Add semantic validation that the expression of the switch operator has a type as per the requirements of a switch governing type; otherwise, generate a compile time error.

2. Add new compiler diagnostics for argument list validations. For example:
    - Ensure that the number of expressions in values is one greater than the number of expression in labels; otherwise, generate a compile time error.
    - Ensure that the labels are all compile time constants with implicit conversions to the switch governing type. If not, generate required compile time errors.
3. Validate that the types of the expressions in Values are implicitly convertible to a common type Z, which is the type of the expression.

These items are left as an exercise for the reader. For further guidance on implementing a new semantic error in the compiler code base, refer to recipe, *Implementing a new semantic error in the C# compiler code base*, in `Chapter 8`, *Contribute Simple Functionality to Roslyn C# Compiler Open Source Code*.

We also added basic stub implementations for the following pieces, which need further enhancements:

1. `IOperation` support the switch operator: This will involve creating a new `OperationKind` (http://source.roslyn.io/#Microsoft.CodeAnalysis/Operations/IOperationKind.cs,bf7324631c03b2e7) for the switch expression, adding a new interface, say `ISwitchChoiceExpression`, with the following API shape and then implementing this interface on the `BoundSwitchOperator`.

```
/// <summary>
/// Represents a C# switch operator.
/// </summary>
/// <remarks>
/// This interface is reserved for implementation by its
associated APIs. We reserve the right to
/// change it in the future.
/// </remarks>
public interface ISwitchChoiceExpression : IOperation
{
  /// <summary>
  /// Switch expression to be tested.
  /// </summary>
  IOperation SwitchExpression { get; }

  /// <summary>
  /// List of labels to compare the switch expression against.
  /// </summary>
  ImmutableArray<IOperation> SwitchLabels { get; }
```

```
            /// <summary>
            /// List of values corresponding to the labels.
            /// </summary>
            ImmutableArray<IOperation> SwitchValues { get; }
        }
```

2. Add lowering support for the switch operator: This is covered in the next recipe.
3. Add flow analysis support for the switch operator: This is not covered in this book, but should be implemented to ensure we report proper flow analysis diagnostics in code involving the switch operator.

Implementing lowering/code generation support for a new C# language feature

Lowering is an intermediate phase that executes after binding and transforms high level bound trees into simplified bound trees. These simplified bound trees are provided to the **Code Generation** phase and converted into MSIL and emitted into a .NET assembly. This section will enable you to add the lowering support for a new C# language feature: Switch operator (`?::`). This will enable you to write, compile, and correctly execute C# programs with the new operator. For details on the intended functionality of this operator, read the section, *New language feature: Switch Operator (?::)* at the start of this chapter. For details on the grammar and syntax definitions for this operator, read the first recipe of this chapter, *Designing syntax and grammar for a new C# language feature*.

Getting Started

You need to ensure that you have enlisted and built Roslyn sources with *VS2017* tag on your machine. For further guidance, refer to the recipe *Setting up Roslyn enlistment* in `Chapter 8`, *Contribute Simple Functionality to Roslyn C# Compiler Open Source Code*.

Additionally, the following three git commits on your enlistment to get the syntax definitions, parser support and binder support, respectively, and build `CSharpCodeAnalysis` project:

- https://github.com/mavasani/roslyn/commit/4b50f662c53e1b9fc83f81a819f29d11b85505d5
- https://github.com/mavasani/roslyn/commit/24144442e4faa9c54fe2a4b519455a1a45c29569
- https://github.com/mavasani/roslyn/commit/7a666595c8bf8d5e8c897540ec85ae3fa9fc5236

How to do it...

1. Open `Roslyn.sln` in Visual Studio 2017
2. Copy the method implementations for `VisitSwitchOperator` and `RewriteSwitchOperator` from the attached code sample source file `CSharpCodeAnalysis\LocalRewriter_SwitchOperator.cs` and paste them into source file `%REPO_ROOT%\src\Compilers\CSharp\Portable\Lowering\LocalRewriter\LocalRewriter_SwitchOperator.cs`.
3. Build project `csc.csproj` to generate `%REPO_ROOT%\Binaries\Debug\Exes\csc\csc.exe` with our local changes.
4. Create a new source file, say `test.cs`, with the following source code:

    ```
    class Class
    {
     public static void Main(string[] args)
     {
       System.Console.WriteLine(args.Length ?: [0, 1, 2] : ["Zero", "One", "Two", "More than two"]);
     }
    }
    ```

5. Compile this source file with locally built `csc.exe` and verify that the build succeeds.

Design and Implement a New C# Language Feature

6. Run the generated executable `test.exe` with a different number of arguments and verify the corresponding outputs are as expected from the switch operator.

```
Administrator: Developer Command Prompt for VS 2017

c:\roslyn>c:\roslyn\Binaries\Debug\Exes\csc\csc.exe test.cs
Microsoft (R) Visual C# Compiler version 42.42.42.42424
Copyright (C) Microsoft Corporation. All rights reserved.

c:\roslyn>test.exe
Zero

c:\roslyn>test.exe arg1
One

c:\roslyn>test.exe arg1 arg2
Two

c:\roslyn>test.exe arg1 arg2 arg3
More than two

c:\roslyn>
```

7. Execute the `ildasm.exe test.exe` command and verify the MSIL for the generated executable contains sequential checks of the switch expression against the list of labels and conditional branches to the corresponding values:

```
.method public hidebysig static void Main(string[] args) cil managed
{
  .entrypoint
  // Code size 51 (0x33)
  .maxstack 8
  IL_0000: nop
  IL_0001: ldarg.0
  IL_0002: ldlen
  IL_0003: conv.i4
  IL_0004: brfalse.s IL_0027
  IL_0006: ldarg.0
  IL_0007: ldlen
  IL_0008: conv.i4
  IL_0009: ldc.i4.1
  IL_000a: beq.s IL_0020
  IL_000c: ldarg.0
  IL_000d: ldlen
  IL_000e: conv.i4
  IL_000f: ldc.i4.2
  IL_0010: beq.s IL_0019
  IL_0012: ldstr "More than two"
  IL_0017: br.s IL_001e
```

Chapter 9

```
IL_0019: ldstr "Two"
IL_001e: br.s IL_0025
IL_0020: ldstr "One"
IL_0025: br.s IL_002c
IL_0027: ldstr "Zero"
IL_002c: call void [mscorlib]System.Console::WriteLine(string)
IL_0031: nop
IL_0032: ret
} // end of method Class::Main
```

You can view all the source changes made in this recipe at https://github.com/mavasani/roslyn/commit/2c1ec4dc60ab0a64b7e9c01d1ec9a1fbcaa611da.

How it works...

In this recipe, we added basic lowering support for the switch operator (?:), which enabled us to compile and execute source code with this new operator and give expected runtime results. Note that this is not an optimal implementation of the lowering/code generation phase for this operator, and requires further work to generate optimized MSIL. This is left as an exercise for the reader.

The C# lowering phase is responsible for transforming the initial bound tree from the binder into a simpler bound tree that can be operated by the code generation phase. The code generation phase operates on the lowered bound tree and transforms it into MSIL. In this recipe, we added lowering support for the switch operator that rewrites a switch operator into nested conditional branches.

Let's take an example to clarify the lowering algorithm. Consider the switch expression used in our recipe:

```
args.Length ?: [0, 1, 2] : ["Zero", "One", "Two", "More than two"]
```

This operator gets rewritten into following lowered (pseudo)code:

```
args.Length == 0
   jump to label Val0
args.Length == 1
   jump to label Val1
args.Length == 2
   jump to label Val2
result = "More than two"
   jump to label Exit
Val2:
```

[281]

```
    result = "Two"
       jump to label Exit
 Val1:
    result = "One"
       jump to label Exit
 Val0:
    result = "Zero"
       jump to label Exit
 Exit:
```

We walk through each constant and compare the value of the expression against this constant. If it succeeds, we jump to a label and evaluate the corresponding switch operator value, load it into the result, and jump to the exit label. If the check fails, then we recursively operate on the remaining labels and values, until the expression doesn't match any constant and we evaluate the last (default) value.

Let's now walk through the details of the code added in the lowering phase that implements the preceding algorithm. `LocalRewriter` type implements the bound tree lowering/rewrite. This type is essentially an implementation of `BoundTreeRewriter` (http://source.roslyn.io/#q=BoundTreeRewriter), which uses a visitor pattern to visit the entire bound tree. It has an overridable *VisitXXX* method for every bound node to convert it into a simpler rewritten bound node and return the rewritten node. We override the `VisitSwitchOperator` method as follows:

```
/// <summary>
/// Rewrite switch operator into nested conditional operators.
/// </summary>
public override BoundNode VisitSwitchOperator(BoundSwitchOperator node)
{
  // just a fact, not a requirement (VisitExpression would have rewritten otherwise)
  Debug.Assert(node.ConstantValue == null);

  var rewrittenExpression = VisitExpression(node.Expression);
  var rewrittenLabels = node.Labels.SelectAsArray(l => VisitExpression(l));
  var rewrittenValues = node.Values.SelectAsArray(l => VisitExpression(l));
  var rewrittenType = VisitType(node.Type);
  var booleanType = _compilation.GetSpecialType(SpecialType.System_Boolean);

  return RewriteSwitchOperator(
    node.Syntax,
    rewrittenExpression,
    rewrittenLabels,
    rewrittenValues,
    rewrittenType,
```

```
    booleanType);
}
```

A general requirement and pattern of bound tree rewriter is to first visit each of the child nodes of the bound node and use the rewritten child nodes for the core rewrite functionality. We first rewrite the switch expression, then the labels, values, and the expression type. We also fetch the well-known System.Boolean type to be used in the rewrite helper. We pass all these values into the core rewrite method, RewriteSwitchOperator:

```
private static BoundExpression RewriteSwitchOperator(
  SyntaxNode syntax,
  BoundExpression rewrittenExpression,
  ImmutableArray<BoundExpression> rewrittenLabels,
  ImmutableArray<BoundExpression> rewrittenValues,
  TypeSymbol rewrittenType,
  TypeSymbol booleanType)
{
  Debug.Assert(rewrittenLabels.Length >= 1);
  Debug.Assert(rewrittenLabels.Length + 1 == rewrittenValues.Length);

  var label = rewrittenLabels[0];
  var consequence = rewrittenValues[0];
  var condition = new BoundBinaryOperator(label.Syntax,
BinaryOperatorKind.Equal, rewrittenExpression, label, null, null,
LookupResultKind.Viable, booleanType);
  BoundExpression alternative = rewrittenLabels.Length > 1 ?
    RewriteSwitchOperator(syntax, rewrittenExpression,
rewrittenLabels.RemoveAt(0), rewrittenValues.RemoveAt(0), rewrittenType,
booleanType) :
    rewrittenValues[1];
  return new BoundConditionalOperator(label.Syntax, condition, consequence,
alternative, null, rewrittenType);
}
```

The rewrite method first validates that we are operating on a switch operator with one or more labels, and the count of values is one more than the count of the values (otherwise we would have generated a binding error and the lowering phase wouldn't have executed).

This method uses a recursive approach to rewrite the switch operator. We first generate a BoundBinaryOperator with the == operator. The rewrittenExpression is the left of the operator, and the first label in the rewrittenLabels is the right. This forms our condition bound node. The first value in rewrittenValues list is the consequence.

If we have more than one `rewrittenLabels`, then we recursively invoke `RewriteSwitchOperator` using only the remaining `rewrittenLabels` and `rewrittenValues` except the first ones in each list, and this becomes the `alternative`. Otherwise, the second label in the current `rewrittenValues` list becomes the alternative.

Finally, we use the preceding `condition` (`BoundBinaryOperator`), `consequence` (first rewritten value) and `alternative` (recursive rewrite of rest the of the expression) to create a `BoundConditionalOperator condition ? consequence : alternative` and return that as the final rewritten node.

As the lowered bound tree has no new bound node kind, we did not require the adding of any new codegen support (it already handled conditional branches). Refer to the `CodeGenerator` (http://source.roslyn.io/#Microsoft.CodeAnalysis.CSharp/CodeGen/CodeGenerator.cs,8838d807a9a1d615) type for any implementation details of the code generator.

Writing unit tests for C# parsing, binding, and codegen phases

This section will enable you to add unit tests for a new C# language feature: Switch operator (?::). For details on the intended functionality of this operator, read the section, *New language feature: Switch Operator (?::)*, at the start of this chapter.

C# compiler has the following set of unit test projects in Roslyn.sln:

- `CSharpCompilerSyntaxTest`: This unit tests for parsing and syntax errors.
- `CSharpCompilerSemanticTest`: This unit tests for semantic errors and semantic model APIs.
- `CSharpCompilerSymbolTest`: This unit tests for symbols defined in the compiler layer.
- `CSharpCommandLineTest`: This unit tests for the compiler's command line options.
- `CSharpCompilerEmitTest`: This unit tests for the code generation phase that verifies the generated MSIL.

In this section, we will add unit tests to `CSharpCompilerSyntaxTest`, `CSharpCompilerSemanticTest` and `CSharpCompilerEmitTest` for parsing, binding, and codegen support, respectively.

Getting Started

You need to ensure that you have enlisted and built Roslyn sources with *VS2017* tag on your machine. For further guidance, refer to the recipe, *Setting up Roslyn enlistment* in `Chapter 8`, *Contribute Simple Functionality to Roslyn C# Compiler Open Source Code*.

Additionally, the following four git commits on your enlistment to get the syntax definitions, parser support, binder support, and lowering support for the new operator and build `CSharpCodeAnalysis` project:

- `https://github.com/mavasani/roslyn/commit/4b50f662c53e1b9fc83f81a819f29d11b85505d5`
- `https://github.com/mavasani/roslyn/commit/24144442e4faa9c54fe2a4b519455a1a45c29569`
- `https://github.com/mavasani/roslyn/commit/7a666595c8bf8d5e8c897540ec85ae3fa9fc5236`
- `https://github.com/mavasani/roslyn/commit/2c1ec4dc60ab0a64b7e9c01d1ec9a1fbcaa611da`

How to do it...

1. Open `Roslyn.sln` in Visual Studio 2017.
2. Open source file `<%REPO_ROOT%>\src\Compilers\CSharp\Test\Syntax\Parsing\ExpressionParsingTests.cs`.
3. [Parsing Test] Add the following new unit test at the end of the source file:

```
[Fact]
public void TestSwitchExpression()
{
 var text = @"expr ?: [0, 1, 2] : [""Zero"", ""One"", ""Two"", ""More than two""]";
 var expr = SyntaxFactory.ParseExpression(text);

 Assert.NotNull(expr);
 Assert.Equal(SyntaxKind.SwitchExpression, expr.Kind());
 Assert.Equal(text, expr.ToString());
 Assert.Equal(0, expr.Errors().Length);

 var switchExpr = (SwitchExpressionSyntax)expr;
 Assert.NotNull(switchExpr.Expression);
 Assert.Equal("expr", switchExpr.Expression.ToString());
```

```
            Assert.NotNull(switchExpr.QuestionColonToken);
            Assert.False(switchExpr.QuestionColonToken.IsMissing);

            Assert.NotNull(switchExpr.Labels.OpenBracketToken);
            Assert.False(switchExpr.Labels.OpenBracketToken.IsMissing);
            Assert.Equal(3, switchExpr.Labels.Arguments.Count);
            Assert.Equal("0", switchExpr.Labels.Arguments[0].ToString());
            Assert.Equal("1", switchExpr.Labels.Arguments[1].ToString());
            Assert.Equal("2", switchExpr.Labels.Arguments[2].ToString());
            Assert.NotNull(switchExpr.Labels.CloseBracketToken);
            Assert.False(switchExpr.Labels.CloseBracketToken.IsMissing);

            Assert.NotNull(switchExpr.ColonToken);
            Assert.False(switchExpr.ColonToken.IsMissing);

            Assert.NotNull(switchExpr.Values.OpenBracketToken);
            Assert.False(switchExpr.Values.OpenBracketToken.IsMissing);
            Assert.Equal(4, switchExpr.Values.Arguments.Count);
            Assert.Equal(@"""Zero""",
         switchExpr.Values.Arguments[0].ToString());
            Assert.Equal(@"""One""",
         switchExpr.Values.Arguments[1].ToString());
            Assert.Equal(@"""Two""",
         switchExpr.Values.Arguments[2].ToString());
            Assert.Equal(@"""More than two""",
         switchExpr.Values.Arguments[3].ToString());
            Assert.NotNull(switchExpr.Values.CloseBracketToken);
            Assert.False(switchExpr.Values.CloseBracketToken.IsMissing);
        }

        CreateCompilationWithMscorlib(source).VerifyDiagnostics();
        }
```

4. Build the test project `CSharpCompilerSyntaxTest` and execute the unit test on a command-line console using the command line copied from the project's `Debug` property page and appending `-method` switch for the newly added unit test:

```
<%USERS_FOLDER%>\.nuget\packages\xunit.runner.console\2.2.0-
beta4-build3444\tools\xunit.console.x86.exe
"<%REPO_ROOT%>\Binaries\Debug\UnitTests\CSharpCompilerSyntaxTes
t\Roslyn.Compilers.CSharp.Syntax.UnitTests.dll" -html
"<%REPO_ROOT%>\Binaries\Debug\UnitTests\CSharpCompilerSyntaxTes
t\xUnitResults\Roslyn.Compilers.CSharp.Syntax.UnitTests.html" -
noshadow -method
Microsoft.CodeAnalysis.CSharp.UnitTests.ExpressionParsingTexts.
TestSwitchExpression
```

Chapter 9

5. Verify the unit test passes successfully:

```
c:\roslyn>C:\Users\mavasani\.nuget\packages\xunit.runner.console\2.2.0-beta4-build3444\tools\xunit.console.x86.exe "c:\r
oslyn\Binaries\Debug\Dlls\CSharpCompilerSyntaxTest\\Roslyn.Compilers.CSharp.Syntax.UnitTests.dll" -html "c:\roslyn\Binar
ies\Debug\Dlls\CSharpCompilerSyntaxTest\\xUnitResults\Roslyn.Compilers.CSharp.Syntax.UnitTests.html" -noshadow -method M
icrosoft.CodeAnalysis.CSharp.UnitTests.ExpressionParsingTexts.TestSwitchExpression
xUnit.net Console Runner (32-bit .NET 4.0.30319.42000)
  Discovering: Roslyn.Compilers.CSharp.Syntax.UnitTests
  Discovered:  Roslyn.Compilers.CSharp.Syntax.UnitTests
  Starting:    Roslyn.Compilers.CSharp.Syntax.UnitTests
  Finished:    Roslyn.Compilers.CSharp.Syntax.UnitTests
=== TEST EXECUTION SUMMARY ===
  Roslyn.Compilers.CSharp.Syntax.UnitTests  Total: 1, Errors: 0, Failed: 0, Skipped: 0, Time: 0.289s

c:\roslyn>
```

If you get a `DirectoryNotFoundException`, ensure that the test results directory exists on the machine:
`<%REPO_ROOT%>\Binaries\Debug\UnitTests\CSharpCompilerSyntaxTest\xUnitResults`.

6. [Binding Test] Open source file `<%REPO_ROOT%>\src\Compilers\CSharp\Test\Semantic\Semantics\BindingTests.cs`

7. Add the following new unit test to the source file:

```
[Fact]
public void TestSwitchExpressionBinding()
{
 var source =
@"
class Class
{
 public static void Main(string[] args)
 {
  System.Console.WriteLine(args.Length ?: [0, 1, 2] : [""Zero"",
""One"", ""Two"", ""More than two""]);
 }
}
";
 var compilation = CreateCompilationWithMscorlib(source);
 compilation.VerifyDiagnostics();

 var tree = compilation.SyntaxTrees[0];
 var model = compilation.GetSemanticModel(tree);

 var switchExp =
(SwitchExpressionSyntax)tree.GetRoot().DescendantNodes().Where(
```

```
            n => n.IsKind(SyntaxKind.SwitchExpression)).Single();
             Assert.Equal(@"args.Length ?: [0, 1, 2] : [""Zero"", ""One"",
            ""Two"", ""More than two""]", switchExp.ToString());
             var symbolInfo = model.GetSymbolInfo(switchExp);
             Assert.Null(symbolInfo.Symbol);
             var typeInfo = model.GetTypeInfo(switchExp);
             Assert.NotNull(typeInfo.Type);
             Assert.Equal("string", typeInfo.Type.ToString());

             symbolInfo = model.GetSymbolInfo(switchExp.Expression);
             Assert.NotNull(symbolInfo.Symbol);
             Assert.Equal("System.Array.Length",
            symbolInfo.Symbol.ToString());

             typeInfo = model.GetTypeInfo(switchExp.Expression);
             Assert.NotNull(typeInfo.Type);
             Assert.Equal("int", typeInfo.Type.ToString());

             Assert.Equal(3, switchExp.Labels.Arguments.Count);
             var constantValue =
            model.GetConstantValue(switchExp.Labels.Arguments[0].Expression
            );
             Assert.True(constantValue.HasValue);
             Assert.Equal(0, constantValue.Value);
             typeInfo =
            model.GetTypeInfo(switchExp.Labels.Arguments[0].Expression);
             Assert.NotNull(typeInfo.Type);
             Assert.Equal("int", typeInfo.Type.ToString());

             Assert.Equal(4, switchExp.Values.Arguments.Count);
             constantValue =
            model.GetConstantValue(switchExp.Values.Arguments[0].Expression
            );
             Assert.True(constantValue.HasValue);
             Assert.Equal("Zero", constantValue.Value);
             typeInfo =
            model.GetTypeInfo(switchExp.Values.Arguments[0].Expression);
             Assert.NotNull(typeInfo.Type);
             Assert.Equal("string", typeInfo.Type.ToString());
            }
```

8. Build the test project `CSharpCompilerSemanticTest` and execute the unit test on a command line console by using the command line copied from the project's `Debug` property page and appending `-method` switch for the newly added unit test:

   ```
   <%USERS_FOLDER%>\.nuget\packages\xunit.runner.console\2.2.0-
   beta4-build3444\tools\xunit.console.x86.exe
   "<%REPO_ROOT%>\Binaries\Debug\UnitTests\CSharpCompilerSemanticT
   est\Roslyn.Compilers.CSharp.Semantic.UnitTests.dll" -html
   "<%REPO_ROOT%>\Binaries\Debug\UnitTests\CSharpCompilerSemanticT
   est\xUnitResults\Roslyn.Compilers.CSharp.Semantic.UnitTests.htm
   l" -noshadow -method
   Microsoft.CodeAnalysis.CSharp.UnitTests.Semantics.BindingTests.
   TestSwitchExpressionBinding
   ```

9. Verify the unit test passes successfully.
10. [CodeGen Test] Open source file `<%REPO_ROOT%>\src\Compilers\CSharp\Test\Emit\CodeGen\CodeGenTests.cs`.
11. Add the following new unit test to the source file:

    ```
    [Fact]
    public void TestSwitchExpressionCodeGen()
    {
     string source = @"
    class Class
    {
     public static void Main(string[] args)
     {
      System.Console.WriteLine(args.Length ?: [0, 1, 2] : [""Zero"",
    ""One"", ""Two"", ""More than two""]);
     }
    }";

     var compilation = CompileAndVerify(source, options:
    TestOptions.DebugExe);
     compilation.VerifyIL("Class.Main", @"
    {
     // Code size 51 (0x33)
     .maxstack 2
     IL_0000: nop
     IL_0001: ldarg.0
     IL_0002: ldlen
     IL_0003: conv.i4
     IL_0004: brfalse.s IL_0027
     IL_0006: ldarg.0
    ```

Design and Implement a New C# Language Feature

```
            IL_0007: ldlen
            IL_0008: conv.i4
            IL_0009: ldc.i4.1
            IL_000a: beq.s IL_0020
            IL_000c: ldarg.0
            IL_000d: ldlen
            IL_000e: conv.i4
            IL_000f: ldc.i4.2
            IL_0010: beq.s IL_0019
            IL_0012: ldstr ""More than two""
            IL_0017: br.s IL_001e
            IL_0019: ldstr ""Two""
            IL_001e: br.s IL_0025
            IL_0020: ldstr ""One""
            IL_0025: br.s IL_002c
            IL_0027: ldstr ""Zero""
            IL_002c: call ""void System.Console.WriteLine(string)""
            IL_0031: nop
            IL_0032: ret
        }
        ");
        }
```

12. Build the test project `CSharpCompilerEmitTest` and execute the unit test on a command-line console by using the command line copied from the project's `Debug` property page and appending `-method` switch for the newly added unit test:

```
<%USERS_FOLDER%>\.nuget\packages\xunit.runner.console\2.2.0-
beta4-build3444\tools\xunit.console.x86.exe
"<%REPO_ROOT%>\Binaries\Debug\UnitTests\CSharpCompilerEmitTest\
xUnitResults\Roslyn.Compilers.CSharp.Emit.UnitTests.html" -
noshadow -method
Microsoft.CodeAnalysis.CSharp.UnitTests.CodeGen.CodeGenTests.Te
stSwitchExpressionCodeGen
```

Chapter 9

13. Verify the unit test passes successfully.

You can also execute the unit tests inside Visual Studio using the **Test Explorer** window, but the test discovery for *Roslyn.sln* is quite slow due to thousands of unit tests across the solution. Hence, you might have to wait for a few minutes before you can execute the first unit test.

You can view all the source changes made in this recipe at https://github.com/mavasani/roslyn/commit/ca1b555aef3d3f5dbe4efecda3580822d382a56f.

10
Command-Line Tools Based on Roslyn API

In this chapter, we will cover the following recipes:

- Writing an application based on the Compiler Syntax API to parse and transform source files
- Writing an application based on the Compiler Semantic API to display diagnostics and overload resolution results
- Writing an application based on the Compiler Analyzer API to execute diagnostic analyzers and display analyzer diagnostics
- Writing an application based on the Workspaces API to format and simplify all source files in the solution
- Writing an application based on the Workspaces API to edit projects in a solution and display project properties

Introduction

This chapter enables developers to write command-line tools using the Roslyn compiler and workspaces API to analyze and/or edit C# code. The article at (`https://github.com/dotnet/roslyn/wiki/Roslyn%20Overview`) provides a very good introduction to the Roslyn APIs at each of these layers.

We will provide you a gist from the article:

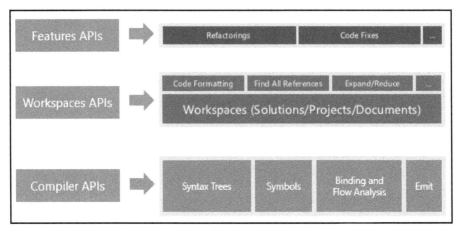

- **Compiler API**: The compiler layer contains the object models that correspond with information exposed at each phase of the compiler pipeline, both syntactic and semantic. The compiler layer also contains an immutable snapshot of a single invocation of a compiler, including assembly references, compiler options, and source code files. There are two distinct APIs that represent the C# language and the Visual Basic language. These two APIs are similar in shape but tailored for high fidelity to each individual language. This layer has no dependencies on Visual Studio components.
- **Workspaces API**: The Workspaces layer contains the Workspaces API, which is the starting point for doing code analysis and refactoring over entire solutions. It assists you in organizing all the information about the projects in a solution into a single object model, offering you direct access to the compiler layer object models without needing to parse files, configure options, or manage project to project dependencies. This layer has no dependencies on Visual Studio components.

Writing an application based on the Compiler Syntax API to parse and transform source files

In this section, we will write a C# console application based on Roslyn Compiler APIs to parse a given source file into a syntax tree, and then perform the following syntax transformations:

- Edit all the class declarations with no explicit accessibility modifier to add an internal modifier.
- Add documentation comment syntax trivia to all public class declarations with no documentation comments.
- Remove empty class declarations with no members.

Getting started

You will need to have the Visual Studio 2017 Community Edition installed on your machine to execute this recipe. You can install a free Community Edition from: https://www.visualstudio.com/thank-you-downloading-visual-studio/?sku=Community&rel=15.

How to do it...

1. Open Visual Studio and create a new C# console application targeting .NET Framework 4.6 or higher, say `ConsoleApp`.
2. Install the `Microsoft.CodeAnalysis.CSharp` NuGet package (as of this writing, the latest stable version is *2.1.0*). For guidance on how to search and install the NuGet package to a project, refer to the recipe *Searching and installing analyzers through the NuGet package manager* in `Chapter 2`, *Consuming Diagnostic Analyzers in .NET Projects*.
3. Replace the source code in `Program.cs` with the source code from the attached code sample `\ConsoleApp\Program.cs`.
4. Build the project.
5. Open a Visual Studio developer command prompt, change the directory to the project root directory, and execute `bin\Debug\ConsoleApp.exe` with no arguments.

6. Verify the output shows incorrect usage: `Usage: ConsoleApp.exe <%file_path%>`
7. Create a text file, say `test.cs`, with the following code at the project root directory:

```
// Class with no accessibility modifier
class C1
{
  void M() {}
}

// Public class with no documentation comments
public class C2
{
  void M() {}
}

// Empty class with no members
public class C3
{
}
```

8. Now, execute the application with `test.cs` as the argument: `bin\Debug\ConsoleApp.exe test.cs`.
9. Verify the expected transformed source is displayed in the output:

```
C:\Users\mavasani\Documents\Visual Studio 2017\Projects\ConsoleApp\ConsoleApp>bin\Debug\ConsoleApp.exe
Usage: ConsoleApp.exe <%file_path%>

C:\Users\mavasani\Documents\Visual Studio 2017\Projects\ConsoleApp\ConsoleApp>bin\Debug\ConsoleApp.exe test.cs
Transformed source:

// Class with no accessibility modifier
internal class C1
{
  void M() {}
}

// Public class with no documentation comments
/// <summary>TODO: Add doc comments</summary>
public class C2
{
  void M() {}
}

C:\Users\mavasani\Documents\Visual Studio 2017\Projects\ConsoleApp\ConsoleApp>
```

How it works...

In this recipe, we wrote a C# console application based on Roslyn Compiler API to parse and transform source text. As mentioned earlier, our application demonstrates three core syntax operations on the parsed tree: edit, add, and remove. Let's walk through the code and understand how we implemented these operations:

```
public static void Main(string[] args)
{
  // Parse arguments to get source file.
  var filePath = ParseArguments(args);
  if (filePath == null)
  {
    return;
  }

  // Parse text into SyntaxTree.
  var tree = Parse(filePath);
  var root = (CompilationUnitSyntax)tree.GetRoot();

  // Transform syntax tree to edit/add/remove syntax.
  root = EditClassDeclarations(root);
  root = AddDocCommentsToClassDeclarations(root);
  root = RemoveEmptyClassDeclarations(root);

  Console.WriteLine("Transformed source:" +
Environment.NewLine);
  Console.WriteLine(root.ToFullString());
}
```

The `Main` method invokes individual methods to perform the following operations:

- `ParseArguments` to scan for the input file to parse and transform.
- Read the text from this source file and `Parse` it into a syntax tree.
- Get the compilation unit root of the parsed tree and perform the following transformations on the root:
    - `EditClassDeclarations` : To add internal modifier to class with no accessibility modifier.
    - `AddDocCommentsToClassDeclarations` : To add stub documentation comments to public class with no documentation comments.
    - `RemoveEmptyClassDeclarations` : To remove class declarations with no members.
- Display the transformed text on the console.

Command-Line Tools Based on Roslyn API

The `ParseArguments` method expects a single argument, which must be a full path to an existing file on the disk. Otherwise, it displays an error and bails out returning null.

```
private static string ParseArguments(string[] args)
{
  if (args.Length != 1)
  {
    Console.WriteLine(@"Usage: ConsoleApp.exe <%file_path%>");
    return null;
  }

  if (!File.Exists(args[0]))
  {
    Console.WriteLine($"File '{args[0]}' does not exist");
    return null;
  }

  return args[0];
}
```

The `Parse` method reads the file contents from the input file and parses it using the parsing API `CSharpSyntaxTree.ParseText`.

```
private static SyntaxTree Parse(string filePath)
{
 var text = File.ReadAllText(filePath);
 return CSharpSyntaxTree.ParseText(text);
}
```

The `EditClassDeclarations` method walks the descendant nodes of the root to find all class declaration nodes whose modifier list has no accessibility modifier (public, private, internal, or protected).

```
private static CompilationUnitSyntax
EditClassDeclarations(CompilationUnitSyntax root)
{
  // Get class declarations with no accessibility modifier.
  var classDeclarations = root.DescendantNodes()
    .OfType<ClassDeclarationSyntax>()
    .Where(c => !c.Modifiers.Any(m =>
SyntaxFacts.IsAccessibilityModifier(m.Kind())));

  // Add modifier to these class declarations and replace in the original tree.
    return root.ReplaceNodes(classDeclarations,
    computeReplacementNode: (o, n) => AddModifier(n));
}
```

Then it invokes the `ReplaceNodes` API on the root syntax node to replace each such class declaration with an updated node returned by the `AddModifier` helper. This helper adds a new internal modifier at the start of the current modifier list of the class declaration. It also takes care of moving any existing leading trivia of the class declaration to the new modifier and adds a whitespace trivia after the new modifier:

```
private static ClassDeclarationSyntax AddModifier(ClassDeclarationSyntax classDeclaration)
{
  var internalModifier = SyntaxFactory.Token(SyntaxKind.InternalKeyword)
    .WithTrailingTrivia(SyntaxFactory.Whitespace(" "));
  if (classDeclaration.HasLeadingTrivia)
  {
    // Move leading trivia for the class declaration to the new modifier.
    internalModifier =
internalModifier.WithLeadingTrivia(classDeclaration.GetLeadingTrivia());
    classDeclaration = classDeclaration.WithLeadingTrivia();
  }

  var newModifiers = classDeclaration.Modifiers.Insert(0, internalModifier);
  return classDeclaration.WithModifiers(newModifiers);
}
```

The `AddDocCommentsToClassDeclarations` method walks the descendant nodes of the root to find all class declaration nodes whose modifier list has a public accessibility modifier and its first token has no leading documentation comment trivia.

```
private static CompilationUnitSyntax
AddDocCommentsToClassDeclarations(CompilationUnitSyntax root)
{
  // Get public class declarations with no documentation comments.
  var classDeclarations = root.DescendantNodes()
    .OfType<ClassDeclarationSyntax>()
    .Where(c => c.Modifiers.Any(m => m.Kind() == SyntaxKind.PublicKeyword) &&
    !c.GetFirstToken().LeadingTrivia.Any(IsDocumentationComment));

  // Add stub documentation comment to these class declarations and replace
in the original tree.
  return root.ReplaceNodes(classDeclarations,
    computeReplacementNode: (o, n) => AddDocumentationComment(n));
}
```

Then, it invokes the `ReplaceNodes` API on the root syntax node to replace each such class declaration with an updated node returned by the `AddDocumentationComment` helper. This helper creates an XML summary element with a `TODO` comment and creates a single line documentation comment with this stub summary element and adds this at end of the current leading trivia for the class declaration.

```
private static ClassDeclarationSyntax
AddDocumentationComment(ClassDeclarationSyntax classDeclaration)
{
 var summaryElement =
SyntaxFactory.XmlSummaryElement(SyntaxFactory.XmlText("TODO: Add doc
comments"));
 var documentationComment =
SyntaxFactory.DocumentationComment(summaryElement);
 var newLeadingTrivia = classDeclaration.GetLeadingTrivia()
   .Add(SyntaxFactory.Trivia(documentationComment))
   .Add(SyntaxFactory.EndOfLine(Environment.NewLine));
   return classDeclaration.WithLeadingTrivia(newLeadingTrivia);
}
```

The `RemoveEmptyClassDeclarations` method walks the descendant nodes of the root to find all class declaration nodes which have no members declarations (methods, fields, nested types, and so on) and then invokes the `ReplaceNodes` API on the root syntax node to remove all such declarations.

```
private static CompilationUnitSyntax
RemoveEmptyClassDeclarations(CompilationUnitSyntax root)
{
 // Get class declarations with no members.
 var classDeclarations = root.DescendantNodes()
   .OfType<ClassDeclarationSyntax>()
   .Where(c => c.Members.Count == 0);

 // Remove these class declarations from the original tree.
 return root.RemoveNodes(classDeclarations,
SyntaxRemoveOptions.KeepNoTrivia);
}
```

Writing an application based on the Compiler Semantic API to display diagnostics and overload resolution results

In this section, we will write a C# console application based on Roslyn Compiler APIs to create a compilation from the given source file and then perform the following semantic analyses:

1. Compute and display the compilation diagnostics that would be produced by the C# compiler if the file were to be compiled.
2. Compute the **symbol info** for each invocation (method call) in the source file and display the following semantic information for each call:
    1. Overload resolution result (https://msdn.microsoft.com/en-us/library/aa691336(v=vs.71).aspx): Success or failure reason.
    2. If overload resolution succeeded, the method symbol bound to the invocation.
    3. Otherwise, if overload resolution failed and we have one or more candidate symbols, then display each candidate symbol.

Getting started

You will need to have the Visual Studio 2017 Community Edition installed on your machine to execute this recipe. You can install a free Community Edition from https://www.visualstudio.com/thank-you-downloading-visual-studio/?sku=Community&rel=15.

How to do it…

1. Open Visual Studio and create a new C# console application targeting .NET Framework 4.6 or higher, say `ConsoleApp`.
2. Install the `Microsoft.CodeAnalysis.CSharp` NuGet package (as of this writing, the latest stable version is *2.1.0*). For guidance on how to search and install NuGet package to a project, refer to the recipe *Searching and installing analyzers through the NuGet package manager* in `Chapter 2`, *Consuming Diagnostic Analyzers in .NET Projects*.
3. Replace the source code in `Program.cs` with the source code from the attached code sample `\ConsoleApp\Program.cs`.

4. Build the project.
5. Open a Visual Studio developer command prompt, change the directory to the project root directory, and execute `bin\Debug\ConsoleApp.exe` with no arguments.
6. Verify the output shows incorrect usage: `Usage: ConsoleApp.exe <%file_path%>`.
7. Create a text file, say `test.cs`, with the following code at the project root directory:

```
class C1
{
 void F()
 {
  M1();
  M2(0);
  M2(null);
 }

 void M1()
 {
 }

 void M2()
 {
 }

 void M2(int x)
 {
 }
}
```

8. Now, execute the application with `test.cs` as the argument: `bin\Debug\ConsoleApp.exe test.cs`.
9. Verify the expected diagnostics and invocation semantics with overload resolution results are displayed in the output:

```
Administrator: Developer Command Prompt for VS 2017

C:\Users\mavasani\Documents\Visual Studio 2017\Projects\ConsoleApp\ConsoleApp>bin\Debug\ConsoleApp.exe test.cs
Number of diagnostics: 1
(7,8): error CS1503: Argument 1: cannot convert from '<null>' to 'int'

Invocation: 'M1()'
  Overload resolution result: Succeeded
  Method Symbol: void C1.M1()

Invocation: 'M2(0)'
  Overload resolution result: Succeeded
  Method Symbol: void C1.M2(int x)

Invocation: 'M2(null)'
  Overload resolution result: OverloadResolutionFailure
  2 candidate symbols:
    Candidate Symbol: void C1.M2()
    Candidate Symbol: void C1.M2(int x)

C:\Users\mavasani\Documents\Visual Studio 2017\Projects\ConsoleApp\ConsoleApp>
```

How it works...

In this recipe, we wrote a C# console application based on the Roslyn Compiler API to create a compilation and analyze and display the diagnostics and overload resolution semantics for invocation expressions. These operations are very similar to what a C# compiler would do when compiling the source code. Let's walk through the code and understand how we implemented these operations:

```
public static void Main(string[] args)
{
 // Parse arguments to get source file.
 var filePath = ParseArguments(args);
 if (filePath == null)
 {
  return;
 }

 // Parse text and create a compilation.
 var compilation = CreateCompilation(filePath);

 // Display diagnostics in the compilation.
 DisplayDiagnostics(compilation);

 // Display semantic information about invocations in the file.
 DisplayInvocations(compilation);
}
```

The Main method invokes individual methods to perform the following operations:

- `ParseArguments` to scan for the input file to parse and transform.
- `CreateCompilation` to create a C# compilation from a parsed syntax tree created with the text from this source file.
- `DisplayDiagnostics` to compute the compiler diagnostics and then display them.
- `DisplayInvocations` to analyze each invocation (method call) in a syntax tree and display the overload resolution result and bound symbols.

Implementation of `ParseArguments` is identical to the one in the previous recipe, *Writing an application based on Compiler Syntax API to parse and transform source files*. Refer to the *How it works...*, section of that recipe for further explanation on this method.

The `CreateCompilation` method first reads the file contents from the input file and parses it using the parsing API `CSharpSyntaxTree.ParseText`. Then, it creates a metadata reference for the system assembly (corlib) using the location of the assembly containing the object type. It creates compilation options with output kind `DynamicallyLinkedLibrary` (`.dll`) and uses these inputs to create a C# compilation:

```
private static Compilation CreateCompilation(string filePath)
{
 var text = File.ReadAllText(filePath);
 var tree = CSharpSyntaxTree.ParseText(text);
 var systemAssembly =
MetadataReference.CreateFromFile(typeof(object).Assembly.Location);
 var options = new CSharpCompilationOptions(outputKind:
OutputKind.DynamicallyLinkedLibrary);
 return CSharpCompilation.Create("TestAssembly",
   syntaxTrees: new[] { tree },
   references: new[] { systemAssembly },
   options: options);
}
```

The `DisplayDiagnostics` method computes the compilation diagnostics using the `Compilation.GetDiagnostics` API and then displays the diagnostic count and string representation of each diagnostic.

```
private static void DisplayDiagnostics(Compilation compilation)
{
 var diagnostics = compilation.GetDiagnostics();
 Console.WriteLine($"Number of diagnostics: {diagnostics.Length}");
 foreach (var diagnostic in diagnostics)
 {
```

```
    Console.WriteLine(diagnostic.ToString());
   }

   Console.WriteLine();
 }
```

The `DisplayInvocations` method first gets the semantic model for the syntax tree in the compilation. Then, it iterates over the descendant nodes of the root to get all `InvocationExpressionSyntax` nodes. For each such invocation, it queries the symbol info of the expression from the semantic model. The symbol info contains information about the semantics of the invocation. We display the overload resolution success/fail result based on whether or not the candidate reason is `CandidateReason.None`. Then, we display the bound symbol or candidate symbols for the success and failure cases, respectively:

```
private static void DisplayInvocations(Compilation compilation)
{
 var tree = compilation.SyntaxTrees.Single();
 var semanticModel = compilation.GetSemanticModel(tree);
 var invocations =
tree.GetRoot().DescendantNodes().OfType<InvocationExpressionSyntax>();
 foreach (var invocation in invocations)
  {
   Console.WriteLine($"Invocation: '{invocation.ToString()}'");
   var symbolInfo = semanticModel.GetSymbolInfo(invocation);

   var overloadResolutionResult = symbolInfo.CandidateReason ==
CandidateReason.None ? "Succeeded" : symbolInfo.CandidateReason.ToString();
   Console.WriteLine($" Overload resolution result:
{overloadResolutionResult}");

   if (symbolInfo.Symbol != null)
   {
    Console.WriteLine($" Method Symbol:
{symbolInfo.Symbol.ToDisplayString(SymbolDisplayFormat.MinimallyQualifiedFo
rmat)}");
   }
   else if (!symbolInfo.CandidateSymbols.IsDefaultOrEmpty)
   {
    Console.WriteLine($" {symbolInfo.CandidateSymbols.Length} candidate
symbols:");
    foreach (var candidate in symbolInfo.CandidateSymbols)
    {
     Console.WriteLine($" Candidate Symbol:
{candidate.ToDisplayString(SymbolDisplayFormat.MinimallyQualifiedFormat)}")
;
    }
   }
```

```
        Console.WriteLine();
    }
}
```

Writing an application based on the Compiler Analyzer API to execute diagnostic analyzers and display analyzer diagnostics

In this section, we will write a C# console application based on Roslyn Compiler APIs that loads the given analyzer assembly, executes all diagnostic analyzers defined in this assembly on a given source file, and outputs all the reported analyzer diagnostics.

Getting started

You will need to have the Visual Studio 2017 Community Edition installed on your machine to execute this recipe. You can install a free Community Edition from https://www.visualstudio.com/thank-you-downloading-visual-studio/?sku=Community&rel=15.

How to do it...

1. Open Visual Studio and create a new C# console application targeting .NET Framework 4.6 or higher, say `ConsoleApp`.
2. Install the `Microsoft.CodeAnalysis.CSharp` NuGet package (as of this writing, the latest stable version is *2.1.0*). For guidance on how to search and install the NuGet package to a project, refer to the recipe *Searching and installing analyzers through the NuGet package manager* in `Chapter 2`, *Consuming Diagnostic Analyzers in .NET Projects*.
3. Replace the source code in `Program.cs` with the source code from the attached code sample `\ConsoleApp\Program.cs`.
4. Add a C# class library project targeting .NET Framework 4.6 or higher to the solution, say *Analyzer*.
5. Install the `Microsoft.CodeAnalysis` NuGet package to this project (as of this writing, the latest stable version is *2.1.0*).

6. Replace the source code in `Class1.cs` with the diagnostic analyzer source code from the attached code sample `\Analyzer\Class1.cs`. This file contains the code for the default symbol analyzer that reports a diagnostic for type names containing any lowercase characters.
7. Build the solution.
8. Open a Visual Studio developer command prompt, change the directory to the project root directory of `ConsoleApp`, and execute `bin\Debug\ConsoleApp.exe` with no arguments.
9. Verify the output shows incorrect usage: `Usage: ConsoleApp.exe <%analyzer_file_path%> <%source_file_path%>`.
10. Create a text file, say `test.cs`, at the project root directory of `ConsoleApp` with the following code:

    ```
    class ClassWithLowerCase
    {
    }

    class OuterClassWithLowerCase
    {
     class NestedClassWithLowerCase
     {
     }
    }

    class CLASS_WITH_UPPER_CASE
    {
    }
    ```

11. Now, execute the application with a relative path to analyzer assembly and `test.cs` as the arguments: `bin\Debug\ConsoleApp.exe ..\..\..\Analyzer\bin\Debug\Analyzer.dll test.cs`.
12. Verify that the expected analyzer diagnostics are displayed in the output:

    ```
    Number of diagnostics: 3
    (1,7): warning CSharpAnalyzers: Type name 'ClassWithLowerCase'
    contains lowercase letters
    (5,7): warning CSharpAnalyzers: Type name
    'OuterClassWithLowerCase' contains lowercase letters
    (7,9): warning CSharpAnalyzers: Type name
    'NestedClassWithLowerCase' contains lowercase letters
    ```

How it works...

In this recipe, we wrote a C# console application based on the Roslyn Compiler API to load and execute diagnostic analyzers from an analyzer assembly and report the diagnostics reported by the analyzers. These operations are very similar to what the C# compiler would do when you compile source files with /analyzer:<%analyzer_file_path%> command line switch. Let's walk through the code and understand how we implemented these operations:

```
public static void Main(string[] args)
{
 // Parse arguments to get analyzer assembly file and source file.
 var files = ParseArguments(args);
 if (files.analyzerFile == null || files.sourceFile == null)
 {
  return;
 }

 // Parse source file and create a compilation.
 var compilation = CreateCompilation(files.sourceFile);

 // Create compilation with analyzers.
 var compilationWithAnalyzers =
CreateCompilationWithAnalyzers(files.analyzerFile, compilation);

 // Display analyzer diagnostics in the compilation.
 DisplayAnalyzerDiagnostics(compilationWithAnalyzers);
}
```

The Main method invokes individual methods to perform the following operations:

- `ParseArguments` to scan for:
    - Analyzer assembly file.
    - Input source file on which the analyzers will be executed.
- `CreateCompilation` to create a C# compilation from parsed syntax tree created with the text from the input source file.
- `CreateCompilationWithAnalyzers` to create a compilation instance with diagnostic analyzers from the given analyzer assembly file attached to it.
- `DisplayAnalyzerDiagnostics` to execute the analyzers to compute the analyzer diagnostics and then display them.

Implementation of `ParseArguments` and `CreateCompilation` is identical to the one in the previous recipe, *Writing an application based on Compiler Syntax API to parse and transform source files*. Refer to the *How it works...*, section of that recipe for further explanation on these methods.

The `CreateCompilationWithAnalyzers` method takes the compilation and the analyzer assembly as the parameters:

```
private static CompilationWithAnalyzers
CreateCompilationWithAnalyzers(string analyzerFilePath, Compilation
compilation)
{
 var analyzerFileReference = new AnalyzerFileReference(analyzerFilePath,
new AnalyzerAssemblyLoader());
 var analyzers = analyzerFileReference.GetAnalyzers(LanguageNames.CSharp);
 var options = new CompilationWithAnalyzersOptions(
   new AnalyzerOptions(ImmutableArray<AdditionalText>.Empty),
   onAnalyzerException: (exception, analyzer, diagnostic) => throw
exception,
   concurrentAnalysis: false,
   logAnalyzerExecutionTime: false);
 return new CompilationWithAnalyzers(compilation, analyzers, options);
}
```

First, it creates `AnalyzerFileReference` (http://source.roslyn.io/#q=AnalyzerFileReference) with the analyzer file path and an instance of the analyzer assembly loader (`IAnalyzerAssemblyLoader` - details later in the section (http://source.roslyn.io/#q=IAnalyzerAssemblyLoader)). It invokes the `AnalyzerReference.GetAnalyzers` API (http://source.roslyn.io/#q=AnalyzerReference.GetAnalyzers) on this analyzer file reference to load the analyzer assembly with the given analyzer assembly loader, and then create instances of the diagnostic analyzers defined in this assembly.

It creates a default set of `CompilationWithAnalyzersOptions` (http://source.roslyn.io/#q=CompilationWithAnalyzersOptions) for configuring the analyzer execution. The possible options include:

- `AnalyzerOptions`: Analyzer options contain the set of additional non-source text files that are passed to the analyzers. In this recipe, we use an empty set. You can read more about additional files at https://github.com/dotnet/roslyn/blob/master/docs/analyzers/Using%20Additional%20Files.md.
- `onAnalyzerException` delegate: Delegate to be invoked when an analyzer throws an exception. In this recipe, we just re-throw this exception.

- `concurrentAnalysis`: Flag to control whether the analyzers should be run concurrently or not. In this recipe, we default this to false.
- `logAnalyzerExecutionTime`: Flag to control whether the relative execution times for each analyzer should be tracked. If set to true, then this data can be requested for each analyzer using the public API `CompilationWithAnalyzers.GetAnalyzerTelemetryInfoAsync` (http://source.roslyn.io/#q=CompilationWithAnalyzers.GetAnalyzerTelemetryInfoAsync). This returns an `AnalyzerTelemetryInfo`, which has a property named `ExecutionTime` (http://source.roslyn.io/#q=AnalyzerTelemetryInfo.ExecutionTime). In this recipe, we default this to false.

Finally, the method creates and returns a `CompilationWithAnalyzers` (http://source.roslyn.io/#Microsoft.CodeAnalysis/DiagnosticAnalyzer/CompilationWithAnalyzers.cs,7efdf3edc21e904a) instance with the given compilation, analyzer file reference, and options.

We briefly mentioned our custom `AnalyzerAssemblyLoader` passed into the `AnalyzerFileReference` constructor above. It is implemented in our code as follows:

```
private class AnalyzerAssemblyLoader : IAnalyzerAssemblyLoader
{
  void IAnalyzerAssemblyLoader.AddDependencyLocation(string fullPath)
  {
  }

  Assembly IAnalyzerAssemblyLoader.LoadFromPath(string fullPath)
  {
    return Assembly.LoadFrom(fullPath);
  }
}
```

This analyzer assembly loader handles loading the analyzer assembly using the .NET APIs for assembly loading on the executing platform. In this recipe, we use .NET Framework API `Assembly.LoadFrom` (https://msdn.microsoft.com/en-us/library/system.reflection.assembly.loadfrom(v=vs.110).aspx) to load the assembly from the given path.

We ignore the callbacks to add analyzer dependency locations in our custom `AnalyzerAssemblyLoader`, as our test analyzer assembly has no dependencies. We can enhance this assembly loader to track these locations and handle assembly loading for dependencies.

Chapter 10

DisplayAnalyzerDiagnostics takes the CompilationWithAnalyzers instance created earlier and executes the analyzers on the underlying compilation using GetAnalyzerDiagnosticsAsync API. It then walks through all the analyzer diagnostics and outputs the message for each diagnostic, with the line and column information:

```
private static void DisplayAnalyzerDiagnostics(CompilationWithAnalyzers compilationWithAnalyzers)
{
 var diagnostics = compilationWithAnalyzers.GetAnalyzerDiagnosticsAsync(CancellationToken.None).Result;
 Console.WriteLine($"Number of diagnostics: {diagnostics.Length}");
 foreach (var diagnostic in diagnostics)
 {
  Console.WriteLine(diagnostic.ToString());
 }

 Console.WriteLine();
}

 return newSolution;
}
```

> You can invoke the CompilationWithAnalyzers.GetAnalysisResultAsync (http://source.roslyn.io/#q=CompilationWithAnalyzers.GetAnalysisResultAsync) public API to get a more fine-grained view of the analysis results. The returned AnalysisResult (http://source.roslyn.io/#Microsoft.CodeAnalysis/DiagnosticAnalyzer/AnalysisResult.cs,86a401660972cfb8) allows you to get separate syntax, semantic, and compilations diagnostics reported by each diagnostic analyzer and also allows you to get the analyzer telemetry info for each analyzer.

Writing an application based on the Workspaces API to format and simplify all source files in the solution

In this section, we will write a C# console application based on Roslyn Workspaces APIs to load a C# solution into a workspace and then perform the following operations:

1. Format the solution to change tabs to white spaces with a custom indentation size. This is a syntactic code refactoring.
2. Simplify the solution to change local declarations to have an explicit type specification instead of var. This is a semantic code refactoring.

You can read the XML documentation comments and implementation details for the Formatter and Simplifier for additional information on these operations at: `http://source.roslyn.io/#Microsoft.CodeAnalysis.Workspaces/Formatting/Formatter.cs,f445ffe3c814c002` and `http://source.roslyn.io/#Microsoft.CodeAnalysis.Workspaces/Simplification/Simplifier.cs,1d256ae3815b1cac`, respectively.

Getting started

You will need to have the Visual Studio 2017 Community Edition installed on your machine to execute this recipe. You can install a free Community Edition from `https://www.visualstudio.com/thank-you-downloading-visual-studio/?sku=Community&rel=15`.

How to do it...

1. Open Visual Studio and create a new C# console application targeting .NET Framework 4.6 or higher, say `ConsoleApp`.
2. Install the `Microsoft.CodeAnalysis.CSharp.Workspaces` NuGet package (as of this writing, the latest stable version is *2.1.0*). For guidance on how to search and install NuGet package to a project, refer to the recipe *Searching and installing analyzers through the NuGet package manager* in `Chapter 2`, *Consuming Diagnostic Analyzers in .NET Projects*.

3. Replace the source code in Program.cs with the source code from the attached code sample \ConsoleApp\Program.cs.
4. Build the project.
5. Open a Visual Studio developer command prompt, change the directory to the project root directory and execute bin\Debug\ConsoleApp.exe with no arguments.
6. Verify the output shows incorrect usage: Usage: ConsoleApp.exe <%solution_file_path%>.
7. Create a new C# console application, say TestSolution, and add one implicitly typed and one explicitly typed local declaration to the Main method (note the indent size of 4):

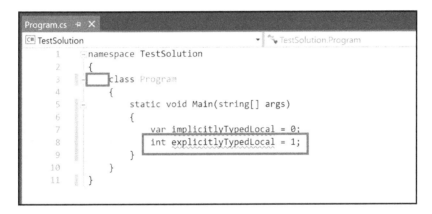

8. Now, execute the application with full path to TestSolution.sln as the argument: bin\Debug\ConsoleApp.exe <%test_solution_path%>.
9. Verify the console output:

```
Loading solution '<%test_sln_path%>'...
Formatting solution...
Simplifying solution...
Solution updated.
```

10. Verify the new contents of the source file in *TestSolution now* has an indent size of 2 and no explicitly typed local declarations:

```
Program.cs
TestSolution                                        TestSolution.Program
 1    namespace TestSolution
 2    {
 3        class Program
 4        {
 5            static void Main(string[] args)
 6            {
 7                var implicitlyTypedLocal = 0;
 8                var explicitlyTypedLocal = 1;
 9            }
10        }
11    }
```

How it works...

In this recipe, we wrote a C# console application based on Roslyn Workspaces API to format and simplify all the source files in a solution. These operations are very similar to what a Visual Studio IDE would do when you apply formatting and simplification quick fixes after setting the corresponding tools options. Let's walk through the code and understand how we implemented these operations:

```
public static void Main(string[] args)
{
 // Parse arguments to get solution.
 var slnPath = ParseArguments(args);
 if (slnPath == null)
 {
  return;
 }

 // Create workspace.
 MSBuildWorkspace workspace = MSBuildWorkspace.Create();

 // Open solution within the workspace.
 Console.WriteLine($"Loading solution '{slnPath}'...");
 Solution solution = workspace.OpenSolutionAsync(slnPath).Result;

 // Format the solution.
 solution = FormatSolution(solution, workspace.Options);

 // Simplify the solution.
```

```
    solution = SimplifySolution(solution, workspace.Options);

    // Apply changes.
    ApplyChanges(workspace, solution);
}
```

The `Main` method invokes individual methods to perform the following operations:

- `ParseArguments`: To scan for the input file to parse and transform.
- `MSBuildWorkspace.Create`: To create a workspace and `Workspace.OpenSolutionAsync` to load the given solution in the workspace.
- `FormatSolution`: To format all the documents in the solution.
- `SimplifySolution`: To simplify all the documents in the solution.
- `ApplyChanges`: To apply the formatting and simplification changes to the workspace and persist these to the disk.

Implementation of `ParseArguments` is identical to the one in the recipe, *Writing an application based on Compiler Syntax API to parse and transform source files*. Refer to the *How it works...*, section of that recipe for further explanation on this method.

`MSBuildWorkspace` (http://source.roslyn.io/#q=MSBuildWorkspace) is a custom implementation of the core Roslyn Workspace, which uses the MSBuild (https://docs.microsoft.com/en-us/visualstudio/msbuild/msbuild) project model for loading the solution/project files and allows reading and writing individual documents in the projects.

The `FormatSolution` method formats all documents in the solution. First, it modifies the options to prefer whitespace over tabs, with an indentation size of 2 (default is 4):

- `FormattingOptions.UseTabs`: Value set to `false`.
- `FormattingOptions.IndentationSize`: Value set to 2.

```
private static Solution FormatSolution(Solution originalSolution, OptionSet options)
{
  Console.WriteLine("Formatting solution...");

  // Prefer whitespaces over tabs, with an indentation size of 2.
  options = options
    .WithChangedOption(FormattingOptions.UseTabs, LanguageNames.CSharp, false)
    .WithChangedOption(FormattingOptions.IndentationSize, LanguageNames.CSharp, 2);

  Solution newSolution = originalSolution;
```

```
    foreach (var documentId in originalSolution.Projects.SelectMany(p =>
p.DocumentIds))
    {
      Document document = newSolution.GetDocument(documentId);

      // Format the document.
      Document newDocument = Formatter.FormatAsync(document, options).Result;

      // Update the current solution.
      newSolution = newDocument.Project.Solution;
    }

    return newSolution;
  }
```

It keeps track of the current solution snapshot in newSolution, which is initialized to originalSolution. It then iterates over all the documents in the solution and does the following:

- Format the document by invoking Formatter.FormatAsync public API (http://source.roslyn.io/#q=Formatter.FormatAsync) with the current document and options.
- Update newSolution to point to the solution of the formatted newDocument.

Note how we can't simply iterate over originalSolution.Projects or project.Documents because it will return objects from the unmodified originalSolution, not from the newSolution. We need to use the ProjectId/DocumentIds (that don't change) to look up the corresponding snapshots in the newSolution.

Finally, it returns the newSolution after all documents have been formatted.

The SimplifySolution method simplifies all documents in the solution. First, it modifies the options to prefer implicitly type local declaration, that is, user var over explicit type specification, by setting SimplificationOptions.PreferImplicitTypeInLocalDeclaration to true:

```
  private static Solution SimplifySolution(Solution originalSolution,
OptionSet options)
  {
    Console.WriteLine("Simplifying solution...");

    // Prefer 'var' over explicit type specification.
    options =
options.WithChangedOption(SimplificationOptions.PreferImplicitTypeInLocalDe
```

```
claration, true);

  Solution newSolution = originalSolution;
  foreach (var documentId in originalSolution.Projects.SelectMany(p =>
p.DocumentIds))
  {
    Document document = newSolution.GetDocument(documentId);

    // Add simplification annotation to the root.
    var newRoot =
document.GetSyntaxRootAsync().Result.WithAdditionalAnnotations(Simplifier.A
nnotation);

    // Simplify the document.
    Document newDocument =
Simplifier.ReduceAsync(document.WithSyntaxRoot(newRoot), options).Result;

    // Update the current solution.
    newSolution = newDocument.Project.Solution;
  }

  return newSolution;
}
```

`SimplifySolution` has very identical implementation to the `FormatSolution` method for iterating the documents, simplifying them by invoking `Simplifier.ReduceAsync` public API (http://source.roslyn.io/#q=Simplifier.ReduceAsync), storing the latest snapshot in `newSolution` after processing each document, and finally returning the new solution snapshot at the end. It has one important difference though. `Simplifier.ReduceAsync` only processes nodes with a special syntax annotation: `Simplifier.Annotation` (http://source.roslyn.io/#q=Simplifier.Annotation). Hence, before invoking this API, we add this syntax annotation to the root of the document.

The `ApplyChanges` method invokes the `Workspace.TryApplyChanges` public API (http://source.roslyn.io/#q=Workspace.TryApplyChanges) with the new solution snapshot to apply the changes in the solution snapshot to the workspace. This also causes the `MSBuildWorkspace` to persist these changes onto the disk:

```
private static void ApplyChanges(Workspace workspace, Solution solution)
{
  // Apply solution changes to the workspace.
  // This persists the in-memory changes into the disk.
  if (workspace.TryApplyChanges(solution))
  {
    Console.WriteLine("Solution updated.");
  }
```

```
    else
    {
      Console.WriteLine("Update failed!");
    }
}
```

Writing an application based on the Workspaces API to edit projects in a solution and display project properties

In this section, we will write a C# console application based on Roslyn Workspaces APIs to load a C# solution into a workspace and then perform the following operations:

- Display project properties such as project file path, output file path, project language, assembly name, reference count, document count, and so on.
- Add a new project to the solution.
- Remove an existing project from the solution.
- Edit project to add a project reference.

Getting started

You will need to have the Visual Studio 2017 Community Edition installed on your machine to execute this recipe. You can install a free Community Edition from https://www.visualstudio.com/thank-you-downloading-visual-studio/?sku=Community&rel=15.

How to do it…

1. Open Visual Studio and create a new C# console application targeting the .NET Framework 4.6 or higher, say `ConsoleApp`.
2. Install the `Microsoft.CodeAnalysis.CSharp.Workspaces` NuGet package (as of this writing, the latest stable version is *2.1.0*). For guidance on how to search and install the NuGet package to a project, refer to the recipe *Searching and installing analyzers through the NuGet package manager* in `Chapter 2`, *Consuming Diagnostic Analyzers in .NET Projects*.

3. Replace the source code in `Program.cs` with the source code from the attached code sample `\ConsoleApp\Program.cs`.
4. Build the project.
5. Open a Visual Studio developer command prompt, change the directory to the project root directory, and execute `bin\Debug\ConsoleApp.exe` with no arguments.
6. Verify the output shows incorrect usage: `Usage: ConsoleApp.exe <%solution_file_path%>`.
7. Create a new C# class library solution, say `TestSolution`, and add one more class library project, say `ClassLibrary`, to the solution. Now, execute the application with full path to `TestSolution.sln` as the argument: `bin\Debug\ConsoleApp.exe <%test_solution_path%>`.
8. Verify the console output shows the project properties for the initial solution with two projects, `TestSolution` and `ClassLibrary`:

```
C:\Users\mavasani\Documents\Visual Studio 2017\Projects\ConsoleApp\ConsoleApp>bin\Debug\ConsoleApp.exe "c:\users\mavasani\documents\visual studio 2017\Projects\TestSolution\TestSolution.sln"
Loading solution 'c:\users\mavasani\documents\visual studio 2017\Projects\TestSolution\TestSolution.sln'...
Project count: 2
 Project: TestSolution
   Assembly name: TestSolution
   Language: C#
   Project file: c:\users\mavasani\documents\visual studio 2017\Projects\TestSolution\TestSolution\TestSolution.csproj
   Output file: c:\users\mavasani\documents\visual studio 2017\Projects\TestSolution\TestSolution\bin\Debug\TestSolution.dll
   Documents: 3
   Metadata references: 9
   Project references: 0

 Project: ClassLibrary
   Assembly name: ClassLibrary
   Language: C#
   Project file: c:\users\mavasani\documents\visual studio 2017\Projects\TestSolution\ClassLibrary\ClassLibrary.csproj
   Output file: c:\users\mavasani\documents\visual studio 2017\Projects\TestSolution\ClassLibrary\bin\Debug\ClassLibrary.dll
   Documents: 3
   Metadata references: 9
   Project references: 0

Press any key to continue...
```

9. Press any key to continue and note the following operations were performed: add project to solution, remove project from solution, and edit existing project (add project reference).

```
Press any key to continue...

Adding project 'AddedClassLibrary'...
Removing project 'ClassLibrary'...
Adding project reference from 'AddedClassLibrary' to 'TestSolution'...
Press any key to continue...
```

10. Press any key to continue and verify the solution now contains two projects `TestSolution` and `AddedClassLibrary`, and there is a project reference from `AddedClassLibrary` to `TestSolution`:

```
Project count: 2
 Project: TestSolution
    Assembly name: TestSolution
    Language: C#
    Project file: c:\users\mavasani\documents\visual studio 2017\Projects\TestSolution\TestSolution\TestSolution.csproj
    Output file: c:\users\mavasani\documents\visual studio 2017\Projects\TestSolution\TestSolution\bin\Debug\TestSolution.dll
    Documents: 3
    Metadata references: 9
    Project references: 1
 Project: AddedClassLibrary
    Assembly name: AddedProjectAssembly
    Language: C#
    Project file:
    Output file:
    Documents: 0
    Metadata references: 0
    Project references: 0

C:\Users\mavasani\Documents\Visual Studio 2017\Projects\ConsoleApp\ConsoleApp>
```

How it works...

In this recipe, we wrote a C# console application based on Roslyn Workspaces API to perform various operations on a projects in a solution: add, remove, edit, and display project properties. The rich Workspaces APIs provide you with a powerful object model for analyzing and editing projects and documents in a solution. Let's walk through the code and understand how we implemented these operations:

```
public static void Main(string[] args)
{
  // Parse arguments to get solution.
```

```
string slnPath = ParseArguments(args);
if (slnPath == null)
{
 return;
}

// Create workspace.
MSBuildWorkspace workspace = MSBuildWorkspace.Create();

// Open solution within the workspace.
Console.WriteLine($"Loading solution '{slnPath}'...");
Solution solution = workspace.OpenSolutionAsync(slnPath).Result;

// Display project properties.
DisplayProjectProperties(solution);

// Add project AddedClassLibrary.
WaitForKeyPress();
solution = AddProject(solution, "AddedClassLibrary");

// Remove project ClassLibrary.
solution = RemoveProject(solution, "ClassLibrary");

// Add project reference from AddedClassLibrary to TestSolution.
solution = AddProjectReference(solution, referenceFrom:
"AddedClassLibrary", referenceTo: "TestSolution");

// Display project properties.
WaitForKeyPress();
DisplayProjectProperties(solution);
}
```

The Main method invokes individual methods to perform the following operations:

- `ParseArguments`: To scan for the input file to parse and transform
- `MSBuildWorkspace.Create`: To create a workspace and `Workspace.OpenSolutionAsync` to load the given solution in the workspace
- `DisplayProjectProperties`: To display common properties for all projects in a solution.
- `AddProject`: To add a new project to the solution
- `RemoveProject`: To remove an existing project from a solution
- `AddProjectReference`: To add a project reference to an existing project in a solution

Implementation of `ParseArguments` is identical to the one in the recipe, *Writing an application based on Compiler Syntax API to parse and transform source files*. Please refer to the *How it works...*, section of that recipe for further explanation on this method.

`MSBuildWorkspace` (http://source.roslyn.io/#q=MSBuildWorkspace) is a custom implementation of the core Roslyn Workspace, which uses the MSBuild project model for loading the solution/project files, and allows reading and writing individual documents in the projects.

`DisplayProjectProperties` displays common project properties such as project name, language, assembly name, references, documents, and so on:

```
private static void DisplayProjectProperties(Solution solution)
{
 Console.WriteLine($"Project count: {solution.Projects.Count()}");

 foreach (var project in solution.Projects)
 {
  Console.WriteLine($" Project: {project.Name}");
  Console.WriteLine($" Assembly name: {project.AssemblyName}");
  Console.WriteLine($" Language: {project.Language}");
  Console.WriteLine($" Project file: {project.FilePath}");
  Console.WriteLine($" Output file: {project.OutputFilePath}");
  Console.WriteLine($" Documents: {project.Documents.Count()}");
  Console.WriteLine($" Metadata references:
{project.MetadataReferences.Count()}");
  Console.WriteLine($" Project references:
{project.ProjectReferences.Count()}");
  Console.WriteLine();
 }

 Console.WriteLine();
}
```

The `AddProject` method creates a barebones `ProjectInfo` (http://source.roslyn.io/#q=ProjectInfo) with the given `projectName`, a unique Project ID, version stamp, assembly name, and C# language name:

```
private static Solution AddProject(Solution originalSolution, string
projectName)
{
 Console.WriteLine($"Adding project '{projectName}'...");
 var projectInfo = ProjectInfo.Create(
  id: ProjectId.CreateNewId(),
  version: new VersionStamp(),
  name: projectName,
  assemblyName: "AddedProjectAssembly",
```

```
    language: LanguageNames.CSharp);
   return originalSolution.AddProject(projectInfo);
 }
```

It then invokes the `Solution.AddProject` API (http://source.roslyn.io/#q=Solution.AddProject) to add a new project with the created project info to the solution.

The `RemoveProject` method removes an existing project with the given `projectName` from the solution. It uses the `Solution.RemoveProject` API (http://source.roslyn.io/#q=Solution.RemoveProject) to remove the project:

```
 private static Solution RemoveProject(Solution originalSolution, string
 projectName)
 {
  Console.WriteLine($"Removing project '{projectName}'...");
  var project = originalSolution.Projects.SingleOrDefault(p => p.Name ==
 projectName);
   return originalSolution.RemoveProject(project.Id);
 }
```

The `AddProjectReference` method adds a project reference from the given `referenceFrom` project to the given `referenceTo` project. It searches for existing projects in the solution with the given names, creates a `ProjectReference` (http://source.roslyn.io/#Microsoft.CodeAnalysis.Workspaces/Workspace/Solution/ProjectReference.cs,944b5173649705e4) with project ID for the `referenceFrom` project, and uses the `Solution.AddProjectReference` (http://source.roslyn.io/#q=Solution.AddProjectReference) to add the required reference.

```
 private static Solution AddProjectReference(Solution originalSolution,
 string referenceFrom, string referenceTo)
  {
  Console.WriteLine($"Adding project reference from '{referenceFrom}' to
 '{referenceTo}'...");
  var projectReferenceFrom = originalSolution.Projects.SingleOrDefault(p =>
 p.Name == referenceFrom);
  var projectReference = new ProjectReference(projectReferenceFrom.Id);
  var projectReferenceTo = originalSolution.Projects.SingleOrDefault(p =>
 p.Name == referenceTo);
   return originalSolution.AddProjectReference(projectReferenceTo.Id,
 projectReference);
 }
```

Index

.editorconfig file
  using, for code style rule configuration 140

A

analyzer framework
  reference 158
analyzer project, Visual Studio
  creating 11, 19
  debugging 11, 19
  executing 11, 19
analyzer project
  NuGet package, publishing 54
  publishing, for VSIX 54
  unit test, creating 53
  unit tests, writing 46
analyzers
  configuration, Rule Set editor used 79
  configuration, ruleset file used 79
  configuring, in Solution explorer in Visual Studio 71, 75
  configuring, Rule Set editor used 76
  configuring, ruleset file used 76
  installing, through NuGet package manager 58
  searching, through NuGet package manager 58
  viewing, in Solution explorer in Visual Studio 71, 75
API surface maintenance
  with public API analyzer 145, 149
application, based Compiler Syntax API
  writing, for parsing source files 295, 300
  writing, for transformation of source files 295, 300
application, based on Compiler Analyzer API
  writing, for execution of diagnostic analyzers and display analyzer diagnostics 306, 311
application, based on Compiler Semantic API
  writing, for display of diagnostics and overload resolution results 301, 305
application, based on Workspaces API
  writing, for display of project properties 318, 323
  writing, to edit projects in solution 318
  writing, to format source files in solution 312, 322

B

batch code fixes (FixAll)
  applying, across document 93, 96
  applying, across project 93, 96
  applying, across solution 93, 96
binding/semantic analysis support
  implementing, for C# language feature 270, 276
binding
  reference 255
  unit tests, writing 284
BoundTreeRewriter
  reference 282
BoundTrees 243

C

C# 7.0 tuples
  used, for refactoring source code 105, 112
C# code snippets
  execution, Roslyn scripting API used 225, 229
C# code style rules, built into Visual Studio 2017
  configuring 132, 138
C# compiler code base
  new semantic error, implementing 240, 243
  new syntax error, implementing 235, 238
  unit tests, writing for new error 244
C# interactive session
  initializing, from existing C# project 219
C# interactive window

REPL commands, using 214
script directives, using 214
script sessions evaluation, with keyboard shortcuts 217
script sessions navigation, with keyboard shortcuts 217
C# language feature
  binding/semantic analysis support, implementing 270, 274, 276
  designing 260, 262
  lowering/code generation support 281, 284
  lowering/code generation support, implementing 278
  parser support, implementing 264, 267, 269
  syntax and grammar, designing 258
C# parsing
  unit tests, writing 284
C# script
  evaluating, within Visual Studio interactive window 210, 213
  executing, on Visual Studio developer command prompt using csi.exe 222
  writing 210
C# scripting
  about 209
  reference 209
CIL
  reference 158
Code fix 82
code generation
  reference 256
code style rules
  setting, with third-party StyleCop analyzers 150
CodeFixProvider
  creating, to fix compiler warning 82, 86, 91
  debugging, to fix compiler warning 82, 87, 91
  executing, to fix compiler warning 82, 87, 91
  unit tests, writing 125, 129
codegen phases
  unit tests, writing 284
CodeRefactoringProvider
  creating, for refactoring source code 105, 112
compilation analyzer
  creating, for analysis of whole compilation and report issues 38, 45

Compiler API 294
CompletionProvider
  creating, for providing additional intellisense items 116, 120, 125
configuration-related security vulnerabilities
  identifying, in web applications 159, 161
Contributor License Agreement (CLA)
  reference 251
cross-Site request forgery
  reference 174
cross-site scripting vulnerabilities
  identifying in view markup files in web applications 164
cross-site scripting
  reference 164
csi.exe
  used, for C# script execution on Visual Studio developer command prompt 222
custom FixAllProvider
  creating, to fix issue occurrences across scope 97, 101, 104

D

diagnostic analyzers
  about 9, 57
  stateful analyzers 10
  stateless analyzers 10
Document hyperlink 142

E

EditorConfig
  reference 132, 144
existing C# project
  C# interactive session, initializing 219

F

file analyzers
  reference 11
FindReferences API
  reference 116
flow analysis
  reference 256
Formatter
  reference 312
FxCop analyzers

used, for identifying performance improvements
  to source code 177, 181
FxCop performance rules
  reference 181

G
GitHub
  reference 234
grammar 258

I
incremental live unit test
  executing, with code changes 193, 197
insecure method calls, leading to SQL and LDAP
    injection attacks
  identifying 168, 171
issues, language syntax
  reporting, with syntax node 24, 28
issues, symbol declarations
  reporting, with symbol analyzer 19, 24

L
Lexer 239
Lexer.Lex
  reference 254
lexical analysis
  about 264
  reference 254
licensed enterprise edition
  installation link 198
  reference 186, 201
Lightweight Directory Access Protocol (LDAP) 168
live unit tests (LUT)
  about 183, 185
  options configuration, Tools Options dialog used 205
  results, navigating 191
  results, viewing 191
  running, in Visual Studio for unit test projects
    based on MSTest frameworks 190
  running, in Visual Studio for unit test projects
    based on NUnit 185
  running, in Visual Studio for unit test projects
    based on XUnit 185
  Start/Stop/Pause/Continue/Restart functionality,

  for fine grain control 198, 201
lowering/code generation support
  implementing, for C# language feature 278
lowering
  reference 256

M
method body analyzer
  creating, for analyzing whole method 32, 38
  creating, for issue reporting 32, 38
MSBuild
  reference 315
MSBuildWorkspace
  reference 315
MSTest
  reference 185

N
NuGet package manager
  analyzers, installing 58, 65
  analyzers, searching 58, 65
NuGet package
  publishing, for analyzer project 54, 56
NUnit
  reference 185

P
path tampering
  reference 174
performance improvements, to source code
  identifying, FxCop analyzers used 177, 181
public API analyzer
  used, for API surface maintenance 145, 149
PUMA scan analyzers
  configuration 158
  cross-site scripting (XSS) 158
  injection 158
  password management 158
  reference 163
  validation 158

R
REPL commands
  using, in C# interactive window 214

resolution results
  reference 301
Roslyn API
  reference 293
Roslyn enlistment
  setting up 233
Roslyn issue
  creating, reference 251
Roslyn pull request
  sending, for contribution to C# compiler and VS IDE 251
Roslyn scripting API
  used, for execution of C# code snippets 225, 229
Roslyn Syntax Visualizer
  reference 250
  used, for viewing Roslyn syntax tokens and nodes for source file 247, 249
Roslyn
  reference 232, 233, 256
  source folders and compilers 232
Rule Set editor
  used, for configuring analyzers 76, 79
ruleset file
  used, for configuring analyzers 76, 79
runtime performance 158

S

script directives
  using, in C# interactive window 214
security 158
Semantic Analysis
  reference 255
SemSemanticModel APIs 243
Simplifier
  reference 312
Solution explorer, Visual Studio
  analyzers, configuring 71
  analyzers, viewing 71, 75
  configuring 75
SQL injection
  reference 168
subset of tests, for live execution
  excluding 201, 204
  including 201, 204

Switch Operator 257
switch statement
  reference 257
symbol analyzer
  creating, to report issues about symbol declarations 24
syntax 258
syntax analysis
  about 264
  reference 254
syntax node analyzer
  creating, to report issues about language syntax 28
syntax tree analyzer
  creating, for analysis of source file 32
  creating, to report syntax issues 28, 32

T

third-party StyleCop analyzers
  using, for code style rules 150

U

unit tests
  writing, for analyzer project 46, 53
  writing, for binding 284, 290
  writing, for C# parsing 284, 290
  writing, for CodeFixProvider 125, 129
  writing, for codegen phases 284, 290
unvalidated redirect
  reference 174

V

Visual Studio 2017 community edition
  installation link 210
  reference 306
Visual Studio 2017
  reference 234
Visual Studio developer command prompt
  C# script execution, csi.exe used 222
Visual Studio interactive window
  C# script 213
  C# script, evaluating 210
VS extension gallery
  VSIX analyzers, installing 65
  VSIX analyzers, searching 65, 71

VSIX analyzers
    installing, through VS extension gallery 65, 71
    searching, through VS extension gallery 65, 71
VSIX
    publishing, for analyzer project 54, 56

W

weak password protection and management
    identifying, in web applications 171
weak validation of data
    identifying, from external components to prevent attacks 174, 177

web applications
    configuration-related security vulnerabilities, identifying 159, 161
    cross-scripting vulnerabilities, identifying 167
    cross-site scripting vulnerabilities, identifying in view markup files 164, 167
    weak password protection and management, identifying 171
Workspaces API 294

X

XUnit
    reference 185

Lightning Source UK Ltd.
Milton Keynes UK
UKHW031847250320
360890UK00004B/100